Sticks,
Stones,
Roots
& Bones

About the Author

Stephanie Rose Bird grew up in the tradition of Hoodoo. She has studied and practiced rootwork for over three decades. She is an herbal healer, writer, artist, academic consultant, and independent scholar.

To Write to the Author

If you wish to contact the author or would like more information about this book, please write to the author in care of Llewellyn Worldwide and we will forward your request. Both the author and publisher appreciate hearing from you and learning of your enjoyment of this book and how it has helped you. Llewellyn Worldwide cannot guarantee that every letter written to the author can be answered, but all will be forwarded. Please write to:

Stephanie Rose Bird
℅ Llewellyn Worldwide
2143 Wooddale Drive, Dept. 978-0-7387-0275-9
Woodbury, MN 55125-2989, U.S.A.

Please enclose a self-addressed stamped envelope for reply,
or $1.00 to cover costs. If outside U.S.A., enclose
international postal reply coupon.

Many of Llewellyn's authors have websites with additional information and resources. For more information, please visit our website at:

http://www.llewellyn.com

Sticks, Stones, Roots & Bones

Hoodoo, Mojo & Conjuring with Herbs

Stephanie Rose Bird

Llewellyn Publications
Woodbury, Minnesota

First Edition
Nineteenth Printing, 2023

Book design and editing by Joanna Willis
Cover design by Ellen Lawson
Illustrations on pages 2, 4, 30, and 50 by Llewellyn art department
Illustrations on pages 3, 5, 20, 29, 44, 47, 60, 68, 86, 103, 105, 108, 117, 120, 131–32, 135, 157, 160, 173, 178, 192, 223, and 239 by Stephanie Rose Bird

Credits
"Consider the life of trees . . ." by Cedric Wright from *Cedric Wright: Words of the Earth,* edited by Nancy Newhall. Copyright © 1960 by the Sierra Club. Reprinted by permission of Sierra Club Books.
Excerpts from "Mojo" by Ruth Bass are reprinted with the permission of Scribner, an imprint of Simon & Schuster Adult Publishing Group, from SCRIBNER'S MAGAZINE, VOL. #87, 1930. Copyright © 1930 by Charles Scribner's Sons; copyright renewed © 1958.
"I wish I were her Nubian slave . . ." reprinted from Lise Manniche, *Sacred Luxuries: Fragrance, Aromatherapy, and Cosmetics in Ancient Egypt.* Text © 1999 by Lise Manniche, photographs © 1999 Werner Forman, © 1999 Opus Publishing Limited. Used by permission of the publisher, Cornell University Press.
"The Negro Speaks of Rivers" from *The Collected Poems of Langston Hughes* by Langston Hughes. Copyright © 1994 by the Estate of Langston Hughes. Used by permission of Alfred A. Knopf, a division of Random House, Inc.

Library of Congress Cataloging-in-Publication Data
Bird, Stephanie Rose, 1960–
    Sticks, stones, roots & bones: Hoodoo, mojo & conjuring with herbs / Stephanie Rose Bird.—1st ed.
        p.   cm.
    Includes bibliographical references (p.) and index.
    ISBN 13: 978-0-7387-0275-9
    ISBN 10: 0-7387-0275-7
        1. African American magic. 2. Hoodoo (Cult) I. Title: Sticks, stones, roots, and bones.
    II. Title.

    BF1622.A34B57 2004
    133.4'3'08996073—dc22

                                                                                    2004044129

Llewellyn Publications
A Division of Llewellyn Worldwide Ltd.
2143 Wooddale Drive
Woodbury, MN 55125-2989
www.llewellyn.com
Llewellyn is a registered trademark of Llewellyn Worldwide Ltd.
Printed in the United States of America

Sometimes there is that rare bird,
a voice from the wilderness, that sees and knows.
This is dedicated to such a bird, as he could see from the time I was a girl
that someday I would write this book.

You said you would be a spiritual heavyweight once you passed over to the other side.
Now I see that your prophecy has come true. Blessed Be.

This is dedicated in loving memory to
Carl Nimrod Hunt Malone,
Babawayo of Shango, tender of myths and secrets,
best friend, spiritual midwife, griot, carver, comedian,
drummer extraordinaire formerly of Sun Ra, and much more.

I see Red Cardinal fly and know your spirit still soars.
Thank you for paving the path with smooth stones and sparkling pearls of wisdom.

—Your loving niece for eternity

Contents

Acknowledgments

Although books have the appearance of lone entities, no book is an island, least of all this one. I give thanks for the wisdom of the universe and the path of the divinely feminine; praise be to the great goddess, creator of life itself. The earth, sun, moon, planets, plants, stones, water, and the elements all have played an important role; I have drawn a lot from you, thank you. Those whispers in the night (without doubt they must have been voices of the ancestors), thank you for your age-old wisdom. Blessed be!

From the domain of the spirits to the colorful, dense, live-wire, so-called mundane world of love, energy, and support, now for additional thanks. To use one of your favorite words, I owe a *massive* debt of gratitude to my husband—soul mate, friend, lover, spirit coach, earth friend. You saw to it that I had the shelter, mental space, resources, inspiration, and the wherewithal to put this book together; thank you, love of my life. To our four beautiful children—not only in appearance but also in thought and deed—I thank you for the joie de vivre that you exude and for filling my life with light, joy, and hope. To my parents, who taught me to sow seeds, tend the earth, harvest the fruits, and give back to the earth, I thank you both. To my brothers and sister who shared a charmed upbringing with me out in the woods, thank you for being who you are. To my in-laws, kind and generous wise souls who expand my notion of what family is and what friendship can and should be, thank you for reading my work without complaint, offering critiques, and supporting my artistic ventures and ideas in their myriad forms in your special way.

To my friends who listened patiently and supported this book every step of the way with laughter, joy, and sometimes tears: Ellen Campbell, Chun Hui Pak Arnold, Kathy Shoubaki, Brooke Baron, Linda Shealey, Gail Momenthy, and Ann Blair. Thank you, my rainbow tribe of sisters, for listening, sustaining, sharing, and most of all, for your infinitely caring spirits.

From the art world, I thank my original mentor, Stanley Whitney, who started me on this path toward wisdom. Thanks for teaching us that we can do anything as long as we are seers. Thanks to Renee Williams Jefferson at Wisdom Artist Gallery and Beate Minkovsky at WomanMade Gallery, whose recipes are shared within these pages, for providing a supportive outlet for my botanical crafts. To Chicago artists Marva Pitchford Jolly and Preston Jackson for embedding the spirit of Hoodoo into their sculptural works for all to experience. Thanks to the editors who permit my art and words to come together: Jennifer Barrette, Sally Pinkerton, and Diane Bush. Thanks to Camille White Olson and Dr. Phil Royster for being tireless champions of my art. To Phil and Joan Berman, whose kind patronage of my paintings sustains and affirms my creativity, thank you.

Who would have thought ten years ago that I'd have a full circle of friends and associates that I've never seen face to face. From my desk, I see and honor the light in you. *Namaste.* My personal editor, assistant, friend, and seer extraordinaire, Jannette Giles-Hypes—thank you, my Southern sister, for reading volumes and heaps of my words and sorting through them so that they would eventually come together to make sense. Thank you for spreading love, light, and joy in all that you do in the virtual, spiritual, and everyday world; your friendship and editorial assistance are spiritual blessings. It would seem paltry to only call Marie Brown my agent in light of the amazing relationship we share. Marie, my Harlem sister, thank you for being a friend, supporter, advocate, mentor, and wise woman. Thanks also to all of my other friends at Marie Brown and Associates for your patient assistance. Anne Newkirk Nivens of *Sage Woman* magazine—an e-friend who expanded my vision of friendship, trust, and the circle of sisterhood—thank you, my northern California sister, for giving a space within your pages where I can share my voice. To the other editors who supported my work, thank you sincerely: Robyn Griggs Lawrence, Gretchen Hubert, Dawn Friedman, Jennifer Emick, and Robyn Lakini Skie.

I never gave thought to being published abroad; the Internet made that unfathomable notion a reality. Nadia El-Awady (Egypt), Bob Harris (France), and John Kerr (Australia), thanks for letting my work on African healing traditions cross cultural and geographic boundaries.

Big ups to Michael Fallon, editor of Llewellyn's annual publications, for permitting me the freedom to explore, expand, and create within the pages of *Llewellyn's Herbal Almanac, Magical Almanac,* and *Witches' Spell-A-Day Almanac.* Speaking of Llewellyn, I feel especially grateful to have found an intimate publishing house that supports my work. It's more than just a company; as a writer, I feel like one of the Llewellyn family, a position I honor and cherish. This begins with the couple at the helm: Carl L. Weschcke, president, and Sandra K. Weschcke, secretary and treasurer. A special thanks goes to acquisitions manager Nancy Mostad and acquisitions editor Natalie Harter for their kindness, and acquisitions editor Meg Bratsch for negotiating through an elaborate labyrinth of permissions and rights issues. Joanna Willis, my trusted editor, thanks for "seeing" my work and editing it with a keen eye for detail. Thanks to the art department, especially Lynne Menturweck and Lisa Novak, and the publicity and marketing team: Jerry Rogers, Josie Christopherson, Alison Aten, and Beth Scudder. Thanks also to the people there whose names I don't know, but who have supported my work nevertheless.

This book is built on a foundation of research culled from numerous folks, including Africanists, art historians, historians, Egyptologists, anthropologists, folklorists, herbalists, and most importantly, practitioners. Credits appear on page iv and throughout this book, but there are a few that I need to highlight because of the indelible impression they have made. I pray to the Goddess that I have left no one out. If I have, it is entirely by accident, and I beg your forgiveness for any oversight, as it is unintentional.

I thank every author and editor mentioned in my bibliography. Thanks to those listed in my bibliography who led me down a path of discovery and revelation: Robert Farris Thompson, Lise Manniche, Robert Voeks, Harold Courlander, Daryl Cumber Dance, Harry Middleton Hyatt, Marquetta L. Goodwine, William S. Pollitzer, and Faith Mitchell. Archivist, proprietor, and author Catherine Yronwood used the Internet to bring international attention to Hoodoo, a faith whose following had been waning before her work. Her research gave voice to the collection of practices I was born into; thanks for helping me remember. To the spirit of Scott Cunningham, the passionate scholar whose encyclopedias are a deep reservoir of cross-cultural information—a source at once reliable and enlightening—thank you. Thank you to African wisemen Malidoma Patrice Some, Yaya Diallo, and John Anenechukwu Umeh for telling the story of our traditional beliefs from the heart of the motherland with soul, from the heart. Thank you to Robert Johnson, Muddy Waters, and a full cadre of blues and roots artists for singing Hoodoo into our souls. Thank you to Zora Neale Hurston, for defying categorization; every contemporary hoodoo and African American folklorist owes gratitude to you. Zora blazed the path of Hoodoo with her two feet, shaped the stories into form with her rich brown hands, and seared it into our hearts and souls through magickal words, making it a path never to be forgotten. Thank you, Zora Neale Hurston. Ase!

Introduction

Once upon a time, we were Africans involved in a unique lexicon of beliefs, lore, stories, and customs that were designed to help integrate us into an environment filled with plants, animals, elements, and a complex array of spirits. With the advent of slavery (see Figure 1), the physical bond with the motherland was broken, but like seeds lifted from a ripe plant by wind, we found fertile ground in distant lands elsewhere.

Our beliefs took root in the Americas in slightly altered forms. The freshly sown seedlings took hold strongest in sunny climates reminiscent of the fair conditions in Africa. The various hybrids of African-based religion are now thriving in coastal Brazil, the Dominican Republic, and Cuba in the form of Candomble, Shango, and Santeria, and in Louisiana and Haiti in the form of Vodoun. In the southern United States, Hoodoo took root in Alabama, Mississippi, Georgia, Florida, and North and South Carolina. Hoodoo was established during slavery times using the available plants in the United States and borrowing from the ancient wisdom of the Native Americans.

> *Now keep your hands off a' my mojo,*
> *'cause it sure is lucky to me*
> *Now, keep your hands off a' my*
> *mojo, I wish I had two or three*
> *I wear my mojo above my knee*
> *To keep you from tryin' to hoodoo me*
> *So keep your hands off a' my mojo, if*
> *you ain't got no stuff for me.*
>
> —Leola B. "Coot" Grant and
> "Kid" Wesley Wilson,
> "Take Your Hands off My Mojo"

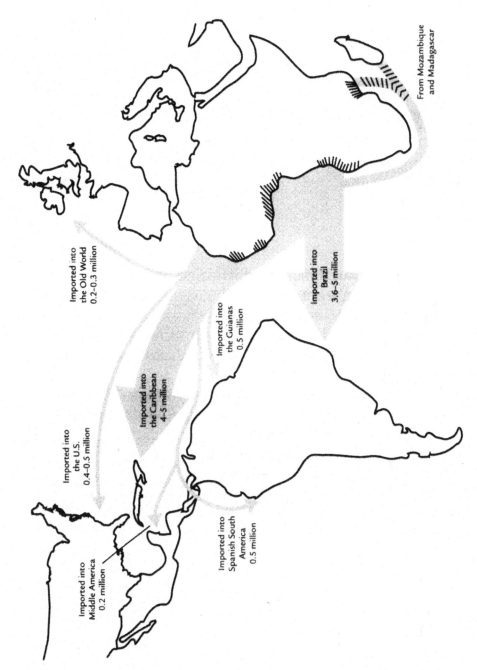

From Mozambique
and Madagascar

Imported into
the Old World
0.2–0.3 million

Imported into
Brazil
3.6–5 million

Imported into
the Guianas
0.5 million

Imported into
the Caribbean
4–5 million

Imported into
the U.S.
0.4–0.5 million

Imported into
Middle America
0.2 million

Imported into
Spanish South
America
0.5 million

Figure 1: Atlantic slave trade 1502–1870.

With immigration and migrations of freed slaves in North and South America, the growth of African-based religions spread from the older cultural centers of Bahia (Brazil), Havana (Cuba), and Yorubaland (Africa) to dynamic industrial centers such as New York City, Miami, Los Angeles, and Chicago (see Figure 2). Some of our traditional practices were transformed into systems that strongly incorporated Catholicism. For example, the elaborate system of saints, priests, priestesses, deities, and ceremonies honored by Catholics is included in Santeria of Spanish-speaking countries and Vodoun of French-speaking areas. Santeria, Shango, and Vodoun are unique blends of Western and non-Western religious rituals, ceremonies, prayers, invocations, and blessings, but they are also open to include the darker side of the spiritual world: jinxes, curses, and hexes.

On the other hand, Hoodoo and Candomble are distinctly American (North and South). Therefore, they are multicultural and reflect strong links between various indigenous groups, Judeo-Christian faiths of the dominant cultures, and West African magickal and medicinal herbalism. They are primarily healing traditions that involve the use of herbs, plants, roots, trees, animals, magnets, minerals, and natural waters combined with magickal amulets, chants, cere-

monies, rituals, and handmade power objects. (Handmade power objects empower the practitioner to take control of his or her own fate, rather than place power in the hands of synchronized deities or religious leaders.)

Since Hoodoo is an American tradition that is widely practiced in the areas my kin are from, it is the primary Africanism that was passed down to me. The word "Hoodoo," however, was seldom spoken by African Americans. They did not really want to name or recognize this eclectic collection of African holdovers that endured

Woman digging roots

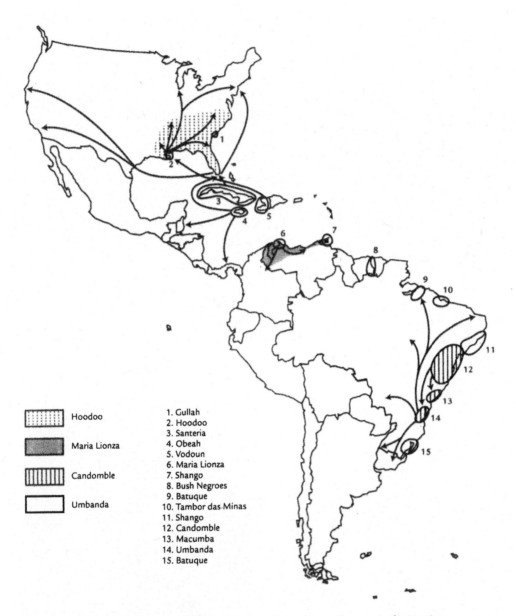

Figure 2: Distribution of African-derived medical and magical systems in the Americas.

Legend:
- Hoodoo
- Maria Lionza
- Candomble
- Umbanda

1. Gullah
2. Hoodoo
3. Santeria
4. Obeah
5. Vodoun
6. Maria Lionza
7. Shango
8. Bush Negroes
9. Batuque
10. Tambor das Minas
11. Shango
12. Candomble
13. Macumba
14. Umbanda
15. Batuque

Source: Robert A. Voeks, *Sacred Leaves of Candomble: African Magic, Medicine, and Religion in Brazil* (Austin, TX: University of Texas Press, 1997), 3.

and reminded us of the Middle Passage and slavery. Popularly called both "Hoodoo" and "Voodoo" by the uninformed, the term is of dubious origins and is most likely the creation of the media as an adulteration of *Vodoun*. The word "Hoodoo" was never spoken in my home, yet its tenets were evident in my upbringing. The term is a useful way to give form to the colorful and specific folkloric beliefs practiced by a wide range of believers, including the Gullah people of Georgia and the Carolinas, Black folk in major metropolitan areas, White folk of the Appalachians, and Native Americans.

Since it is not a religion, Hoodoo has always been practiced by a wide variety of people, regardless of ethnicity or religious affiliation. Its attractiveness lies in the fact that it is natural, nondogmatic, and practical. Primary concerns of hoodoos include blessing the home and keeping the domestic environment peaceful and free of unwanted intrusions, whether they are bad vibes brought about by humans, animals, or spirits. Other concerns are gaining a life mate who is loving and doesn't cheat or abandon his or her spouse, general health and happiness in life, predicting the future, controlling people when necessary and freeing oneself or others from undesired control, using hexing and unhexing, and drawing luck in seeking employment, career advancement, good grades in school, winning money, lucky breaks, or the good fortune of success. In short, Hoodoo is concerned with health, wealth, love, luck, and happiness—concerns to which many people can relate.

The means used to achieve the desired situation is called the *laying of tricks* and *fixing tricks,* which are kin to European witchcraft spells and Gypsy charms. These objects are reminiscent of African herbal bundles. The most common form is a *bag of tricks,* also called a *nation sack, gris-gris, hand, mojo, trick bag, luck ball,* or *flannel,* which employs herbs and other magickal ingredients.

Mojo hand

The use of the terms *my mojo* and *his (or her) bag of tricks* are often included in the lyrics of traditional African American blues songs, particularly those of the legendary Muddy Waters, who is also called the "Hoodoo Man." Unfortunately, the lyrics have been misinterpreted. *Mojo* was interpreted as a metaphysical aura of sexual power or prowess, and the *trick bag* was interpreted as a metaphor for various forms of misleading behaviors. In reality, a mojo and a bag of tricks are one and the same: a bag of charms that serves as an amulet for purposes ranging from attracting a lover and maintaining a relationship to drawing luck or attracting money. These bags are carried close to the person—usually on the thigh, in the bra, or in a special pouch under one's clothing. If someone "steals your mojo," they have stolen your special amulet that holds your hopes and dreams. The mojo is a personalized item that carries your personal energy. Therefore, it is very dangerous—possibly fatal—if it falls into the hands of another, especially if that person is a hoodoo, witch, or conjurer.

In addition to the mojos, a wide variety of herb-based scented oils and incenses are employed in Hoodoo. Oils can be applied to the person, diffused in the air, set out in significant areas of the home, and used to dress candles. Whimsical names abound such as "Van Van Oil," "Black Cat Oil," "Fast Luck Oil," and "Bend Over Oil." Numerous types of herbal incenses are used with equally intriguing names. The incense is burned while chanting, singing, or praying.

Salts have been used for cleansing and healing for thousands of years. They are enjoying a renewed interest by adherents to feng shui philosophy who use it in the same way as Hoodoo practitioners. In these disparate practices, salt is placed on the floor and in corners during spiritual cleansing, and the crystals are used during bathing for curative and restorative purposes. In Hoodoo, sweet waters are also applied to the body and left in bowls to deter or attract spirits and humans. In Hoodoo, divination is achieved using other natural materials (such as crystals, tea leaves, coffee grounds, animal bones, water gazing, crystal gazing, and seashells) as oracles to predict the future. Dream interpretation, controlling dreams through lucid dreaming, and astral projection are also important activities. Ancestral and natural spirits are acknowledged, invoked, and utilized for protection, predictions, healing, curses, and blessings.

The most striking features of African-based belief systems have been passed down through the generations. They shape Hoodoo and are shared in this book for the development and affirmation of personal strength, self-determination, connection to nature, awareness of the environment, and connection to our past.

Television, movies, and commerce tend to sap the vibrancy out of authentic experience. Sadly, the practice of Hoodoo went out of favor after it was commercialized and trivialized by the media and nonbelievers, but this creative practice of African American folklore deserves to be preserved and continued. During the earlier half of the twentieth century, Hollywood and unscrupulous businesses were captivated by the commercial and lucrative possibilities of Hoodoo and Vodoun. Today, there are precious few suppliers of truly herbal Hoodoo products and supplies. There are fewer still who will openly admit to practicing these beliefs, owing in large part to the "pagan" stigma that might be attached to it by fundamentalist Christians. Ingredients can be store bought (I have listed some suppliers and practitioners in appendix B), but for true authenticity, create as many of the recipes and formulas by hand as possible. Doing it yourself lets you add your own finesse, personal touches, and unique cultural traditions as you lay your tricks. Remember, Hoodoo is based on self-determination and independence, not commerce. Take advantage of the recipes for fixin' your tricks. Through practice and dedication, you will become a true root doctor, conjurer, or hoodoo in your own right.

This book is your practical guide to gaining greater control of the aspects of your life that need attention. Below is a full explanation of the meaning of the title that builds a framework for the rest of the book. The following chapters explain Hoodoo candle rituals, spiritual cleansings, ways to draw luck, dreaming, rituals for love, blessings, altars, psychic warfare, peace, and important rites of passage.

As a contemporary Hoodoo practitioner, I, like my ancestors, am fully aware of the magickal potential of neighboring systems. This book revolves around traditional West African magickal paths, yet in it there is an eclectic collage of wisdom and lore from around the world.

Reading this book is an important step in the spiritual journey to a magickal life. If you need additional help, you will find it at the back of the book where product suppliers, practitioners, sourcebooks, organizations, and a bibliography are listed for further studies.

A Word About Nature

Sticks, stones, roots, and bones—these are the basic ingredients found in any good hoodoo's mojo bag. As we utilize the essential tools for Hoodoo, we must always stay aware of their source: Mother Nature. Being considerate and respectful is key. To enlist her help we need to work closely with the Earth Mother in her various manifestations. To do this we shall endeavor to do the following:

- Listen to her whispers late at night under the light of the moon.

- Hear her calls early in the morning.

- Watch her sigh and undulate with the ebb and flow of the currents.

- Seek out her advice in working our roots.

- Stay mindful of the limitations and gifts when tapping her resources.

> *Cultivating a great respect for nature is the ultimate goal of all the customs concerning the sacred wood.*
>
> —Yaya Diallo and Mitchell Hall, *The Healing Drum*

Most importantly we need to make sure we work *with* nature and not just use what she has to offer us. An easy way to accomplish this is to assure a proper balance of give and take in the relationship. We may utilize the earth's resources, but we should not overuse, cause pain, or destroy her in the process. We must approach the Earth Mother as she exists today, rather than doggedly aligning ourselves with traditions that contribute to the abuse or neglect of nature—this includes animals, the oceans, and fragile plants. By opening our eyes and seeing her in the manner that she exists today, we are working with her and not against her. An important aspect of this book is to help the contemporary conjurer practice as a hoodoo of the twenty-first century.

It is critical that we take into consideration the large population of humans that reside on earth and the effects these numbers have on the Earth Mother's reserves. We need to own up to the urban nature of our existence. Moreover, we must stay mindful of the recent developments in our culture. To stay true to the origins of Hoodoo, we will attempt to incorporate as much of the tradition as possible. As we create this blend, we seek a balance between the old ways, new issues, and technologies. Our goal is to honor the Earth Mother and our ancestors as we work our roots.

In appendix A, you will find lists of endangered species of plants and animals. Please heed this information as you perform your work.

Sticks, Stones, Roots & Bones

So what is the meaning behind the title *Sticks, Stones, Roots & Bones?*

Sticks

Trees are tremendously important to Africans, thus they play an important role in Hoodoo. Trees are the primary teachers of the hoodoo and the hunters, herbalists, and warriors of Africa, as you will learn in chapter 2. Similar to a West African hunter or warrior, a good hoodoo must spend a great deal of time alone with trees in order to learn the secrets and wisdom they wish to share with us.

Tree bark, tree branches, and their leaves and flowers are essential tools of Hoodoo. Metaphorically, trees represent the relationship between the living and the dead (this is true in Africa as well as many other parts of the world). Trees are intricately linked with death, burial, and spiritual connection, as you will see in chapter 14.

There are additional ways in which sticks are important in Hoodoo: the practical and metaphoric senses of *sticking*. Sticking is an adaptation of piercing and scarification rituals. It is the activating motion performed on poppets (sometimes referred to as "Voodoo dolls"), stuffed fabric, or vegetables or fruits that represent humans. (Sometimes even the sticklike herb devil's shoestring is used to represent the

Consider the life of trees.
Aside from the axe, what trees acquire
from man is inconsiderable
What man may acquire from trees is
immeasurable
From their mute forms there flows a
poise, in silence, a lovely sound and
motion in response to wind.
What peace comes to those aware of the
voice and bearing of trees!
Trees do not scream for attention.
A tree, a rock, has no pretense, only a
real growth out of itself, in close
communion with the universal spirit.
A tree retains a deep serenity.
It establishes in the earth not only its
root system but also those roots of
its beauty and its unknown
consciousness.
Sometimes one may sense a glisten of
that consciousness, and with such
perspective, feel that man is not necessarily the highest form of life.

—Cedric Wright

limbs of a human on a poppet.) Sticking and knotting in prescribed amounts on certain days fixes magickal bundles and mojo bags. Hoodoo jobs and tricks often involve sticking in one way or another—whether it be sticking a poppet, sticking thread into a bundle or piece of fabric ritualistically, or sticking by our magick until our tricks work.

> *When a family comes to settle some-where, this stone is the first object placed on the new homesite. It symbolizes unity and reminds family members of humility, of freedom from greed, and of their descent from the ancestors.*
>
> —Yaya Diallo and Mitchell Hall,
> *The Healing Drum*

Stones

Stones are often taken for granted. The role of minerals and stones in African and African American magickal systems has been severely underestimated. In the book *From My People: 400 Years of African American Folklore* by Daryl Cumber Dance, the carrying of a beauty pebble (quartz crystal) is indicated in a firsthand account as the primary way of identifying a hoodoo or conjurer.

Stones seem to be inert, yet they are actually reservoirs of history, karma, and energy. Each type of stone has its own frequency and unique ability to aid conjur craft. First of all, however, the rock needs to be charged.

There are several ways to charge a rock. Some people bury them and dig them up repeatedly until they feel a noticeable change in the energy of the stone. Others simply place the stone out in the sun for three to seven days, again checking periodically for changes. Still others use special water soaks combined with sun. They place the stone out in the sun for three to seven days and then soak it in salt-water for another few days. Whichever method you choose, once the stone is charged, it is under your control. You should wrap it in a piece of silk and keep it near your person so it understands your energy flow and desires. Charged stones are essential conjuring tools with unique applications and functions. In the following chapters you will encounter ways of using many different types of stones in mojo bags, potions, rituals, and for tricks.

Fossils—Fossils are some of the most sacred gifts of the Great Mother. Fossils are bones of sorts, remnants of life in times that we can only read about. To charge these, hold them in your hands or put them on your altar to give a very special energy to your work. Try to use a selection from places of importance to you. I have some wonderful specimens from the Mississippi riverbed that are the frozen image of a primeval palm leaf.

Amber—Amber seems rocklike, but it is actually fossilized tree resin. With its golden tone and sunny appearance, it is likened to Sun Ra, the Egyptian sun god. This resin often has insects trapped inside of it, giving us a brief glimpse of ancient life frozen in time. Amber is always warm to the touch and is good for warming medicine.

Roots

Rootwork is another name for Hoodoo. Rootwork consists of understanding herbalism and then incorporating indigenous wisdom regarding nature. My approach draws heavily upon the herbal wisdom of Africa and Native America. In later chapters you will learn how various societies and groups embody and inspire the hoodoo's rootworking system.

Roots are a vital tool to traditional hoodoos. Roots contain potent juju or good medicine—everything a conjurer desires. Yet many different types of plants are either extinct, endangered, or on an "at risk" list. This must not be underestimated. Plants, like all life on earth, are fragile. They help us, and it is only natural that we should, in turn, look out for them and help maintain their existence in any way possible. Roots are the life source of a plant. Taking the root is not like harvesting berries, flowers, or leaves. Most often roots don't grow back.

Whenever possible, we need to use roots sparingly and judiciously—especially if they come from an endangered plant. Once we tap the root, we have taken a life off this earth; this is a grave responsibility. Find substitutes for roots whenever possible. John the Conqueror root, angelica root, Queen Elizabeth root, and Adam and Eve root are central ingredients in the hoodoo's medicine bag. It is possible to use these gifts sparingly by using chips from the roots, releasing their magickal ingredients into an oil, or pulverizing them into a powder form. Once the roots are extracted into oil or powdered form, other magickal ingredients can be added to accentuate the desired effects. We will learn to do these things and more. Just remember that in order for roots to be our assistants, we must look after them in return for their help. Making sure the necessary plants for our craft are not made extinct is a responsibility that goes along with being an adept conjurer.

Another important aspect of the word *roots* in the title has to do with the orientation of this book. Many books I have read have overt Eurocentric approaches, especially in relation to magickal paths. I have even noticed a tendency within research on Hoodoo by non-Africans to constantly default back to Europe when there isn't an easy answer for the root of a tradition or practice. I seek to present Hoodoo from an African American perspective and trace the roots of this particular magickal path to West Africa and ancient Khemet (Black Egypt).

Now I know some people will scratch their heads in wonder that I would find a connection in what is largely known as Egyptology and Hoodoo, but the commonalities in perspective, orientation, and even ingredients used are astonishing. Furthermore, many West African and African American scholars firmly believe that sub-Saharan peoples migrated to where they now live from Khemet. Judging from their findings and the links between the two cultures, I agree. I am certain from my research that if a default key has to be hit regarding a practice, name, formula, or bit of oral folklore, most certainly the root can be found still intact in either Khemetian beliefs, Ifa practices (of the Yoruba people of Nigeria), or other traditions from the diverse peoples of West Africa—the root and homeland of African Americans and Hoodoo.

Bones

In days of old, bones and animal parts were widely used in conjur craft. And why not? They were plentiful. People hunted regularly and used every part of the animal for food, shelter, warmth, medicine, and magick. Today many animals and plants face extinction. Their habitats are threatened by our continued growth. It would be irresponsible of me to give out recipes and formulas that inspired hundreds or even thousands of people to seek out various animal parts, tradition or not. There is no magick in harming others, human or animal. I do include a few recipes calling for feathers, which should be found or ascertained from a pet store. Some recipes also call for chicken bones or bone meal, but millions of people do still eat chicken and chickens are important sacrificial animals to the hoodoo.

Having said that, I highly recommend using only what you need, and moreover, what you have to spare from your meals. If a friend or family member hunts raccoon or rabbits, then you will have ample raccoon parts for your love potions and rabbit's feet for luck draw. Certain regions of the country have desolate locations that are littered with snakeskins, animal horns, and skulls. Plus, people still do farm and slaughter their own animals. If you need chicken blood, you should consider visiting a chicken farm, because there have been gruesome reports of laypeople fudging the job and causing great harm to the animal. What I am saying is, if you harvest these things ethically, great. If you know someone who harvests ethically, that's cool too. If not, use safe substitutes.

Negative energy is extremely counterproductive to Hoodoo work. Trust me, in a heartbeat things that you send out into the world can get botched up and come riding on the wings of the wind or even a bird and land right back on your doorstep. Of course, if you are a vegetarian or vegan, you will want to pass on these traditions altogether.

Metal

According to author Scott Cunningham, metal is another type of bone. Consider incorporating metal magick more forcefully into your practices. After all, it is a highly important part of Hoodoo.

Silver—From an African perspective, silver represents the sea, the Great Mothers, and the moon. It is helpful for intuitive work, dream quests, and fertility and love tricks. Songhai wisemen believe that the third finger of the left hand is our conduit for spirit power, so a silver ring is placed on this finger to enhance this capacity.

> Metals are the "flesh of the gods and goddesses," the bones of the Earth, manifestations of universal powers.
>
> —Scott Cunningham,
> *Cunningham's Encyclopedia of Crystal, Gem & Metal Magic*

Copper—Copper is a healing metal and a conduit of spiritual healing energy. It is also associated with the goddesses Ishtar, Astarte, Inanna, and Isis. Copper works especially well combined with quartz crystals. Copper pennies are revered in Hoodoo as charms for luck- and money-draw magick. Black folk from the Caribbean and South America are especially fond of copper bracelets and anklets as tools for healing.

Brass—Brass is widely used in Africa. The magickal qualities of brass are similar to gold, but without the vanity. Brass is a good metal for candleholders and for using in love-draw magick.

Iron—Black folks in the Americas have been cooking in seasoned cast-iron skillets for hundreds of years. Iron represents the orisha Ogun, the warrior protector. Since iron is connected to Ogun, it carries some of his fiercely protective characteristics. Nails, rust, and metal filings are several ways that iron is utilized in Hoodoo. Metalsmithing was—and in some cases still is—a highly honored traditional craft in Africa. It was also revered in early African American culture.

Lead—Lead is used for its ability to hold and deliver intent. Graphite pencils, which are reminiscent of lead pencils, are often used in specific written jobs and tricks. Thankfully, graphite pencils are easily available and inexpensive.

Lodestone—Lodestone is central to love, luck, and prosperity work. It is a stone made from magnetite. Similarly, fool's gold or pyrite chips are used in drawing magick, mojos, spiritual baths, and on altars.

Quicksilver—Quicksilver, or mercury, was once widely used for luck spells, but since it is extremely toxic, it is best to avoid it.

This book, then, is a compilation of songs, recipes, tricks, jobs, rituals, spells, stories, recollections, and folklore that revolve around the eclectic magickal path called Hoodoo. This book gives practical, hands-on ways to denote important rites of passage and cycles of life using magickal herbalism and African traditions that are at the very crux of Hoodoo. The chapters contained herein present information, spells, charms, and amulets to deal with the common, everyday concerns and preoccupations of most folk: drawing love, prosperity, and luck.

Hoodoo was almost ridiculed out of existence by those who had no idea what they had stumbled across. Capitalism and commerce also made a huge dent, as the crafting of formulas and recipes require two essential ingredients to work: the TLC (tender loving care) and *ashe* (magickal forces and energies of the universe) that come from personal, at-home brewing.

Recently, there has been a renewal of interest, study, and practice of conjuration and Hoodoo, largely due to a few excellent sites on the Internet. I am grateful that the ancestor and nature spirits found me to be a suitable conduit to contribute to the renaissance of this significant path. I hope reading this book will leave you inspired and well equipped to become involved in continuing the tradition.

chapter 1

Fixin' to Work Roots

Hoodoo began in folks' sheds, basements, and kitchens. It seems as though once it spread into the hands of merchants, the demise of this folkcraft began. The renewed interest of late in Hoodoo, rootwork, and conjuring affords a wonderful opportunity to start fresh from scratch. If you want to be a hoodoo, who else can you depend on to procure the proper ingredients, and blend them at the right time and in the right way to produce the desired results?

Time and Space

Time is one of the main elements needed for rootwork. Luckily, you don't have to run out and buy it. You do, however, need to have some set aside. I can't sugarcoat this for you. Just like a good soup stock, tasty stew, or homemade pie, your herbal brews and fragrant oils will take time and skill to fix them up just right. On average you will need to invest at least an hour for the preparation of your handmade treatment. While recipes that require infusions or distillation will take longer, some treatments are instant. If you crave convenience, the latter are the recipes for you.

One of the main reasons the making of Hoodoo products was relinquished to others was the rise of companies interested in marketing to African Americans. This group of companies, salesmen, and merchants saw an opportunity to profit from the folk beliefs and the lack of time folks faced for mixing their own products. Now, instead of quality products, we are sold inferior blends that often are little more than sweetly scented, colored waters and synthetic oils—a pale memory of the depth and texture the old hoodoos who were well versed in herbalism invested in their roots.

The real deal is, if you want your rootwork to take, you need to be absolutely certain that the roots, berries, beans, and herbs are authentic and that the harvest was correctly timed astrologically according to the effects desired. Many of us are unaccustomed to spending hours in the kitchen, and even less time in the garden or woods. However, if you want to be a good hoodoo, let me help you become reacquainted with the lost art of patience in pursuit of quality. Start slow; take your time, gradually build up your expertise, taste, and skill, and before you know it you'll have all the herbs and equipment needed to formulate a unique repertoire of recipes for your loved ones and yourself.

Clean, organized space is also essential. Having a work space (such as a level table or countertop) clear of clutter for your cookery is very important. Clean space will save you the agony of messy accidents or contaminating your brew after all of the love and care you've put into making it.

Equipment and Tools

In this book I have tried to give ample options in the recipes with consideration for various budgets, time constraints, and geographic locations. This is designed to ease your passage into the art of rootworking as gently and painlessly as possible. Before fixin' to work up a mojo, sachet, wash, or anointing oil, however, you need certain equipment to get started.

Apron

A plastic "splash-proof" apron sold by soap suppliers and chemical shops is highly recommended for protection against the caustic sodium hydroxide used during cold-processed soapmaking. Also consider putting on old clothes to use as smocks or work clothes.

Blender

A blender is used for thorough mixing and liquefying.

Bottles and Jars

Bottles and jars are very important pieces of equipment. I like using recycled bottles as much as possible for shampoo and conditioners. Mouthwash, liquid dish detergent, shampoo, and conditioner bottles, as well as lotion, yogurt, and baby food containers are all useful. Glass storage jars are used mainly for oil infusions and tinctures. Tinted glass ones with spring or cork tops work well.

At times you will want to make special blends as gifts or for stores. There are plenty of specialty container suppliers who carry powder dispensers, spritzers, cologne bottles, flip-top body-wash bottles, and decorative jars with screw tops for this purpose. It's nice now and again to use these decorative containers for yourself—especially the powder dispensers, since powders are essential to hoodoos. Pretty perfume bottles used for storing personal scents also add a nice touch. They can be bought new or at antique shops. There is more information in appendix B about commercial bottle suppliers.

Remember, when using recycled materials, it is very important to sterilize them first by boiling plastic containers and cleaning glass bottles with very hot, soapy water. Rinse and allow to dry before beginning. They can also be sterilized in a dishwasher if you have one.

Cauldron

A cauldron doesn't have to be fancy or bought from a specialty shop; a plain, cast-iron Dutch oven will do. However, if you want to brew your roots in a proper cauldron, there are plenty of suppliers who carry them.

Charcoal Blocks

Buy charcoal blocks in quantity, as they are the most efficient way of burning loose herbal incense. Avoid those that contain saltpeter; it is toxic when burned. (Traditionally, saltpeter was an ingredient used by hoodoos. Sadly, the type sold today is sodium nitrate, a highly combustible substance that is also harmful to the skin, eyes, and lungs.) Pure bamboo charcoals from Japan are available and make a more wholesome alternative.

Chiminea

A chiminea is a portable, miniature fireplace that is generally kept on the patio. This is great for burning incense and for fire rituals if you don't have a fireplace.

Coffee Grinder

A coffee grinder is a convenient way to grind tough spices and roots compared to its ancestor, the mortar and pestle, which requires hand grinding and lots of elbow grease. Watch out though; really tough spices and roots need to be ground by hand or they'll break your coffee grinder. Trust me, I've been through quite a few.

Double Boiler

A double boiler is an indirect way of heating that prevents waxy mixtures, like ointments and candle wax, from cooking too quickly. A double boiler can be improvised by floating a stainless-steel bowl in water in a pot that is slightly larger than the bowl.

Droppers

Droppers are essential for dispensing droplets of essential oils, fragrance oils, body fluids, or other precious liquids that you don't want to waste. Throughout this book I ask that you drop in essential oils, as this is the approach used by good perfumers. It helps ensure that the oils don't clump up; instead, they disperse evenly. See appendix B for suppliers.

Drying Rack

A drying rack is where fresh herbs are hung by their stems to dry. Also, it's an attractive way to display and store dried herbs indefinitely.

Food Processor

Even a mini food processor without all the fancy attachments will do to blend and liquefy ingredients for personal-care recipes.

Freestanding Mixer

A freestanding mixer is convenient, but not essential. It is used for whisking and thoroughly blending ingredients while saving your energy.

Funnel Set

Funnels are used to prevent spills and ease the transfer of liquids, oils, and powders from the bowl or pan to a small-necked bottle (referred to here as *bottling*).

Grater

A Teflon or stainless-steel grater is recommended because it lasts longer and resists sticking and rusting. It is mainly used for shredding beeswax and refining roots.

Kettle

A kettle is used to boil water for infusing herbs.

Measuring Cups

Measuring cups are used to measure both dry ingredients and liquids. Pyrex, tempered glass, and stainless steel work best. Glass and stainless steel are easy to clean completely to prevent cross-contamination of ingredients.

Measuring Spoons

Measuring spoons made of stainless steel with clearly marked measurements etched into the surface are preferred.

Mixing Bowls

Glass, ceramic, or stainless-steel mixing bowls are recommended because they will not become stained from colorants, nor will they harbor bits of leftover ingredients once cleaned properly. Cleanliness is very important because dirty bowls or other equipment will introduce bacteria to your recipes, lessening their longevity and efficacy.

Mortar and Pestle

Recommended for tough spices and roots. See "Coffee Grinder" section above.

Pans

Stainless-steel pans with heavy bottoms work best because they distribute heat evenly and resist burning and overheating. Most importantly, stainless steel stays inert, which prevents contamination and depletion. Contamination and depletion are likely to occur while using cast iron, aluminum, or copper. Make sure you have tight-fitting lids handy as well. They help retain the medicinal qualities of the volatile oils, otherwise these precious substances evaporate.

Stirring Spoon

Stainless-steel stirring spoons are preferred.

Stirring Wand

A stirring wand, usually made of nonreactive glass or ceramic, is used similarly to a cocktail stirrer to blend perfumes while discouraging cross-contamination.

Storage Bins

Storage bins are used to hold dried herbs. Dark glass containers with spring tops or stainless steel is ideal. Keeping light away from the herbs helps them retain their medicinal qualities longer. Some folk store them in brown paper bags, particularly when they are being dried. This works well only if you don't have moths or other pests that might try to eat the herbs.

Stove or Hotplate

A stove or hotplate is used for heating, drying, and simmering brews.

Mortar and pestle

Straining Devices

A straining device can be cheesecloth (muslin) stretched over a preserve or other wide-necked jar and secured with a rubber band or twine. I prefer to use a stainless-steel sieve.

Sun Tea Jars

Glass or plastic sun tea jars are used to brew herbs in sun- or moonlight.

Thermometers

Candy thermometers will work, but a meat probe is my first choice because it will not break as easily. Thermometers are essential when making soap, and are useful for checking temperatures during the creation of creams, salves, and healing balms.

Twine

Twine is good for tying herbs together at the stems before hanging them to dry, and for fixing muslin to a jar for straining. Hemp (marijuana) string is an excellent alternative for its strength and durability.

Whisk

A stainless-steel whisk is preferred.

Gathering and Drying Herbs

Suggestions to Urban Dwellers

For folk living in cities, apartments, or other tight spaces where land comes at a premium price, the primary source for gathering herbs will be specialty catalogs, health-food stores, and the Internet. Even within this commercial arena, the way you go about gathering is critical, and the relationships you develop can be meaningful, educational, and fun. Things to look for are as follows:

- Are the herbs ethically harvested? Be careful about barks and roots. Some, like Little John, are overharvested and face extinction.

- Are the herbs organically grown? This is the safest method for personal-care products and consumables.

- Are the herbs fresh and within their expiration date? They should have a bright color, strong scent, and no mold or mildew.

- Are the prices fair, without excessive markups? Do some research and compare prices.

- Are the herbs usually in stock, available without delays?

- Is the source convenient and practical for you?

- Is a knowledgeable person available to answer your questions?

Start out with a local shop, if possible. Then, as you become comfortable with creating your own brews, you can branch out into wholesale. Buying herbs in bulk saves big bucks! Other options include visiting your local farmer's market, or driving outside the city to support roadside farm stands. If you so choose, you can also grow your favorite herbs in pots on the windowsill, terrace, or even inside using grow lights.

Suggestions to Suburban and Rural Dwellers

If you are fortunate enough to have enough space to grow your own herbs, fruits, and vegetables, the following suggestions are for you. Please remember, when gathering Mother Nature's gifts, approach the plants with respect and thank them for sharing their healing energy with you.

Harvesting Leaves—Look for leaves of a consistent green color without brown or yellow spots. Harvest midmorning after the dew has evaporated. Gather leaves before the plant begins to flower. For plants that have long growing seasons, such as basil or oregano, pinch back the tops to prevent flowering. (Flowering takes energy away from the main body of the plant.) Keep herbs separated by type, and tie the stems loosely together in a bundle with twine or hemp string. Until you are very familiar with all of the herbs, it is best to label the bundles and date them as well. Hang them up to dry immediately after harvesting to prevent mildew or deterioration.

Hang the herb bundles stem up in an area with good circulation away from direct sunlight. The ideal temperature for the first twenty-four hours is ninety degrees, followed by seventy-five to eighty degrees the rest of the time. Most herbal bundles will dry between two to three weeks. Petals and leaves should feel light, crisp, and paperlike. If there are small buds or tiny leaves that may fall off during the drying time, create a roomy muslin bag to encase flowers and leaves and tie it loosely with twine or hemp string at the stems. This is particularly important with seed-dropping plants, such as fennel or sunflowers. When herbs are completely dry, store the whole leaf and stem away from direct sunlight in dark glass or stainless-steel airtight containers.

Harvesting Flowers—Flowers are extremely delicate. Select healthy flowers in the early afternoon during dry weather conditions. Take extra care not to bruise the petals, refrain from touching them, cut from the stem, and allow the flowers to drop into a basket. Dry smaller, more delicate flowers, such as lavender and chamomile, whole. You can hang them upside down tied with twine over a muslin cloth or large bowl or wrapped loosely with muslin to retain dried buds.

Use fresh flowers in the home whenever possible. You may also freeze them in an ice cube tray filled with spring water.

Harvesting Seeds—Collect seeds on a warm, dry day. Seeds need to dry in a warm, airy environment. Make provisions to catch the quickly drying seeds by placing a bowl or box underneath the hanging plants.

Harvesting Bark—Bark peels easiest on damp days. Choose a young tree or bush and, if possible, one that has already been pruned, cut, or taken down naturally by wind or stormy conditions to prevent damage or even death to the plant. Stripping too much bark from a tree will kill it. A thoughtful approach to Mother Nature's gifts is essential. Bark may harbor insects or moss, so wash it first and allow it to dry flat on waxed paper in a location that is well ventilated and away from direct sunlight.

Harvesting Roots—Roots are ready for collecting after the autumn harvest. Dig up roots after their plant has begun to wither and die. Extract the whole root while trying not to bruise it. Like bark, roots need to be cleaned before they are dried, and they also require ethical harvesting. Cut roots into small sections and dry in an oven set between 120 and 140 degrees. Turn and check them regularly; roots should feel light and airy like sawdust when fully dried. For marshmallow root, peel away the top layer of skin before drying in this manner.

Harvesting Berries—To harvest berries, use the same procedure as for bark. But remember, berries and fruits take a long time to dry—about twice as long as leaves. You will know when they are fully dry because they will become very light, wrinkled, and reduced in size by nearly half. Turn them frequently and check for leaking juices. Replace the paper they're drying on often to prevent the growth of bacteria or mold.

Storage

Since the flavors and volatile oils of herbs mix readily, store herbs separately. Label and date sterile tinted glass or stainless-steel containers and keep in a cool, dark place. The final quality of your herbs depends on how well they are stored and prepared.

Extraction Techniques

Decoctions

A decoction is the extraction of medicines from roots, bark, or berries. This is done by simmering the items in a covered pan of water over medium-low heat for thirty minutes to five hours, depending on the toughness of the herb.

Infusions

Infusions are either water- or oil-based. Both are designed to extract the volatile oils from the tender parts of herbs. Water-based infusions are *teas,* also called *tisanes* or *brews*. They are made by pouring boiling, distilled water over the herb and keeping it covered for thirty minutes to one hour.

Oil-based infusions are created by loosely packing herbal materials into a sterilized container, then pouring oil over the plants. Types of oils commonly preferred include olive oil, sunflower oil, almond oil, and safflower oil. Cover the container tightly, keep it away from direct sunlight, and give the jar a whirl every day for four to six weeks (depending on desired strength).

Tinctures

A tincture is the extraction of medicinal qualities from herbs using alcohol such as vodka, grain alcohol, rum, or ethanol.* The concentrations of volatile oils are greater in tinctures than in infusions or decoctions. A sterilized container with a cork or other tight-fitting top is filled to the top with loosely packed herbal material and pure alcohol. (Do not use rubbing alcohol as it is too harsh and drying for face and hair treatments, and smells so strong that it will overpower any attempts of scenting.) Place on a sunny windowsill and swirl gently every day for four to six weeks. Strain off the herbs or flowers and decant into a sterilized tinted bottle.

Specialties—Variations can be created by following the tincture procedure but replacing the alcohol with different liquids. Vinegar makes an acidic extract. Four Thieves Vinegar, a popular Hoodoo formula, uses garlic vinegar. Macerated† buds or flower petals added to vegetable glycerine makes an emollient, scented extract, and honey poured over macerated buds or petals produces a delicately scented, edible, emollient tincture that is terrific in love potions or in edible body rubs.

A Note About Animism

Knowing the proper harvesting, drying, handling, and extracting techniques is essential to Hoodoo, but there is more to conjur craft than the merely technical. Throughout this book will you find invocations that call upon ancestral or spiritual helpers, including a multicultural selection of goddesses and gods. Moreover, often within a trick or job you are given a chant or asked to recite a magickal

---

*Certain suppliers sell actual alcohol blends used in perfumery and the herbalism industry. Check appendix B for resources. Restrictions apply and make these professional-grade alcohols prohibitive for most, thus my recipes feature types more widely available.

†Maceration helps release the volatile oils and delicate scents of buds and flowers. To macerate buds, mash them up in a mortar with a pestle or pulse for thirty seconds in a mini food processor.

poem as you work your roots. Why? Speaking directly to the pot, fire, candle, and herb is essential. Remember, Hoodoo has strong roots in African animistic philosophy. Animistic philosophy considers each element or aspect of nature as being alive. Natural objects—whether they be stick, stone, root, or bone—have a universal energy force within them to which we are all connected. To simply use herbs, flowers, stones, bones, fire, or water without paying homage to its life force insults the spirits. I have included incantations and tricks to help get your jobs done right, and you should also feel free to make up your own.

chapter 2

It's in the Bag

Nothing makes my blood boil quicker than hearing the Austin Powers character perpetuate the myth that the word *mojo* is synonymous with sexuality. The glazed look, sophomoric grin, and gleam in his eye when he mentions his "mojo" is insulting. Numerous blues singers include the word *mojo* in their lyrics, but few people who aren't familiar with Hoodoo culture understand what a mojo hand is.

"Got My Mo-Jo Working"
by Preston Foster
Recorded by Ann Cole, Muddy Waters, et al.

I got my mo-jo working but it just won't work on you.
I got my mo-jo working but it just won't work on you.
I want to love you so till I don't know what to do.

I got my black cat bones all pure and dry,
got a four-leaf clover all hanging high.
I got my mo-jo working but it just won't work on you.
Oh, I want to love you so till I don't know what to do.

Got my hoodoo ashes all around your bed,
got my black snake boots underneath your head.
I got my mo-jo working but it just won't work on you.
Oh, I want to love you so till I don't know what to do.

I got a gypsy woman giving me advice,
got some red hot tips I have to keep on ice.
I got my mo-jo working but it just won't work on you.
Oh, I want to love you so till I don't know what to do.

I got my rabbit's foot, I know it's working right,
got your strand of hair, I keep it day and night.
I got my mo-jo working but it just won't work on you.
Oh, I want to love you so till I don't know what to do.

People of African descent have been looked upon as having a strong sense of sexual being, and perhaps this has led to confusing "mojo" with "sexuality." Now, don't get me wrong. A mojo can certainly be used to enhance sexual attraction, but that is only one of its multiple purposes. To thoroughly understand the meaning of a mojo, it is necessary that we turn away from popular culture and look instead to the root source: Mother Africa.

African Concepts

Ashe

Ashe is the invisible power of nature. Ashe is present inside herbal products and natural objects. Herbal teas, incense powders, spiritual washes, healing balms, healing soaps, healing charms, medicine bundles, and even the purposefully spoken word all contain ashe. The Igala people of Nigeria, for example, consider any type of plant life to be filled with medicinal powers. Medicines, whether designed to address spiritual or physical complaints, are believed to derive their power from ashe.

Consumable products (such as tea, washes, soap, and powders) are effective, yet they lack the long-term strength encapsulated in a *power object*. Power objects can be shields, masks, sculptures, amulets, or charms. Each type of power object is a conglomeration of different elements of ashe.

Both the Bamani Komo society masks and Boli figurative sculptures are encrusted with feathers and quills. The mystical powers of the bird and porcupine are bound and invited to share its ashe with the object. Encrustation is the result of feeding the power object. Food is important, for it sustains the life of the power object. Feeding may consist of ground stones or plants; leaves; feathers; ground bones; powerful animal skins, teeth, sexual organs, or horns; chicken blood; semen; or saliva.

Nkisi

Kongo power figures are called *nkisi* (*minkisi*, singular). Nkisi incorporate in them elements of the land, sky, water, or a combination of these. Nkisi (also called *charms*) are powered by nature spirits. They help people heal and they can serve as a safe spot or hiding place for the soul. They might contain seashells, feathers, nuts, berries, stones, bones, leaves, roots, or twigs. Nkisi are as diverse and plentiful as the illnesses that exist on earth.

The Yaka, Kongo, Teke, Suku, and Songhai (see Figure 3) pack a cavity in the belly of their sculptures with a wide array of ashe-containing materials: bones; fur; claws; dirt from an elephant's footprint; crocodile teeth, scales, and sex organs; lightning excreta (things touched by lightning); bones, flesh, and nail clippings of sorcerers; remnants of suicide victims and of warriors. The figurines are then covered with the skins of power animals: water buffalo, wild cats, lizards, antelope, and birds. They are also decorated with raffia, cloth, bells, beads, metal, and nails.

Nkisi nkondi

The best examples of these magickal figures or *accumulative sculptures* come from central Africa. The Yaka, Suku, and Kongo peoples prepare sachets made from either shells, baskets, pots, bottles, food tins, plastic bags, or leather bags. The medicine bags are then charged with an infinite variety of

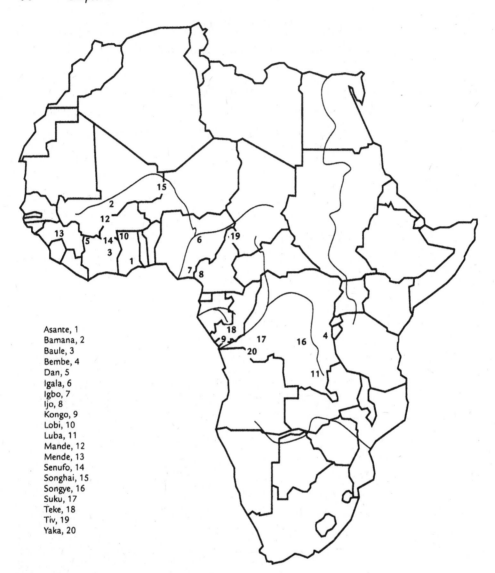

Asante, 1
Bamana, 2
Baule, 3
Bembe, 4
Dan, 5
Igala, 6
Igbo, 7
Ijo, 8
Kongo, 9
Lobi, 10
Luba, 11
Mande, 12
Mende, 13
Senufo, 14
Songhai, 15
Songye, 16
Suku, 17
Teke, 18
Tiv, 19
Yaka, 20

Figure 3: African language groups.

natural materials (although some are manmade, including glass and gunpowder). In *Flash of the Spirit,* Robert Farris Thompson describes the interior of power bags as looking through clear water at the bottom of a river. Thompson compares the bags to a miniature universe.

Nkisi Nkondi—Nkisi nkondi is a type of figure that nails are inserted into to bind its powers. Leaves and other medicines, combined with various elements, increase the strength of each. Each ingredient has an action on humans; the bringing together of various natural forces is the source of healing.

Ne Kongo, a cultural hero, carried the first healing medicines (nkisi) with him from heaven to earth. He prepared the medicines in a clay pot set on top of three stones or termite mounds. His actions founded the expertise that a healer (*nganga*) developed to dispense medicine. The healer's therapy involves the proper mixture of plants and elements.

Masters of Jiridon

Learning the proper way to mix plants and the elements takes many lessons. The lessons are not taught through an apprenticeship with a human as much as they are learned directly from the trees and plants themselves. *Jiridon* is the science of the trees. To learn jiridon, the seeker—whether hunter, warrior, or shaman—must spend ample time alone in the wilderness observing the workings of nature, including the expressions of animals and the whispers of the trees.

In early African American historical accounts, there are written records of people who spoke the language of the trees. They were called *tree whisperers*. Tree whisperers in the United States spend time living with and studying a single tree.

Tree whisperers are highly observant. They listen attentively to the reactions a tree has to things like the lashing of wind and to sunny, warm days. Eventually tree whisperers can hear the tree speaking quite clearly to them. The tree teaches those who will listen to be masters of jiridon. Masters of jiridon are also master herbalists and adept ecologists.

The following is an intriguing, first-person account of this ancient practice collected by Ruth Bass, a white Mississippian, in 1930. While Ruth Bass was very interested in Hoodoo and conjuration, some of her side comments reflect the cultural bias prevalent at that time. Yet her passion for the subject matter resulted in this very special story, which will transport you to a different space and time.

> In these swamp-lands I have often found traces of the old magic called tree-talking. Here magic becomes a still more imponderable thing and carries with it a philosophy that is more or less pantheistic. It had its

roots in the friendship of the jungle man for the mysterious, animated, and beautiful world in which he lived. The swamp people, like the jungle men, recognize life in everything about them. They impart a consciousness and a wisdom to the variable moods of material things, wind, water, trees.

Details are vague and hard to find, but, so far as I have been able to ascertain, the basis of tree-talking is the cultivation of a friendship with a certain tree—any tree of any species will do . . . It is simply magic, a magic that is still found in the Bayou Pierre swamp-land today. Among my acquaintances I number one tree-talker. The other conjurers point to Divinity when I mention tree-talking. More than once I have visited his cabin on the edge of the swamp, burning with curiosity, and I learned nothing tangible. I resolved to try again and on a warm afternoon in autumn I followed the swamp path along the bayou until I found him—and what he lived by.

Old Divinity sat on the little front porch of his cabin at the very edge of the swamp. It was late October, dry and still with a low-hanging sky. Leaves were beginning to drift from the big water-oak that dominated his clean-swept yard. A frizzly cock and three varicolored hens scratched and clucked in the shriveled leaves under a fig-tree near the porch. Six white pigeons sat in a row on the roof sunning their ruffled feathers. A brown leaf, whirled from the oak by a sudden gust of wind, fell on Divinity's knee. He laid a gnarled old hand on the leaf and held it there. A swarm of sulphur-yellow butterflies floated by. Silently, aimlessly, purposefully, they drifted eastward. Divinity sighed.

. . .

"Bes'tuh stay in one place an' take whut de good Lawd sends, lak a tree." Here was my chance, it seemed.

"Yes, there's something of magic about a tree. I've heard that, for whoever can understand, there's a thing called tree-talking, ever hear of it, Divinity?"

"Did Ah! Ma gran'mammy brung tree-tawkin' from de jungle. Ah's from a tree-tawkin fambly, an' Ah ain't be livin' undah this watah oak evah since ah surrendah foh nuthin'." I felt that I was near to looking into that almost inscrutable Negro soul. Here were pages of precious folk-knowledge and all of it in danger of passing with ninety-six-year-old Divinity. What could I say to draw out a bit of his jungle lore? I said nothing.

The old man fumbled through his numerous pockets for his sack of home-mixed tobacco and clay pipe. A flame flared up from his match, then the fragrance of burning deer-tongue slipped away in the soft air. Divinity rubbed his dry old hands together. I was afraid to seem too eager. Silence lay between us. Suddenly there came from the swamp pines and cypresses that crowded upon the little clearing, a soft murmur, a sound like the whimper of a company of comfortless creatures passing through the trees. We felt no wind and there was no perceptible movement in the treetops; but the gray swamp-moss swayed gently as though it were endowed with the power of voluntary motion.

"Heah dat? If yo heah murmurin' in de trees when de win' ain't blowin' dem's perrits. Den effen yo know how tuh lissen yo kin git dey wisdom."

"Spirits of what, Divinity?"

"Why, de sperrits ob trees! Dey rustle de leaves tuh tract tenshun, den dey speaks tuh yo."

"So trees have spirits, have they?"

"Cose dey does." The old man withered me with a glance, puffed out a cloud of fragrant smoke and proceeded, in his slow old voice, to tell me a few things about spirits. Everything has spirit, he told me. What is it in the jimson-weed that cures asthma if it isn't the spirit of the weed? What is that in the buckeye that can drive off rheumatism unless it's spirit? Yes, he assured me, everything has spirit. To prove it he could take me to a certain spring that was haunted by the ghost of a bucket. Now if that bucket didn't have a spirit where did its ghost come from? To Divinity man is only a rather insignificant partaker in the adventure called life . . . To him it is stupid to think of all other things as being souless, insensitive, dead. "Is eberything cept'n man daid den? Dat redburd yondah—" A cardinal, like a living flame, flashed into a dark pine. "Dat black bitch ob yourn—what she got?" Old Divinity hit home. I stroked the soft head the old spaniel rested on my knee.

. . .

"It's a pity more men don't know this," I agreed, half to myself. "Yessum. It's a sho pity," Divinity agreed, half to himself. Then I asked Divinity how men could learn this truth of his. He assured me that some men were born with it, though most people had to find it out for themselves.

"What about you, Divinity, were you born with wisdom, or did you learn it?"

"Me? Ah's de gran'son ob a witch," he answered proudly. "An' Ah's bawn wid a veil ovah ma face. A pusson what bawn wid a veil is er dub-ble-sighter." A double-sighter, he told me gravely, was a person who had two spirits, one that wanders and one that stays in the body. He was "strong in de haid." Divinity told me seriously, mixing great truths with sheerest fancy, he could see the wind . . .

The sun was reddening in the west. A breeze had sprung up, bring-ing a continual soft murmur from the swamp trees. Old Divinity sat silent. His pipe had gone out. No wonder he sat and thought of death, so lonely and so old, with no one to look to.

"Do you get very lonely, Divinity, now that all your children are gone?"

"No'm. When Jessmin, ma baby, lef', Ah felt sad at fust, but now Ah sets an' tawks tuh mase'f, er de trees an' de win' . . . Bettah tuh stay in one place an' take what de good Lawd sen', lak a tree . . ."

Dusk was creeping through the swamp. I rose to go . . . "Winter! Ah, winter, touch that little cabin lightly," I wished, as I turned through the darkening swamp, and left the old, old grandson of a witch sitting on his porch, while a lone killdeer called up the wind. Mojo? Call it what you will. The magic of the swamp had come upon me. I found myself talking with the wind!

Bilongo and Mooyo

The Bamana of western Sudan use power objects, such as medicine bags, that are imbued with ashe for addressing various ills. These objects are used to express power as warriors, to fight supernatural malaise, and to foil evil intentions. The bags contain *bilongo* (medicine) and a *mooyo* (soul).

New World Mojo Bags—Enslaved Kongo and Angolan medicine people brought the concepts of bilongo and mooyo together in the New World in *mojo bags*. The mojo bags are prepared by a specialist akin to a *nganga* (priest/priestess) called a *rootworker* or *conjurer* in Hoodoo practice. The objects within each bag guide the spirits to understand the reason their help is sought.

Materials with particularly strong ashe, such as dirt from human or animal footprints, are placed in a flannel bag, which is referred to simply as a *flannel* or, more commonly, a *mojo bag*. (This practice, called *foot track magick*, survived slavery and is alive in American Hoodoo.) Other materials encased in a mojo include ephemera associated with the dead: coffin nails, ground bones, or graveyard dirt. The objects—whether stick, stone, root, or bone—have a corresponding spirit and particular medicine ascribed to it. To mix the various parts properly, recipes and techniques called *daliluw* are used. Herbal chemistry is involved, but some daliluw require rituals during preparation. The ritual enhances the daliluw by activating or controlling the energies that animate the world.

New World nkisi go by a variety of names: *mojo, hand, flannel, toby,* and *gris-gris* are a few. Whatever the name, one thing that they are not is a simple metaphor for a sex organ or sexuality. Sorry, Austin.

Feeding the He, Feeding the She—I love feeding my *he* and my *she*. What are these objects of my affection? A male and female pair of matched lodestones. The he is typically masculine, with his slightly pointed, phallic shape. The she is rounded in the way of a woman's belly or breasts. The two need to match up so that not only is one male and the other female in shape, but one also needs a positive draw while the other should be negative or receptive.

So what's the deal? The he and the she are central to the art of Hoodoo and often associated with mojos. It is through the magnetic power of these two stones and their powerful attraction to one another that we are able to draw what we need to us. So when you purchase a pair of lodestones, make sure they are from a manufacturer who cares enough to make sure you truly have a male-female/positive-negative pair (see appendix B).

Because mojo bags are alive with ashe and contain a mooyo, they must be fed. To do this, sprinkle the appropriate feeding powder over the contents of the mojo. This gives the bag a magickal charge. American hoodoos feed their mojos powdered herbs, magnetic sand, herbal oils, dusts, and foot track dirt—in combination or singly as needed. The owner of the bag must continue to feed it periodically to sustain its life force. This feeding is coordinated carefully to days connected with the gods and goddesses. Likewise, feed your lodestones each week with magnetic sand on a corresponding day and moon suitable to the job at hand.

Mojos have many purposes. The following is a sampling of mojo medicine bags.

FAST LUCK MOJO

Green drawstring flannel
Feathers
1 whole nutmeg

Red lodestone
8 dimes

Feeding Powder
1 tablespoon ground
   five-finger grass

2 tablespoons magnetic sand
1 tablespoon ground nutmeg

Put the feathers, nutmeg, lodestone, and dimes in the flannel.

To make the feeding powder, mix together the five-finger grass, magnetic sand, and nutmeg in a small metal or glass bowl. Feed immediately with one teaspoon of the powder and repeat on Sundays as needed.

MONEY DRAW MOJO

This recipe uses John the Conqueror root, which is named for a legendary slave who showed remarkable courage and strength in the face of adversity. John the Conqueror root is an essential ingredient in the hoodoo's medicine bag as it embodies the survival spirit of our people. This bag is designed not only to draw money, but to help win court cases and to bring luck in games of chance.

Green drawstring flannel
8 whole cloves
8 whole allspice
1 parrot feather

1 small piece peridot (bead or
   stone), charged
1 John the Conqueror root
1 whole nutmeg

Feeding Powder
⅛ cup powdered John the
   Conqueror root

¼ cup powdered chamomile flowers
4 drops chamomile essential oil

Place the cloves, allspice, feather, peridot, John the Conqueror root, and nutmeg into the flannel.

To make the feeding powder, combine the John the Conqueror root and chamomile powders in a small metal or glass bowl. Sprinkle the chamomile oil over the powder. Feed your mojo with one teaspoon of this powder each Thursday.

STAY AWAY FROM ME MOJO

This is to fight off folks who just don't understand the meaning of "no," and to fend off evil intentions or stalkers.

Orange drawstring flannel
Pinch of cascara sagrada bark chips
3 senna pods
Stay Away Powder (recipe follows)

Pinch of graveyard dirt (see note)
1 piece of dragon's blood
1 piece of black onyx

Place the cascara sagrada bark, senna pods, graveyard dirt, dragon's blood, and onyx in the flannel. Bury the bag for one week.

Meanwhile, make the Stay Away Powder. After one week, feed the bag with one teaspoon of this powder. Feed on Mondays as needed. Carry the bag on your person.

Note: See chapter 6 for more information and a substitute for graveyard dirt.

STAY AWAY POWDER

¼ cup chicken bone meal (see note)
⅛ cup powdered nettles

⅛ cup powdered verbena
5 drops patchouli essential oil

Mix the chicken bone meal, nettles, and verbena together in a small metal or glass bowl. Sprinkle the patchouli oil over this mixture.

Note: You can obtain chicken bone meal either from a garden center or grind dry chicken bones yourself.

PEACEFUL HAND

Bad vibes at work, tension at school, arguments at home—they all take their toll. This recipe combines herbs, roots, and stones with peaceful correspondences.

Purple or red flannel
3 myrrh pieces
4 frankincense tears
Pinch of dried chamomile flowers

Pinch of dried angelica root
1 amethyst stone, charged
Peace Powder (recipe follows)

Place the myrrh, frankincense, chamomile, angelica, and amethyst in the flannel.

Make the Peace Powder. Feed immediately with one teaspoon of the powder and repeat on Sundays as needed.

PEACE POWDER

¼ cup pulverized lavender buds
¼ cup powdered violet leaves

3 drops angelica essential oil
2 drops lavender essential oil

Mix the lavender buds and violet leaves together in a small metal or glass bowl. Sprinkle the angelica and lavender oils over the mixture.

ATTRACTION MOJO

This recipe is for when you want to shine, stand out, or draw folks near. Good for job interviews, dating, public speaking, and competitions.

Yellow or orange flannel
Whole dried lime
Pinch of lemon verbena
1 small charged citrine stone

Small pair of male and female
  lodestones
2 dried calendula flowers
Attraction Powder (recipe follows)

Place the lime, lemon verbena, citrine stone, lodestones, and calendula in the flannel.

Make the Attraction Powder. Feed immediately with one teaspoon of this powder and repeat on Sundays as needed.

ATTRACTION POWDER

⅛ cup powdered orange rind
⅛ cup powdered damiana
¼ cup magnetic sand

4 drops attar of roses
2 drops bitter almond essential oil
3 drops sweet orange essential oil

Mix together the orange and damiana powders in a small metal or glass bowl. Add the magnetic sand. Sprinkle the oils over the mixture.

UNHEX MOJO

Red or purple flannel
1 John the Conqueror root

1 piece of agate, charged
Pinch of dried St. John's wort

Feeding Powder

2 tablespoons powdered hyssop
2 tablespoons powdered rosemary
1 teaspoon powdered angelica root

3 drops attar of roses or quality rose fragrance oil
3 drops frankincense essential oil

Place the John the Conqueror root, agate, and St. John's wort into the flannel.

To make the feeding powder, mix together the hyssop, rosemary, and angelica in a small metal or glass bowl. Add the attar of roses and frankincense oil one drop at a time, stirring between each drop.

Sprinkle on one teaspoon of the powder and repeat on the day of the sun (Sundays) as needed.

Nation Sacks

We end this chapter with the nation sack. A woman's nation sack is strictly "women's business." If a man should touch the sack, he will meet with ill fortune. Nation sacks typically act as protection for women and children; sometimes they are used to draw love.

Nation sacks were once only found in the area of Memphis, Tennessee. They grew into prominence there in the early twentieth century. Yet the nation sack is full of Africanisms, and stems from the secret women's societies of certain West African tribes. There are numerous secret societies in Africa (both male and female), many of which negotiate between the human and the spirit world. If anyone were to reveal the secrets that bind the group, they, like the man who touches a nation sack, will live to regret it.

The following song by Robert Johnson mentions a nation sack. Robert Johnson was a prominent Delta blues singer who frequently mentions Hoodoo practice in his songs. Johnson claims to have sold his soul to the devil to become the great singer and musician that he was.

"Come on in My Kitchen"
(excerpt from Take 1)
by Robert Johnson

Mmm mmm mmm mmm mmm mmm
mmm mmm mmm mmm mmm
Mmm mmm mmm mmm mmm
mmm mmm mmm mmm
You better come on
in my kitchen
babe, it's goin' to be rainin' outdoors

Ah, the woman I love
took from my best friend
Some joker got lucky
stole her back again
You better come on
in my kitchen
baby, it's goin' to be rainin' outdoors

Oh-ah, she's gone
I know she won't come back
I've taken the last nickel
out of her nation sack
You better come on
in my kitchen
babe, it's goin' to be rainin' outdoors

Oh, can't you hear that wind howl?
Oh-y, can't you hear that wind howl?
You better come on
in my kitchen
baby, it's goin' to be rainin' outdoors

Part of the power of the nation sack is secrecy. Another significant feature is that when it is used to draw love, often a photograph, fingernail or hair clippings, pieces of clothing, and even semen from the man are included in the sack. Secrecy combined with the act of hunting and gathering appropriate yet difficult-to-obtain materials for the sack build intensity that produces a particularly potent charm.

LOVE DRAW NATION SACK

Think hard before doing this trick; you'll have difficulty getting rid of this man or woman after working it!

Red flannel
Pair of male and female blue
    lodestones
1 piece of orris (Queen Elizabeth)
    root

5 dried red rosebuds
5 pennies
Personal items from the person
    you are drawing to you (see note)

Feeding Powder
2 tablespoons powdered lemon
    verbena
Handful of crumbled rose petals

3 drops attar of roses
3 drops lavender essential oil
2 drops angelica essential oil

Place the lodestones, orris root, rosebuds, pennies, and personal items in the flannel.

To make the feeding powder, blend together the ingredients in the order given: lemon verbena, rose petals, attar of roses, lavender oil, and angelica oil. Feed immediately and on the day of Venus and Oshun (Fridays) as needed.

Ladies, keep this sack in your bra, under your garter belt, or under your belt. It must remain private and untouched by others!

Note: This can be a tiny photograph, lock of hair, a button, or soil from the bottom of the person's shoes.

chapter 3

The Broom in Hoodoo

The humble broom holds an elevated position in African and African American folklore, magicko-religious beliefs, and spiritual practices. Most folks are familiar with our reverence for the broom because of its prominent role in traditional African American weddings. The jumping of the broom ceremony, for example, has been embraced as a vestige of Black heritage. Yet, looking into the elaborate broom etiquette and customs of early African Americans and hoodoos only provides a partial understanding of the role of the broom. For an in-depth understanding of the relationship between brooms and Black folks, we must journey much further back in time. Tracing the broom's usage back across the Atlantic sheds the brightest light on its complex articulation in African and African American culture.

Brooms and Africans

In our mundane lives, we take brooms for granted. They are there when we need them—in fact, they always seem to have been there. Magickally, brooms are often thought of in terms of European witchcraft: wild rides under the full moon and sexually charged sabbat rituals. While Europeans have a venerable history and a genuine fondness for broom magick and broommaking that goes all the way back to the Middle Ages, broom corn itself originated in central Africa.

Broom corn (*Sorghum vulgare technicum*) is also called *sorghum*. Sorghum is a stiff grass and is used extensively in the production of molasses. Molasses is a significant ingredient in African American magick and is the sacrificial offering to the goddess Oya and god Shango. Molasses also plays a key role in African American soul food cooking, most notably in the preparation of baked beans and gingerbread.

Broom corn is related to palm and raffia, other highly valued materials and commodities used in West African ceremony, ritual, and art. Palm is used for a number of purposes: food, wine, oil, soap, housing, basketry, crafts, ceremony, and ritual. Dragon's blood, a resin from palm trees, is also used in Hoodoo as a potent incense. It is filled with powerful intent and is capable of serious juju.

Raffia and palm fibers or fronds are symbolically interchangeable in magicko-religious practice. They, along with natural grasses, broom, and dragon's blood resin, represent the wild, untamed nature of the forest. As such, they are denizens

of power, for grasses embody and contain the living spirits of the forest.

Sub-Saharan Africans (the primary ancestors of African Americans) don't concern themselves with taming or controlling nature. *Nature* isn't really a word found in the primary traditional languages of West Africa. Instead, the word *wilderness* prevails as both a place and a concept.

The Negotiators

The gifted negotiators who mediate between the wilderness spirits and civilized society are hunters and metalsmiths, and to some extent healers, diviners, and warriors. Since so many tribes, clans, groups, and societies live in very close proximity to the wilderness (or forest, bush, or savannah), a strict separation between what is considered wild and civilized is enforced. Yet the hunter, metalsmith, healer, diviner, and warrior regularly cross the boundaries that separate these distinct worlds, helping their commu-

Home cleansing broom

Powerful Hoodoo Grasses

Van Van is a popular name for various Hoodoo formulas. The primary source of Van Van's scent and spiritual power is either palmarosa, citronella, lemon grass, or ginger, grasses of the *Cymbopogon* (Sprerg.) genus and the Poaceae family. These aromatic grasses flourish on lands where our people have traditionally thrived. These grasses, used alone or combined, form the herbal base of Van Van and Chinese Wash (see page 58).

Khus Khus is another popular name for Hoodoo blends. It is so named because of one of its chemical components, khusinol. Khus Khus refers to vetiver, as vetiver is called *Khus* in older books. Vetiver has a deep, earthy, relaxing aroma. Chemically it acts as a fixative; spiritually it strengthens and adds sensuality. In present-day India, oil from the wild vetiver grass is used to make a perfume called *Ruh Khus*, or "Oil of Tranquility."

You will discover a variety of spellings for vetiver, including *vertivert* and *vertiver*. To be certain of the authenticity of the vetiver used in recipes for Khus Khus, look for the botanical name *Chrysopogon zizanioides* (L.) Roberty, not *Vetiveria zizanioides* (L.) Nash or *Andropogon muricatus* Retz.

nities integrate the power of nature into their daily lives. (For more on this topic, refer to chapter 6.)

Generally, these arbitrators recognize and honor the subgroups of beings that reside in the wilderness. These beings are somewhat akin to the fairies or pixies of northern Europe, yet they are believed to be more grotesquely misshapen. They are human inversions of sorts, and even walk and do other things backwards.

Some species of the forest folk in particular are either invoked or repelled by broomlike, grass-clad masqueraders. These include the following:

Bori: Bori are a high-population species who live in various habitats of the Hausa people. They look somewhat like humans, but have hoofed feet. They also shapeshift readily and are known to be fond of taking the form of snakes.

Eloko: Eloko are people-eating dwarves that live among the Nkundo people of Zaire. They live in the hollows of trees in densely forested areas. Eloko blend in well with their environment since they are covered in grass and their clothing is made from leaves. These dwarves are minute and green and easily mistaken for grass. If that happens though, they become infuriated. Only a hunter's magickal prowess can dispel an angered eloko.

Dodo: The dodo is another forest spirit that hangs with the Hausa people. This is another species of shapeshifter that often takes on the form of snakes. The dodo are ravenously hungry for human flesh and can become angered quite easily. The very mention of the metal iron dispels them.

Abatwa: Abatwa are much smaller than the common fairy. They hide under a blade of grass; they sleep inside anthills. Typically, the entire species rides into a village on a single horse. They murder their victims with poisoned arrows.

It is only on rare occasions and for specific reasons that these types of spirits of the wilderness are invited to be a part of civilized society. These occasions include annual performances, harvest festivals, fertility rites, and purification activities—including sweeping.

Forest spirits are believed to cower around the doors of human beings' homes, waiting for discarded food, drinks, or clothing to bring to their own villages and families. It is frowned upon by villagers to sweep dirt out the front door or even to throw wash water there because it would encourage the spirits' presence. To repel or dispel tiny spirits who hang about doorways and stoops, both are meticulously cleansed on a daily basis using spiritually charged herbs and special waters (this procedure is shared in the next chapter). The cleansing of doorways and front stairs is prevalent in many parts of West Africa and exercised by many practitioners of Vodoun and Hoodoo in the African diaspora.

The Go society has a mask and costume called a *Ga Wree Wree*. The Ga Wree Wree is a fierce symbol of the powers that lurk within the forest. The mask contains leopard teeth and raffia and it is primarily red—the essential color of life force (blood). The huge bell-shaped skirt of the costume is made entirely of raffia. A Ga Wree Wree performer walks or sits immersed in the grassy folds of the skirt.

According to unwritten law, a Ga Wree Wree is a creature that oversees and then passes judgment on the activities of the community.

The Dan people of the Ivory Coast have their own masks and costumes, which almost always feature grass (such as raffia) to indicate the power of the forest: *Wo Puh Gle* is a talking entertainer, while *Yeh to Gle* is an authority figure. The Kuba of Zaire are renowned for their ability to transform raffia into cloth. They also fabricate raw forest materials such as *makadi* (leaflets from a palm tree) into costumes. The Boma clan of Ijo village in Rivers State, Nigeria, has a time of the year when costumed performers

Raffia-clad Nigerian dancer

wear a mask of natural raffia and other forest material. The performer moves from one end of the town to another like a gigantic broom, sweeping the community clean of its annual build-up of pollution, whether it be spiritual or physical. These groups and many others throughout West Africa have a vital tradition of wearing costumes constructed of natural grasses and straw to enhance their otherworldly duties.

These examples highlight a strong appreciation for broom, grass, straw, and raffia as parts of African ritual. Ritualistic use of natural materials allows us to see them as "other," or distinct from normal day-to-day life. A fear of brooms remained intact well after enslavement; as we will see later, respect for the broom was a remarkable characteristic of early African American life. A peek into the Yoruban orisha Obaluaiye brings greater understanding of the fear and foreboding that brooms incite.

Obaluaiye

Obaluaiye is a fierce god who has the power to either create epidemics like small-pox, or heal them as he sees fit. Obaluaiye's scarlet-clad followers are feared and dreaded. It is believed that devotees of Obaluaiye can strike down people who walk around at high noon under the bright sun.

Epidemic-causing diseases like smallpox are dispensed by Obaluaiye when he feels the need to raise the consciousness of society. When the fierce god is angered or appalled by society, he uses his special broom to spread *yamoti* (sesame seeds) on the earth. The seeds are spread by an ever-widening, concentric sweeping motion. As his broom touches the dirt, dust rises into the air. The seeds ride on the sweeping winds and hit people hard, leaving horrible pockmarks in their wake. The horrific tool of Obaluaiye is a magickal broom called a *shashara.*

In Benin, worship of Obaluaiye is called *Sakpata.* Sakpata worshippers are also in Cuba and Brazil. The shashara (brooms) of Cuba are extraordinarily beautiful. Reflecting their Dahomean style, the brooms have a special magickal handle covered with a blood-red cloth and heavily embroidered with intricate cowry shell patterns. In Bahia, Brazil, the broom is called *ja,* whereas in the Dahomean language it is *ha.* The ja is exalted to the level of nobility. The whisk broom transcends utilitarian function, becoming instead an elaborately decorated power object approaching the beauty of finely crafted jewelry.

When Obaluaiye appears in Bahian temples, he doesn't carry a club, arrow, or spear for protection. His single weapon is his ja. Obaluaiye's broom is paraded about with flowing movements by his followers; this weapon is at once beautiful and terrifying. The motions can suggest both the dispersal of disease-causing sesame seeds and the sweeping away of them.

The Bahian shashara is an unusual, yet potent royal scepter. The fierceness of forest energy is further enhanced by the *ade iko* (all-raffia crown) and the complementary *ewu iko* (all-raffia gown) worn by devotees. These are filled with the dual powers of Obaluaiye and the spirits of the forest.

Nana Buku, whose followers live north of Fon, Benin, is Obaluaiye's mother. Her symbolic image sits on a baobab tree shrine. She is represented by a conical piece of earth, which wears the clothing of the spirits: raffia. She appears to be a large, benevolent whisk broom.

The broom is a powerful tool with many uses. The gods and goddesses who animate it with their powers make the broom an object that can generate luck, domestic bless, purification, destruction, disease, despair, and sadly, even death.

Brooms and African Americans

I remember when I was a girl that broom straw was respected for its curative powers by my family. For example, my ears were pierced using a needle and thread by my aunt. The thread was knotted and left in my ear for six weeks of healing. Then a tiny piece of broom straw was singed and inserted into my ear for another six to eight weeks. The broom straw was believed to form a core, thus sealing off the hole so that the pierced ear would never close. This special process of piercing, knotting, and inserting broom straw was used to fight infection and scarring.

In the book *Folklore from Adams County Illinois,* several other ways that broom straw is used for healing are described. Primarily, broom straw is cited as a potent herb that can be used for lancing warts. Broom straw is then placed on top of the lanced wart in the shape of a cross to encourage complete healing.

Folklore from Adams County Illinois is but one volume in Dr. Harry Middleton Hyatt's exhaustive research into Hoodoo, African American, and European American folkloric traditions, customs, and beliefs. In this early Hyatt book, an entire chapter is devoted to brooms and sweeping. A few of the entries that describe the wild, unpredictable quality of brooms are quite telling of their connection to West African beliefs, and Mande beliefs in particular. The Mande language survived slavery in a creolized form by the Gullah people of the Carolina lowlands, so it is no wonder that Mande beliefs regarding brooms have flourished in Hoodoo and the African American community at large. Georgia's sea coast islands and the Carolina lowlands together hold a vital link to African America's connection with tribal West Africa and is one of the major bases for Hoodoo (see Figure 4 and Tables 1 and 2).

Brooms should be treated with respect. Several of Hyatt's informants warn that resting a broom improperly invites injury, pain, or loss. In particular, resting a broom on the bed is believed to cause the sleeping person to die. Broom straws should be stored facing upward. Storing a broom with its straws resting on the floor brings bad luck.

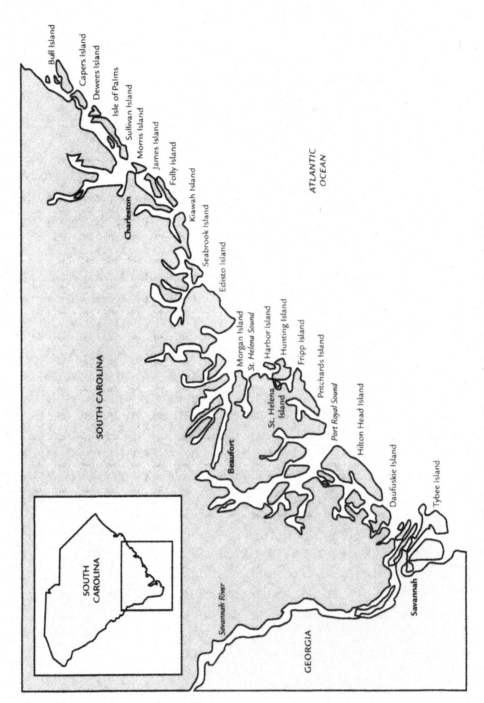

Figure 4: The Sea Coast Islands of Georgia and South Carolina where the Gullah people settled.

TABLE 1

Enslaved Africans Imported from Africa and the West Indies into Charleston, South Carolina, 1807–1816

Coastal region	Cargoes with count	No. of slaves	Cargoes without count	Total cargoes	Total slaves (est.)	% of subtotal With others	% of subtotal Without others
Senegambia	113	14,419	30	143	18,093	15.8	19.7
Sierra Leone	34	5,225	2	36	5,533	4.8	6.0
Windward Coast	85	12,925	22	107	15,879	13.8	17.3
Gold Coast	73.5	10,597	12	85.5	12,268	10.7	13.4
Bight of Benin	5	1,162	1	6	1,394	1.2	1.5
Bight of Biafra	10	2,171	1	11	2,303	2.0	2.5
Angola	133	33,103	11	144	35,812	31.2	39.0
Mozambique-Madagascar	2	473	0	2	473	0.4	0.5
Others*	107.5	17,232	36	143.5	23,033	20.1	
Subtotal	563	97,307	115	678	114,788	100.0	99.9
West Indies†	187	6,605	2	189	6,676		
Total	750	103,912	117	867	121,464		

*Refers to Africa; no specific region is identified.

†Does not include the many ships that brought fewer than 10 slaves and is thus an underestimate.

Source: Marquetta L. Goodwine and Clarity Press Gullah Project, eds., *The Legacy of Ibo Landing: Gullah Roots of African American Culture* (Atlanta, GA: Clarity Press, Inc., 1998), 56.

TABLE 2
African Origins of Practices of Blacks on Georgia Coast

Region	Major tribes	Traits		Citations	
		No.	%	No.	%
Senegambia		2	0.8	40	2.8
Sierra Leone	Mandingo	5	2.0	19	1.4
Windward Coast	Vai	6	2.5	37	2.6
Gold Coast	Ashanti	69	28.4	310	22.1
Bight of Benin	Dahomey	76	31.3	425	30.3
	Yoruba				
	Ewe				
Bight of Biafra	Ibo	58	23.9	336	24.0
	Ibibio				
	Fang				
Congo-Angola	Mpongwe	27	11.1	235	16.8
	Bantu				
Subtotal		243	100.0	1,402	100.0
West Africa		24		134	
Total		267		1,536	

Note: Traits and citations for Nigeria have been divided equally between the Bight of Benin and the Bight of Baifra. Percentage is based on subtotal and excludes West Africa.

Source: Marquetta L. Goodwine and Clarity Press Gullah Project, eds., *The Legacy of Ibo Landing: Gullah Roots of African American Culture* (Atlanta, GA: Clarity Press, Inc., 1998), 64.

How a broom is approached is also a subject of much lore. If you step over a broom or if it falls as you start to leave, you may expect death to follow. Carrying a broom inside a house is a sign that death is coming to descend on the family.

However, proper handling of a broom brings luck, happiness, and prosperity. If you go to look at a home for rent or purchase, informants advise you to carry your broom under your arm or even throw it into a window so it enters before you do. Holding your personal broom under your arm is also a shield against arguments and domestic unrest. If arguments or fights occur, go outside with the

"New Orleans Superstitions"

"The Negro's terror of a broom is of very ancient date—it may have an African origin. It was commented upon by Moreau de Saint-Mery in his work on San Domingo, published in 1796. 'What especially irritates the Negro,' he wrote, 'is to have a broom passed over any part of his body. He asks at once whether the person imagined that he was dead, and remains convinced that the act shortens his life.'

"Very similar ideas concerning the broom linger in New Orleans. To point either end of a broom at a person is deemed bad luck; and many an ignorant man would instantly knock down or violently abuse the party who should point a broom at him. Moreover, the broom is supposed to have mysterious power as a means of getting rid of people. 'If you are pestered by visitors whom you would wish never to see again, sprinkle salt on the floor after they go, and sweep it out by the same door through which they have gone and they will never come back.' To use a broom in the evening is bad luck: *balayer le soir, on balaye sa fortune* (to sweep in the evening is to sweep your good luck away), remains a well-quoted proverb . . ."

Reprinted from the book *A Treasury of Afro-American Folklore* by Harold Courlander. Copyright © 1976, 1996 by Harold Courlander. Appears by permission of the publisher, Marlowe & Company.

broom tucked under your arm and throw it inside the door. The first thing to enter a new home should be your broom.

The etiquette and superstitions described by the so-called "Negroes" in *Folklore from Adams County Illinois* is intricate. It is also consistent with the findings reported by Lafcadio Hearn in the above sidebar ("New Orleans Superstitions," originally published in 1886) and also found by Moreau de Saint-Mery in San Domingo, such as the following:

- If you sweep while you have company, you are sending bad luck toward your guests. Sweeping when you have company is a sign of bad manners and means you want the company to leave.

- Sweeping after dark will bring sorrow, poverty, and bad luck.

- Sweeping dirt out the front door is ill advised. Dirt either goes out the back, or it is discarded in running water or buried. (Most forest spirits, after all, are believed to not be able to cross running water.)

- A person hit by a broom will be arrested or will have other forms of bad fortune.

- A broom falling across a doorway indicates that you are about to step into an unknown, foreign, or strange territory. When an accidental fall of the broom occurs, it is best to walk the way the nature spirits do: backwards.

Even the days when sweeping occurs should be carefully considered. Sweeping is not advised on the day of the moon/Isis (Monday) or the day of Astarte/Yemoya-Olokun/Oshun/Venus/Erzulie (Friday). Bad luck is ensured for an entire year if you dare sweep on New Year's Day.

> Sweeping out of the door after sundown is a sure sign that you are sweeping somebody's soul out.
>
> —Ruth Bass, "Mojo"
> from interview with hoodoo Old Divinity

Interestingly enough, Chinese folklore concerning brooms is almost identical to the beliefs of Africans and African Americans. Brooms are believed to be posed with a spirit in both cultures. There are many prohibitions regarding the use of brooms. For example, brooms cannot be used for games or cleaning altars. Hitting someone with a broom is thought to bring many years of bad luck to the person hit. Brooms are used to increase gambling luck and for unhexing a person. They are also used in certain rituals and ceremonies.

In light of the dense collection of broom lore in Africa, the Americas, and beyond, jumping the broom makes a lot of sense. For as you jump the broom, you are taking a leap from the wild world of being single into a more settled lifestyle of domesticity. The broom is a symbolic boundary between opposite worlds.

As a hoodoo, never take your broom for granted. Store it with respect. Replace it as soon as it appears to be worn down, and never, ever burn it. You will incur the wrath of the fierce gods and goddesses if you do.

Broommaking is an art form that is currently enjoying a revival. There are several wonderful companies that sell handcrafted brooms (see appendix B). I would advise having a round witch's broom for spiritual cleansing; it is suggestive of the womb of the Great Mother Nana Buku. You can also try the recipe below for making your own ritual whisk broom. The Magickal Whisk Broom is helpful for spiritually cleansing small areas, performing exorcisms, or even getting rid of poltergeists.

WHISK BROOM RITUAL

Magickal Whisk Broom (recipe follows)

Make the Magickal Whisk Broom.

Lay your handmade whisk broom outside in the grass and let it sit overnight under the light of the moon.

First thing in the morning when the broom is covered with dew, sprinkle the blessed waters of nature gently throughout your house. Do this while saying the following incantation:

> Spirits of the wilderness,
> I appeal to you,
>
> Bring into my home
> All that is shiny and new.
>
> Spread hope and prosperity,
> Contained within this dew.
>
> Like this special sunrise,
> May my home life be renewed

When you are finished with the ritual, dismantle the broom. Take off the raffia and hemp and burn them. Return the herbs to the water by tossing them into a stream or river. Bury the string of cowry shells. Step backwards (in the manner of the spirits), turn around, and walk away without looking back.

So it is written, so it is done!

MAGICKAL WHISK BROOM

1 felled branch, about 18" long
  (see note)
Raffia, natural and unbleached
Hemp string, natural and
  unbleached
Cowry shells

Dried stems of purifying herbs
  (one kind or a combination),
  like lavender, artemisia,
  rosemary, peppermint, sage,
  juniper, or hyssop

Sand down any rough parts on the branch. This is the handle of the broom.

To make the brush, affix the herb stems as extensions of the handle. Tie them on with the raffia one layer at a time. Do this until the brush is as thick as desired.

Fix the broom tightly by tying it together using the hemp string.

To decorate the broom handle, thread cowry shells on to the hemp string. Tie this on the handle.

Note: A thick, sturdy branch is best. If you begin hunting for the wood after a fierce storm, so much the better, for then you will have better chances of finding a branch struck by lightning. Lightning is a force connected with the Yorubaland orisha of weather and changes Oya and her consort, god of changes Shango.

In *Spell Crafts,* Scott Cunningham and David Harrington suggest cherry wood for love magick, ebony for protection magick, elder for spirituality and protection, and oak for strength and health. Willow is for opening the way (psychic awareness), and pine is for money, healing, and exorcism. To tap the energies of the water goddesses Yemoya-Olokun and Oshun, use a piece of driftwood.

A JUMPING BROOM

Use this broom in your wedding or handfasting ceremony. Of course, if you don't feel crafty enough for this project, feel free to buy a broom from a reputable broommaker (see appendix B). To incorporate other Hoodoo and diverse African traditions into your wedding, refer to chapters 9, 10, and 11.

1 sturdy, felled branch 3–6' long from a willow, magnolia, myrtle, cherry, or apple tree
Whittling knife
½ cup Blessing Oil (recipe follows)
Dried crone wort, lavender, and hyssop stems (see note)
Dried sweet myrtle stems and leaves
Raffia, natural and unbleached
Hemp string, natural and unbleached
Cowry shells
Orange blossom or rose water
2 cups rain, spring, or holy water
¼ cup coarse sea salt or Dead Sea salt
Hot-melt glue gun

Begin by adding the salt to the rain, spring, or holy water. When the salt has dissolved, add the cowry shells. Soak the shells in the saltwater while you work. Also soak ample hemp string in the orange blossom or rose water.

To make the handle, remove the outer bark of the branch with the whittling knife. Save the bark to use in other recipes or rituals. Rub the skinned branch with the Blessing Oil.

To make the brush, affix one layer of the crone wort, lavender, and hyssop stems to the handle with the raffia. Repeat until the brush is as thick as desired.

Fix the broom tightly by tying it together using the hemp string.

Next, twirl the sweet myrtle around the handle of the broom and affix with the glue gun.

To make the handle decoration, thread the cowry shells onto the hemp string. Finish by tying this on the handle of the broom.

Oil the broom with the Blessing Oil as needed. Shortly before the ceremony, spritz the bristles with rose water or orange blossom water. After the ceremony, bury the broom in the yard where you will live if this is possible. If not, take it to a riverbank or beach and bury it there.

Note: Artemisia vulgaris, Lavandula officinalis, and *Hyssopus officinalis,* respectively.

BLESSING OIL

½ cup rose hip seed, peach kernel,
or apricot kernel oil
2 drops neroli essential oil

3 drops gardenia essential oil
3 drops sandalwood essential oil

Blend all oils together.

Chinese Wash

An ingredient essential to the hoodoo's cleansing arsenal is Chinese Wash. Chinese Wash incorporates the ashe, mysticism, and lore of the broom and wild grasses previously discussed. Chinese Wash is so named because it includes lemon grass as an ingredient, which used to be imported primarily from China.

Chinese Wash was mass-marketed commercially in the thirties, forties, fifties, and sixties to the Black community. Before that time, a similar formula was used by hoodoos to spiritually cleanse their homes. The following is my own recipe for homemade Chinese Wash.

CHINESE WASH

6 ounces unscented liquid Castile
soap
3 ounces Murphy oil soap
6 ounces distilled water
½ teaspoon citronella essential oil
½ teaspoon lemon grass essential oil

7 pieces of broom corn straws
cut to fit inside bottle
Pinch of dried lemon grass, if
available
1 16-ounce glass or clear plastic
bottle, cleaned and dried

Mix the Castile soap, Murphy oil soap, and distilled water in a bowl. Add the essential oils using a dropper, and stir gently to disperse the oils. Pour this through a funnel into the bottle. Add in the broom straws and, if using, the lemon grass. Seal and store in a cool place.

This is a highly concentrated blend. To use, add ¼ cup Chinese Wash to a bucket of water when cleansing the home. (Use more, if desired.)

Yield: 15 ounces
Shelf life: 1 year

Sacudimento

The African spirituality around brooms flourishes in Brazil as well. In his book *Sacred Leaves of Candomble,* scholar Robert Voeks reports on a practice of the Afro-Brazilians wherein a *sacudimento,* or leaf-whipping, is administered by a *pai* or *mae de santo* (high priest or high priestess). The sacudimento is made from leaves and twigs gathered, bundled, and used as a makeshift broom. The handcrafted broom is used in a gentle or forceful whipping motion (largely dependent on the intuition, personality, and mood of the pai or mae de santo). The whipping motion is designed to purge evil spirits and bad influences that cause disease (mental or physical) in the client. Sacudimento is believed to restore balance and harmony, all-encompassing West African concepts.

Not to make light of this liturgical use of brooms in Candomble, but I'm sure readers from the "old school" of the South will recall well-meaning, high-minded relatives, parents, or babysitters who did the "sacudimento" on their backside from time to time (calling it instead a "switch-whippin'"). They would shout incantations rhythmically (like "Don't ever do that again!") as they sought to restore harmony in their own way. The tough ones, as you may recall, always made the "naughty child" pick a very young, green branch as a switch. Then you would also be the one to have to strip off the bark and leaves from the plant, creating an especially effective whipping broom!

A Spontaneous Broom Ritual

About a week ago I had one of those Fridays that we all just dread: a deadline had rolled around and I had no inspiration to complete the project that was due. Lately I had been enjoying watching the abundant sunshine dance across the leaves in my backyard, dappling them with bright light, but that morning was dominated by rain. Dreary rain poured down, and the house and my office were covered in clutter.

Suddenly there was a call—whispers barely audible over the raindrops. They were the voices of Mujaji and Hara Ke, two African rain goddesses. "Come outside," they chanted in unison,

> Igba ogogo mmili *literally translates as "dancing waters." Ogogo is an excitedly playful washing of one's body as the rain falls, and without collecting the said rainfalls into any vessel or container.*
>
> —John Anenechukwu Umeh, *After God Is Dibia,* vol. 2

and so I did. Twirling about in the rain, I soaked in the sweet waters the two rain goddesses wanted to share.

As one type of spiritual union suggests another, I came inside and tossed my favorite incense onto a white-hot charcoal: ground copal and frankincense, dried lavender, cedar needles, and a smattering of pink rose petals. The fire was the perfect counterpoint, as my drenched body was becoming chilled. I let the thick smoke of the incense and resinous aroma lick over my body, infiltrate the computer, sweep across my black desk, and smudge my chair.

Unwittingly I had partaken in a traditional African ceremony. This was invigorating, but it seemed as though more participants were required. My eyes went to my broom. I gazed at it and thought, *Surely she could play a role.* I encouraged the broom to become a makeshift tree: broom corn as leaves and branches, and the handle a sleek, straight trunk.

I brought the broom outside. Mujaji and Hara Ke hit it hard and then began sliding down the handle, bouncing off the floor. My witch's broom seemed to eagerly

Herbal spiritual healing broom

devour the much-needed drink provided by the goddesses. Meanwhile, I returned indoors to inhale more heavenly scent.

After a time I brought the broom back inside. I sprinkled the raindrops from the broom onto my work chair, desk, and floor. I sat the broom upright so that once more she could shapeshift into a tree, and rainwater slid down the trunk.

I treated this newly created rain puddle gingerly since the water it consisted of was sacred. I swept the water in a spiraling shape until I had worked out to the perimeter of the room. Then I used a mop treated with orange blossom water to spread its gentility. By then my Blessing Incense was spent, my room was kissed by the goddesses, and my energy, inspiration, and urge to move forward at last had returned.

No wonder; brooms are inhabited by spirits. Mine is imbued with the spirits of the hearth. Rain, dew, and tears of creation goddesses activate my broom's spirit. Bringing the wilderness together with the element of water helped shift my mood from one of complacency to one of action.

Considering the deep history of brooms and sweeping, its symbolic implications, and the ability of brooms to aid with tricks and jobs, it is likely to continue to be an important element within Hoodoo and Black American cultures in general well into the future.

The next chapter contains a series of procedures, recipes, rituals, and tricks for cleansing your body and your home. Carry them out with the knowledge of the mystical powers of the broom.

chapter 4

Cleaning Rituals and Spirit Washes

In Hoodoo there is a deep awareness of the types of energies and vibrations that can be tracked into the home, so an entire area of this practice is dedicated to *foot track magick*. There are many different ways for bad energies to be brought into the home: from the entry path, to the threshold, mailbox, and even the innocent residents of the home. The following is an account recorded by Lafcadio Hearn in his article "New Orleans Superstitions" (originally published in *Harper's Weekly* in 1886, and reprinted in *A Treasury of Afro-American Folklore* by Harold Courlander).

It illustrates African American use of domestic charms and how spiritual cleansing rituals are used to banish negative energy. In the story, a homeowner in the old quarter neighborhood of Spanish Town discovers a young woman spreading a leaf charm on her property.

> *And he showed me a pure river of water of life, clear as crystal, proceeding out of the throne of God and of the Lamb.*
>
> —Revelation 22:1

Just as she had dropped the last leaf the irate French woman rushed out with a broom and a handful of salt, and began to sweep away the leaves, after having flung salt both upon them [the leaves] and upon the little Negress. The latter actually screamed with fright, and cried out, *"Oh, pas jete plis dispel apres moin, madame! pas bisoin jete dispel apres moin; mo pas pe vini icite encore."* (Oh, madam, don't throw any more salt after me; you needn't throw any more salt after me; I won't come here any more.)*

While the leaf charm story shows premeditated, dubious intent, the innocent can also bring negative energy into the home. Children are especially susceptible to attracting negative entities from school, daycare, or the playground. I must stress that these energies are not always brought in through obvious ways like abuse, fights, or arguments. Sources may entail close contact or sympathetic feelings toward a teacher or student who has such entities or vibrations lurking in his or her home.

Varied energies abound in the workplace of yourself and your spouse, particularly if the work is done in multiple residences, such as home renovation, construction, interior design, architecture, gardening, cleaning, childcare, housesitting, or direct sales. Merchandise sales involving the exchange of money by hand, teaching, healthcare, or any other occupation that involves exposure to a wide variety of humans in close range puts you at risk for negative spiritual contact. Even if you are involved in research you should do clearings, since books and papers are great collectors of the energy of those who handle them. In other occupations that seem solitary, you will inevitably encounter negative energy on public transportation, other forms of travel, while socializing, and so on, which attach themselves to you and are then tracked into your home.

Another type of ill intention or negativity is brought into the home in packages and even ordinary mail. I'm not talking about letter bombs, or chain mail, which are obviously hideous and harmful, but mail sent by someone harboring jealousy or ill will toward you or your family. Another type of bad vibe is spread by people who send packages or mail from discordant, hateful, or negative environments.

*Reprinted from the book *A Treasury of Afro-American Folklore* by Harold Courlander. Copyright © 1976, 1996 by Harold Courlander. Appears by permission of the publisher, Marlowe & Company.

So, What's So Special About Salt?

All life comes from the sea. As humans, we begin our lives as fetuses submerged in amniotic fluid, a slightly saline solution. According to John Anenechukwu Umeh, author of *After God Is Dibia,* salt is the solidified tears of God. God was so saddened by the spiritual and physical pollution that populates the earth that his worry and tears formed the great oceans and seas. Because salt is derived from the passion of God, a combination of water and salt is used by *dibia* (Igbo wisemen/healers) to clear all forms of negativity—even hatred.

The goddesses of many cultures play a role in our conception of salt being sacred. This may be a conceptualization of the mystical quality of amniotic fluid, the water of life. The water jar is a symbol of ancient Egyptian goddess Nut. Nut is of the sky—the sun, moon, and stars—and she is also mother to the gods. Her essence pours down rain from the heavens. She is also the milk-giving cow goddess, goddess of the serpents of the primeval waters, fertile pig goddess, bird goddess, and goddess of the underworld. Isis is also the Great Mother goddess of ancient Egypt. The universe and humanities spring from her womb, nourished by her amniotic fluid.

Greek goddess Aphrodite is the daughter produced by heaven and the sea. Sacred baths, ritual bathing, and the spring of renewal are her domain. Aphrodite, the embodiment of the sea, reflects all that is divine in daily life. She is the goddess of the sea and of animals, fertility, rain, and seeds. Astarte of Mesopotamia is the light, guardian of ships, and prayer goddess of the sea, moon, and morning and evening stars. She is the cosmic womb and goddess of fertility.

Venus is Aphrodite and Astarte's Roman counterpart. Her image has been condensed into the goddess of love, but essentially she is a great goddess of the sea. This includes all of the manifestations of the sea, such as fertility, love, nurturance, the cosmic womb, and Great Mother.

Yemoya-Olokun are the great goddesses of the Yoruba in Nigeria (although their devotees are also in the Americas). The duo are considered compassionate and judicious givers and takers of life. In the Yoruban pantheon they are sea mothers who represent the Great Mothers of the universe.

As the essence of both powerful gods and a host of cross-cultural ancient Great Mothers, salt is the substance of purity, cleansing, luck, prosperity, compassion, love, hope, and renewal.

Shopping and trying on shoes or clothing is another way to come into contact with the spirits of others. These energies are strongest with secondhand clothing and objects purchased at estate sales, antique shops, or garage sales, though most can be cleared with smudging or cleansing rituals.

Whether you are self-employed, a homemaker, or work outside the home, living in contemporary times requires you to do ritualistic cleansing to rid your home of the bad vibrations that breed clutter, depression, anger, or despair.

Spiritually Cleansing the Home

The following are suggestions for cleaning your house spiritually. They are given as an extensive ritual, but you can pick and choose what is of interest and do what is needed. Levels of intensity in spiritual cleaning vary with the occasion. An argument that has been resolved already only requires light cleansing, whereas moving into a new place, or a home that has been burglarized, violated, cursed, or visited by unpleasant parties requires extensive cleansing. When moving from a home or changing your office or studio, it is a good idea to take all of your spiritual energy as well as your hair and nail clippings with you by performing a deep cleaning before your departure. This is so no one is able to hex, spread juju, or capture your energy. Naturally, you should also clear your space in this manner after a divorce, break-up, and changing roommates.

HOUSE CLEANING RITUAL

If possible, begin on the waning moon for light jobs or the full moon for serious work.

Step 1: Salt

To start, blend together 1 cup coarse sea salt, 1 cup fine sea salt, and ¼ cup Dead Sea salt (use table salt if other salt is not available). Place a little of this mixture in the corners of each room for purification and protection.

Step 2: Invocation

Invite positive spirits and feed your ancestors by burning either 1 tablespoon pure smoking tobacco, dried sage, cedar, or pine on a piece of hot bamboo charcoal. I use all four successfully. Which you use depends on what the spirits desire and on what is available. Trust your intuition; there are not always hard-and-fast rules to follow.

Step 3: Smudging

Smudging helps banish negative energy and invites positive energy. To banish, light a smudge stick made of sage, lavender, cedar, mugwort, or a blend of herbs. Blow out the fire and allow it to continue to smoke. Beginning at the entrance of your home, wave the smudge stick like a fragrant wand. Make your way to the back door, covering all areas slowly with the smoke. Open the back door and a few windows to let the smoky aroma and negative energy escape.

To invoke, repeat the same process but in reverse and using a sweetgrass braid.

Step 4: Dusting Solutions

The next step is to remove dust. Begin with the ceiling, then the corners of the room, followed by the furniture. Use a natural ostrich duster, if possible. I like using a single eagle or seagull feather for fine work (such as the computer, keyboard, telephone, and other office equipment) to inspire my work and help cultivate meaningful communications and creativity.

When this is done, it is time to attack the dirt and clutter. Sprinkle the natural bristles of an old-fashioned broom with a solution of natural water, sweet water, and essential or fragrance oil. You can make your own or choose from the following:

- **Swift Change:** (*for quick, unexpected changes*) ½ cup lightning water (water captured during a thunder and lightning storm), ¼ teaspoon vetiver essential oil, and ⅛ teaspoon patchouli essential oil
- **Keep Evil at Bay:** ¼ cup rose water, ¼ cup holy water, ½ teaspoon bay essential oil, and ¼ teaspoon lilac fragrance oil

Start at the front door of the house and end at the back door. Sweep out salt from the corners of the room and bring it into the center. Move furniture to be sure all surfaces are cleared. Refresh broom as needed. Save the dust, dirt, and clutter for a ceremonial disposal.

Step 5: Ceremonial Disposal

When a Minianka child is born in Fienso Village, Mali, according to Yaya Diallo and Mitchell Hall (authors of *The Healing Drum*), he or she is placed on a banana leaf outside the home until he or she cries. The banana leaf is a special part of the ceremony that demonstrates whether or not someone is alive (human) or a spirit. Banana leaf paper is commonly found at art supply stores and paper stores.

To ceremoniously dispose of dirt, wrap it in a banana leaf or banana paper and bury it in your yard. For specific needs, see the following:

- For serious work after violence, divorce, separation, or arguments, wrap the dirt and dust in a banana leaf or banana paper, removing any non-degradable objects and junk. Toss the package at a crossroads. Turn around quickly and don't look back.

- For new beginnings, wrap the dirt and dust in a banana leaf or banana paper, removing any nondegradable objects and junk. Toss the package into a river, stream, or the ocean.

- To keep your secrets safe, wrap the dirt and dust in a banana leaf or banana paper, removing any nondegradable objects and junk. Toss the package into the toilet and flush.

Woman conjuring on banana leaf

Step 6: Cleansing Brew

Add 1½ quarts tap water to a large stockpot or cauldron and bring to a boil. Stir in 2 tablespoons dried rosemary, 2 tablespoons dried sage, and 2 tablespoons dried lavender buds (or ⅓ cup of each herb if using fresh) and return to a boil.

Cook for 2 minutes. While cooking, inhale the aromas from the pot and exhale into the pot your healing energy.

Add ½ cup liquid Castile soap or mild dish detergent to the water and stir to mix. Cover and remove from heat. Allow your cleaning brew to infuse and cool.

Once cool, pour the potion through a fine sieve over a catch bowl. Add essential oils or commercial Hoodoo oils to the strained potion and mix well. Choose combinations that match your purpose:

- **All-Purpose Cleaner:** ½ teaspoon rosemary essential oil and ½ teaspoon pine needle essential oil

- **Sickness:** (*for physical or mental illness*) ¼ cup Lourdes water, ½ teaspoon lavender essential oil, and ½ teaspoon eucalyptus essential oil

- **Sunny Days:** (*lifts the spirits, opens the way to mental clarity*) ¼ cup orange blossom water, ½ teaspoon geranium essential oil, and ½ teaspoon orange essential oil

Add the housecleaning brew to a bucket and add water to dilute. Begin spiritual cleaning at the back door. Clean each floor with a mop or sponge, ending at the front of the house. Wash countertops and appliances as well. Pour dirty liquid down the front step or the entry path of the house. Then scrub the front step or entryway with saltwater.

For intensive cleaning and attraction of positive spirits, follow with 1 gallon bluing solution mixed with water. To prepare bluing solution, follow the directions on the package. Use Mrs. Stewart's bluing, Mexican anil balls, or Reckitt's Crown Blue squares, none of which are toxic or dangerous to the natural environment. If bluing is unavailable, sprinkle dried basil leaf on the front and back entry stair or path.

Step 7: Heal-All Furniture Feeding Oil

Fix the following scented oil to feed your woodwork (tables, trim, cabinets, etc.). This blend is designed to enlighten you as you work, helping you sort out the source of the confusion, bad vibes, or negativity cluttering up your home.

Preheat the oven to 190 degrees. In an oven-proof container, stir together 8 ounces oil (almond oil, olive oil, castor oil, or a combination), 1 tablespoon dried rosemary, and 1 tablespoon dried vetiver. Place in the oven and let the herbs release their magickal qualities into the oil by steeping until needed (at least 30 minutes).

When ready, add ½ teaspoon lemon essential oil and ½ teaspoon sweet orange essential oil and mix well. Use with a dusting cloth.

Step 8: Finishing Spray

This step replaces the use of commercial aerosol air fresheners. Mix together the ingredients of the recipe of your choice and put in a spray bottle to spray onto the broom or into the air. You can buy commercially made fragrant waters (such as kananga water or rose water) or else make them yourself. Recipes are at the end of this chapter.

- **Bless This House:** (*general spiritual atmosphere, peaceful home*) ¼ cup holy water, ¼ cup rose water, ½ teaspoon rose fragrance oil

- **Devil Away:** (*troublesome spirits, meddling, gossip*) ¼ cup holy water, ¼ teaspoon each of frankincense, myrrh, and cinnamon leaf essential oils

- **Ancestor Welcoming:** (*unexpected death, bereavement, sorrow*) ¼ cup kananga water, ¼ cup Florida Water (see page 83), ¼ teaspoon each of clary sage and lavender essential oils

- **Chase Away Negative Vibes:** ¼ cup orange blossom water, ¼ cup spring water, ½ teaspoon lemon verbena essential oil, ¼ teaspoon cinnamon essential oil

Step 9: Dress Up

Unless you are moving on to another residence, dress your front door with either a fresh flower, herb, or bay laurel wreath. See the listing below for specific qualities. Also, hang a mirror near the entryway. Clean your entry mirror and all other mirrors with a 50-50 solution of 100-proof vodka and water. Inside the door hang rue or a garlic braid to banish negativity and for protection.

To create your own wreath, arrange fresh flowers and herbs on a straw or grapevine wreath. Affix them to the wreath using natural hemp, twine, or florist wire. Choose the right combinations for the work required:

- **Evil Spirits, Hants (Ghosts), Demonic Possession:** Lilac, peony, snapdragon, and juniper

- **General Cleansing:** Bay, cedar, chamomile, hyssop, iris, lemon verbena, rosemary, and thyme

- **Happiness:** Hyacinth, lavender, and lily of the valley

- **Healing:** Amaranth, bay laurel, carnation, cedar, cowslip, golden seal, heliotrope, pine, rose, rosemary, and violet

- **Hexes:** Galangal, chili peppers, pokeberries, blessed thistle, and vetiver

- **Peace:** Gardenia, morning glory, and violet

- **Power:** Carnation, devil's shoestring, and ginger

- **Spirituality:** Cinnamon, frankincense, and gardenia

- **Strength:** Bay, carnation, pennyroyal, sweet pea, blessed thistle, and lady's mantle

Step 10: Finishing Touches

Walk through the house and throw shiny pennies under the furniture and into the corners of the room. Next, set out lemons in a bowl on the table where you eat for luck and energy. Place fresh, scented flowers in each room. The coins, lemons, and flowers are all pleasing to the spirits and show your ancestors that you notice them and appreciate their favors.

Repeat this ritual as needed. I do it at least every two weeks and sometimes each week.

Spiritually Cleansing the Body

After spiritually clearing your living or work space, it is important to purge the bad vibes, negativity, or spiritual activity you drew to yourself while cleaning. In the following pages, there are three recipes with variations to choose from, including an herbal bath, bath crystals, and bath sachet.

> *Who walks in the mud, at some point must clean his feet.*
>
> —Bahumbu proverb

Sanctify Your Washtub

If you wish, you can begin by sanctifying your tub. Sprinkle a 50-50 combination of baking soda and vinegar in and around the tub. As it bubbles, sprinkle ground sea salt or table salt into the solution. Scrub with a loofah or natural sea sponge until all residue is removed.

Incense

To complete the home clearing and invite a richer spiritual depth to your home, choose one of the following types of pure, sacred incense made from essential oils to burn while you bathe:

- Sandalwood, myrrh, lavender, patchouli, frankincense, or a combination

- Ground frankincense, gum arabic, myrrh, and sandalwood chips

Set a chunk of bamboo charcoal on a natural heat- and fireproof incense burner in the bathroom. Light the charcoal and let it heat thoroughly. (It will turn white in areas.) Then place a pinch of each ingredient on top. (Make sure there is something to catch the ash.) This is the purest type of ceremonial incense and has ancient origins before biblical times.

If you prefer, you can also choose from the wide variety of commercial incenses that can be carefully matched to your specific needs. Refer to appendix B for suggested resources.

Crack open a door or window if possible. Repeat the following hant-clearing chant three times. Take deep cleansing breaths of incense. Emphasize the exhalation to purge and clear yourself and the room of negativity.

Spirits which cling here,
You are not wanted inside.
There is a white light upon you,
From which you cannot hide.
I come to you in the most correct way,
But in my clean and blessed home
You cannot stay.

When you are finished and are draining the tub, recite the following healing blessing:

Like a magnet, I've attracted to me
The good and bad powers that be.
With the strength invested in me,
I ask the bad spirits to depart and let me be.
I come to you in the most correct way,
May graciousness and goodness reign here today.
I call on good forces with power and might,
Let only clarity and brightness remain in my sight.
I call on powers much higher than I,
Shroud me in spiritual goodness and light
From morning to night.
Three times three times three,
Blessed Be!

> *There is no hiding place on the water's surface.*
>
> —Balari proverb

SPIRITUAL BLESSING BATH

2 cups water
¼ cup dried hyssop, lemon verbena, van van (vetiver), or chamomile (or 1 chamomile tea bag), or a combination (see note)
1 cup milk
⅛ teaspoon frankincense essential oil

⅛ teaspoon myrrh essential oil
⅛ teaspoon lavender essential oil
⅛ teaspoon lilac or gardenia fragrance oil
1 quart (32 ounces) warm water
Incense (see page 72)
1 candle (see chapter 5 for help selecting the correct one)

Bring the 2 cups of water to a boil. Add the dried herbs and, if using, the tea bag. Allow the water to return to a boil, then cover and remove from the heat. Steep for 30 minutes.

When finished steeping, strain by pouring through a fine sieve over a bowl.

In a small, separate bowl, mix the milk and oils together. Whisk this into the strained herb infusion, and then add the warm water.

Set the incense and candle on the sink or tub in fireproof holders and light them.

Plug the tub. Using a cup, pour the herbal brew over your head and let it drain down your body. Repeat this process exactly 7, 9, 11, or 13 times, depending on the depth of cleansing desired. For intensive cleansing and healing, repeat this ritual every day for exactly 7, 9, 11, or 13 days.

When finished, drain the tub and extinguish the candle and incense.

Note: Use 1 cup if using fresh herbs.

HEALING BATH CRYSTALS

Sometimes you will encounter a blockage that manifests itself in your body. There may be all manner of complaints: headache, low energy, bodyache, or cramps. For physical manifestations of ill intent, or if you have been taking care of someone who is ill or recently recovered from illness, try this crystal blessing.

2 cups Dead Sea salt, or regular
    sea salt crystals
1 cup Epsom salt

¼ teaspoon peppermint, pine needle,
    lavender, or cedar essential oil (or
    a combination)

Place the salts in a nonreactive, nonabsorbent bowl (glass, ceramic, or stainless steel work well). Sprinkle the essential oil(s) on the salts and stir with a stainless-steel spoon. (Do not use wood, as it will absorb some of the goodness of the oils.)

Use immediately, or, to maximize the effects, bottle and store the crystals for 2 weeks in a wide-mouthed glass jar before using.

To use, begin running a very hot bath. Sprinkle in 1½ cups of the Healing Bath Crystals and swish them around with your hands to encourage them to dissolve into the water. Get in, relax, and enjoy.

Yield: 3 cups, or enough for 2 baths
Shelf life: 3 to 6 months

SPIRIT RENEWAL BATH SACHET

Clearings and battling negativity can easily zap your energy and fray your nerves. To combat fatigue, try this invigorating sachet after cleansing your home. It will renew your psychic resources.

Muslin (cheesecloth) bag (see note)	⅛ teaspoon lavender essential oil
1 teaspoon dried yarrow	⅛ teaspoon rosemary essential oil
1 teaspoon dried chamomile	⅛ teaspoon pine needle essential oil
1 teaspoon dried peppermint	3 tablespoons aloe vera gel
2 tablespoons powdered	2 marigold (calendula) flowers
whole milk	1 teaspoon magnetic sand

Put the yarrow, chamomile, peppermint, and powdered milk into the muslin bag and secure with a rubber band. Hang the sachet under the faucet of your tub and run a hot bath.

In a small bowl, stir the essential oils into the aloe gel. Pour this into the tub, and mix well with your hands to distribute.

Pluck the petals from the marigold flowers into the water. Then sprinkle in the magnetic sand. Get in, relax, and enjoy.

Note: You may also use a ready-made muslin tea bag. See appendix B for suppliers.

Soap

When you bathe, wash your body with African Black soap, Black and White soap, or make your own sacred soap from the recipes below. Use a natural sea sponge for washing the bad vibes away while renewing good spirits.

The following recipes will make enough soap to last at least six months. You may want to share a bar or two with those friends or family members who are in need of blessings and clearing.

> *Let us draw near with a true heart in full assurance of faith, having our hearts sprinkled clean from an evil conscience, and our bodies washed with pure water.*
>
> —Hebrews 10:22

SOUL HEAL SOAP

4 cups melt-and-pour glycerin soap
1 teaspoon shea butter
⅛ teaspoon rose geranium essential oil
⅛ teaspoon lavender essential oil
⅛ teaspoon lime essential oil
Cooking spray, like Pam

8 small lodestones or other favorite rocks, charged
Nonstick muffin tins or soap molds, or Pyrex baking dish
White cloth
Gold cord

Herbal Brew
1 cup distilled water
1 sprig fresh hyssop, or 1 teaspoon dried
1 sprig fresh rosemary, or 1 teaspoon dried

Begin by making the herbal brew. In a small, stainless-steel pan bring the distilled water to a boil. Put the herbs in a small bowl and pour the boiling water over them. Cover and let stand for 30 minutes.

Meanwhile, begin melting the glycerin soap in a double boiler over medium-low heat. (If you don't have a double boiler, float a stainless-steel bowl or clean coffee can in a pot of water.) When the soap is almost all melted, add the shea butter. Once the shea butter is melted, remove from heat.

Strain the herbal brew through a sieve over a catch bowl. Add 2 tablespoons of the brew to the glycerin/shea mixture. Then whisk in the oils one at a time.

Spray the soap molds, muffin cups, or baking dish with the cooking spray. Add a stone to each tin or mold and pour in the soap. Let harden 2 hours.

When ready, pop the soap out of the molds. (If they resist, put in the freezer for 15 to 20 minutes and then try again.) If you are using the baking dish, cut the soap into 8 equally sized bars. Wrap in the white cloth and tie securely with the gold cord.

Yield: 8 4-ounce bars
Shelf life: 1 year

ANGELS ON HIGH SOAP

4 cups melt-and-pour glycerin soap
1 teaspoon castor oil
¼ teaspoon lilac fragrance oil (see note)
¼ teaspoon hyacinth fragrance oil

Cooking spray, like Pam
Nonstick muffin tins, soap molds, or Pyrex baking dish
Silky white cloth
Twine or hemp string

Root Decoction
1 cup distilled water
1 tablespoon ground angelica root

1 tablespoon ground John the Conqueror root

Begin by making the root decoction. In a small, stainless-steel pan, bring the distilled water to a boil. Add the angelica root and John the Conqueror root, cover, and let simmer over medium-low heat for 30 minutes.

Meanwhile, begin melting the glycerin soap in a double boiler over medium-low heat. (If you don't have a double boiler, float a stainless-steel bowl or clean coffee can in a pot of water.) When the soap is almost all melted, add the castor oil and remove from heat.

Strain the root decoction through a sieve over a catch bowl. Add 2 tablespoons of the decoction to the glycerin/castor oil mixture. Then whisk in the fragrance oils.

Spray the soap molds, muffin cups, or baking dish with the cooking spray. Pour in the soap and let harden 2 hours.

When ready, pop the soap out of the molds. (If they resist, put in the freezer for 15 to 20 minutes and then try again.) If you are using the baking dish, cut the soap into 8 equally sized bars. Wrap in the silky white cloth and tie securely with the twine or hemp string in the shape of a cross.

> *Don't you know that you yourselves are God's temple and that God's spirit lives in you?*
>
> —1 Corinthians 3:16

Note: Can substitute ½ teaspoon of your favorite floral perfume for the fragrance oils.

Yield: 8 4-ounce bars
Shelf life: 1 year

Body Oil

If you buy commercially prepared Hoodoo body oil, dilute 1 tablespoon of it in 4 ounces of corn oil, almond oil, or safflower oil. Apply it to damp skin where desired after a cleansing bath.

You can also make your own body oils. This will ensure the proper intent and the right combination of herbs, roots, and leaves are contained in it. Although you may feel awkward at first, relax with the knowledge that you can't beat the personalized attention, care, and love that goes into your homemade Hoodoo brews.

STRENGTHENING BODY OIL

1½ cup mixture of dried, cut, and sifted angelica root, John the Conqueror root, vetiver, lady's mantle, hyssop, lavender, rosemary, and yarrow

2 vitamin E capsules

16 ounces sweet almond oil, sunflower oil, grapeseed oil, safflower oil, or corn oil

½ teaspoon attar of roses

¼ teaspoon geranium essential oil

¼ teaspoon palmarosa essential oil

Place the roots and herbs in a sterilized, 16-ounce jar with a screw-on, spring, or cork top. Add the oil of your choice.

Set the jar on a shelf. Swirl contents once daily for 6 weeks.

After 6 weeks, strain the herbs using a sieve. Finally add the attar of roses, essential oils, and vitamin E. Store away from direct sunlight.

Use when needed. You may anoint the head, wrists, or use on the full body, particularly after healing, cleansing, and clearing.

Yield: Approximately 14 ounces
Shelf life: 6 months

Body Powders

Rev up your power with a Hoodoo powder. Choose a premade powder that matches your intentions from a Hoodoo shop or, better yet, make your own. Choose from the following blends.

COMMANDING POWDER

For tough jobs, strength, and to build courage.

1 teaspoon dried orange peel
2 tablespoons dried marigold
  (calendula) petals
1 teaspoon dried van van (vetiver)
1 tablespoon dried lemon verbena
⅛ teaspoon frankincense
  essential oil
⅛ teaspoon myrrh essential oil

⅛ teaspoon vetiver essential oil
⅛ teaspoon neroli essential oil
5 tablespoons arrowroot (may
  substitute cornstarch)
2 tablespoons baking soda
1 tablespoon ground Queen
  Elizabeth (orris) root

Pulverize the orange peel in a clean coffee grinder or with a mortar and pestle. Add the marigold petals and grind until fine. Add the van van and lemon verbena and continue to refine. Pour into a nonreactive bowl.

Add the oils to the powder and mix with a nonreactive spoon. Add the arrowroot, baking soda, and Queen Elizabeth root and blend well.

Using a funnel, pour the mixture into a bottle with a shaker top or a wide-mouthed jar.

To use, apply to body with a duster or sea sponge.

Yield: Approximately 4 ounces
Shelf life: 6 months

Speaking of Oranges . . .

As we delve into magickal recipes, you will notice the orange has many uses. Sweet orange essential oil comes from ordinary edible oranges (*Citrus sinesis*) and is used mostly for home cleansing. The more potent and complex orange blossom petals of *Citrus bigaradia* or *C. aurantium* are used in neroli or orange blossom water. Petigrain (*C. aurantium*) is also complex. It is made from the leaves and twigs.

HIGH ROAD POWDER

To improve self-esteem, attract good spirits, and lift the spirits.

2 tablespoons dried lavender buds
2 tablespoons dried rose petals
⅛ teaspoon violet fragrance oil
⅛ teaspoon lavender essential oil
⅛ teaspoon attar of roses
5 tablespoons arrowroot (may substitute cornstarch)
2 tablespoons baking soda
1 tablespoon ground Queen Elizabeth (orris) root

Grind the lavender buds and rose petals in a clean coffee grinder or with a mortar and pestle until fine. Put in a nonreactive bowl.

Add the oils to the powder and mix well with a stainless-steel spoon. Then mix in the arrowroot, baking soda, and Queen Elizabeth root.

Using a funnel, pour the mixture into a bottle with a shaker top or a wide-mouthed jar.

To use, apply to body with a duster or sea sponge.

Yield: Approximately 7 ounces
Shelf life: 6 months

Sweet Waters

Seal your body and exude your renewed spirits with cologne or essential oils. Traditional Hoodoo blends include Florida Water, Hoyt's Cologne, or kananga water.

DE-STRESSING FLORAL WATER

The more you think about who may have hexed you, or ponder which uncrossing trick will work best, the more distressed you may become. This coupled with the hazards of everyday life can leave you tired and anxious. Dr. Bach created a wonderful Rescue Remedy, which I always keep near, but way before him folk were using the tenderness of flowers to sway the good spirits and alleviate bothersome thoughts. This is a floral blend that will leave you feeling clear after your spiritual work.

1 cup distilled water
1 tablespoon vegetable glycerin
1 tablespoon honey
½ cup 100-proof vodka
1 tablespoon tincture of benzoin
½ cup rose water
¼ cup orange blossom water

½ teaspoon rose fragrance oil
½ teaspoon geranium essential oil
½ teaspoon lavender essential oil
½ teaspoon lime essential oil
¼ teaspoon petigrain essential oil
¼ cup aromatic organic roses

In a bowl, combine the distilled water, glycerin, and honey and mix well. Add in the vodka and benzoin and let dissolve. Mix in the remaining ingredients in the order given, swirling the blend with each addition.

Decant mixture to a sterilized container with a tightly fitted cap. Store in the refrigerator for two weeks. Swirl contents once daily.

After two weeks, strain the mixture and decant to a spray bottle. Keep refrigerated.

Yield: Approximately 16 ounces
Shelf life: 60 days

FLORIDA WATER

No Hoodoo home is complete without Florida Water. It is used to entice good spirits, feed the ancestors, and dress your altar and yourself.

16 ounces distilled water (see note)
¼ cup 100-proof vodka
6 drops lavender essential oil
2 drops clove bud essential oil
8 drops bergamot essential oil

Add ingredients in the order given to a sterilized glass bottle with a cork top. (Having a clean, dry glass bottle to start with is essential.) Stir to blend and decant to a spray bottle.

Note: Distilled water assures that antibodies and germs, which will decompose the mixture, are not introduced.

Yield: Approximately 18 ounces
Shelf life: 60 days

Fragrant Waters

There are a few popular waters that are frequently used in Hoodoo. Rose water, orange blossom water, lavender water, and kananga water are common.

ROSE WATER

8 drops attar of roses

8 ounces distilled water

Drop the attar of roses into the distilled water. Mix with a stirring wand. Pour through a funnel into a clean, dry bottle. If using as an air freshener, funnel into a spray bottle. Seal and store in the refrigerator.

Variations
    Lavender water: Replace the attar of roses with lavender essential oil.
    Orange blossom water: Replace the attar of roses with neroli essential oil.
    Kananga water: Replace the attar of roses with a higher-grade ylang ylang essential oil.

Yield: 8 ounces
Shelf life: 6 months

BODY PERFUME

16 drops neroli, lavender, or
    higher-grade ylang ylang
    essential oil or attar of roses

8 ounces distilled water
4 tablespoons 100-proof vodka

Drop the attar of roses or essential oil into the distilled water. Mix with a stirring wand. Pour through a funnel into a clean, dry perfume or spray bottle. Seal and store away from sunlight and heat (the bedroom dresser or shelf is fine).

Yield: 8 ounces
Shelf life: 1 year

chapter 5

Harvesting the Gifts of Fire

The holidays should be a heartwarming comfort, yet often they are marred by conflict, anxiety, and tension. The most anxiety-inducing aspect of the holidays is the focus on commercial enterprise with its attendant advertising and solicitation. This builds a whirlwind of negative emotions within us: need grows into desire and quickly spirals into greed. The desire to please can overwhelm the positive aspects of giving.

Autumn Holidays, American Style

It is important to realize that just about every holiday celebrated in the United States has an ancient basis and is largely drawn from indigenous traditions or early agrarian customs. The agrarian aspect is critical, because within these earth-based customs lies a wealth of useful lore, songs, traditions, and recipes that have a deep connection with the Earth Mother and the spirits of nature. Investigating, reinvigorating, and perhaps even borrowing a few of these practices from neighboring societies can return a genuine spirituality to the holidays, making them helpful and even sacred rather than a pain to be dreaded. Hoodoo, with its eclecticism and basis in ritual and ceremony, is the perfect practice to draw upon when adding early American flair to washed-out, overly commercialized holidays.

Autumn is a bittersweet time. We are blessed with the harvest of ripe fruits and vegetables, and the air is electric with fiery orange, red, and yellow leaves, but sadly, our days grow shorter. It is time to begin the journey into ourselves and into our homes. Fittingly, we celebrate Thanksgiving

Maize

to give thanks for our wonderful blessings, a beautiful harvest celebration derived from cultural sharing between Native Americans, European Americans, and African Americans. Many people also observe the advent of fall by celebrating the autumn equinox and All Hallow's Eve, two ancient, nature-based observances that mark the passage of the seasons with an awareness of the cyclical aspect of all forms of life.

In Mexico and the Mexican diaspora, *Los Dias de los Muertos* (The Day of the Dead) is an autumnal ancestral celebration that lasts for several days. On October 27, spirits without any family or friends are treated to jugs of water and pieces of bread placed outdoors to feed their hungry souls. On October 28, those who were killed in accidents or slain are feted outside. The emphasis on outdoor ceremonies is due to both the unsettling idea that the spirits came to pass from life, and the fact that their confused souls may decide to linger in the home if they are invited. All Saints' Day, celebrated November 1, honors the souls of departed children. November 2 is All Souls' Day, a day to display affection and welcoming for the spirits of departed adults. Los Dias de los Muertos helps heal the sorrow of loss through active engagement, festivities, and remembrance.

Whatever your ethnic or cultural background, no doubt you have lost someone dear whose memory could be kept alive through incorporating aspects of Los Dias de los Muertos. Below are suggestions for creating *las ofrendas* (offerings) for your loved ones.

Las Ofrendas

The commemorative flowers used as ofrendas are those that are commonly in season in Mexico during fall: marigolds, cockscombs, and baby's breath.

The Flower-strewn Path—Strewing is an almost forgotten tradition. The only times it is really done is with paper confetti or occasionally during wedding ceremonies. Strewing is an important element in Day of the Dead ceremonies.

In order to get started, collect fresh marigolds from your garden or a local farmer's market. Pluck the petals from the flowers and put them in a large shopping bag or clean, dry bucket. Add potpourri for a more complex scent and form a pathway for the departed to travel from your front door to the altar (see below).

The Altar—Dress a table with a pretty tablecloth that hangs almost to the floor. On top of the table place your departed loved one's favorite fruits, snacks, and soft drinks, and for adults you can add spirits or tobacco if they used these in life. For a child you can add to this a fresh pair of pajamas or clothing and a favorite toy. (On All Saints' Day it is customary for the child's friends to come to the home and play with his or her toys, thereby keeping the departed child's spirit connection in the community alive.)

Place flowers of a type and color that the departed would enjoy. If you'd like, you can add a photograph or two and a few candles. Invite close friends of the departed and family members to add their touches. Arrange the food, flowers, drinks, and other objects in a pleasing, visually rich way. Host a dinner party to celebrate, remember, and heal.

Building an altar of this type is very moving. It is a tender way to keep your ancestors in your home during the holidays rather than falling into a depression over their absence.

Thanksgiving Reconsidered

In parts of Nigeria, the Yoruba people celebrate *Awuru Odo,* a biennial celebration akin to Los Dias de los Muertos. In many traditional cultures that have maintained elements of pagan, animistic spirituality, the ancestors are remembered in a lively and interactive way. The departed are not relegated to an isolated cemetery; instead, they are invited to be a part of the family's daily life.

Thanksgiving affords a wonderful opportunity to engage with one's ancestors in this manner. Try arranging a special place setting for the departed with food and drink. Prepare specific favorite foods for your loved one, then leave an empty chair as an invitation for the departed spirit to join the meal.

Harvesting the Gifts of Fire

It is mid-January, and the lights of Kwanza, Yule, Hanukkah, and Christmas are but a dimmed memory. The days are growing slightly longer, but January in the Midwest is no joke: cold, blue, and gray dominate the frozen landscape, penetrating the soul if permitted. On top of that, today is Monday, and my nest is almost empty of the flurry of activity typical of a young family. Being deprived of light, it is easy for my spirits to take a dive. Rather than staying down low where my spirits currently lie, this Mo(o)nday will be a day centered around my altar. Fire, air, earth, family, and the all-important candles are central to keeping me steady, calm, focused, and balanced.

With curtains drawn and blinds closed, I begin to light the pillars and votives resting on each of my three altars: citrus-scented orange candles to stimulate my energy level; bay-scented green candles as a reminder of the earth's verdant fertility, and so our family will continue to prosper and be in good health; cinnamon-scented red candles for vitality, strength, and love; and white votives to invite the spirit of purity to bless the inception of this week.

Candlemancy is perhaps the most American (in a multicultural sense) of the various aspects of Hoodoo. We have always looked to our neighbors for inspiration and commonalities in our magickal traditions. It is difficult to hear someone say, "Oh, that's Native American," when speaking of sage smudge sticks, or "That's from Japan really, isn't it?" when speaking about specific resins and incenses, because very few cultures have lived for extensive periods of time in complete isolation. Monolithic culture is more of an ideal that supports racism than a reality based in fact. Even before the massive immigrations and the advent of slavery, there were still elaborate trade routes all over the world that made cross-overs in traditions, recipes, and practices inevitable. In the United States when folks huddle together in city neighborhoods, the interchange is swift.

Hoodoo, as a constantly changing form, has looked to and incorporated many traditions, whether they be Jewish, Asian, Native American, South American, or Latino. The most recent explosion has been in our interest in Candomble of Brazil and Latino candlemancy. These traditions use special painted prayer candles in rituals and altars to salute a wide variety of saints.

I grew up with candles in my home and community, so I equate them with family and warmth. Since Advent, our living space has been aglow each dawn and dusk with dressed candles. They've been acting up right funny too—hissing, crackling, starting out sooty and ending with long, tapering flames. For answers to these and other signs my candles attempt to communicate, I turn to the legacy of African American folklore.

One of the most influential candlemancy books to the Hoodoo practice was written in the early forties by Henry Gamache called *A Master Book of Candle Burning: How to Burn Candles for Every Purpose*. Gamache's influences from preceding eras included R. Swinburne Clymer, the Rosicrucians, and spiritualist Paschal Beverly Randolph. Other influential texts include the voluminous interviews of Harry Hyatt, an avocational folklorist who documented an amazing amount of information on Hoodoo, and the slim volumes of work by Anna Riva, readily accessible and omnipresent in the 'hood. Once Anna Riva's books (such as *The Modern Herbal Spellbook* and *Magic with Incense and Powders*) are cross-checked against the cross-cultural works of Scott Cunningham (such as Cunningham's *Magical Herbalism* and *Oils, Incenses and Brews*), the habits, workings, usage, reading, and interpretation of candles gain clarity.

Across these sources there is a consensus regarding the symbolic meanings of color, except for readings on brown and black. To employ candles in rituals, healings, or on your altar, you will need to decide on colors and dressings for your candles.

Candle Colors

White

A white candle is an all-purpose candle, which may provide blessings because of its pure spirit. In Africa, white is the *iwa* (cool) color, thus it is highly symbolic of goodness and balance.

Yellow

Yellow candles are generally used for unhexing, uncrossing, and also bring clarity of thought. Yellow is useful for building confidence, opening the way of premonitions and clairvoyance, movement, travel, intelligence, studying, learning, and eloquence.

Orange

Orange attracts positive energy and desired outcomes, while also stimulating courage.

Red

Because it is the color of blood, red symbolizes vitality, strength, and good health. Red is also used for protection, owing to its relation to the element of fire, and is used in work involving sexuality, attraction, fidelity, and fertility.

Pink

Pink is another "love" color that is perceived as being friendly and creating a pleasing atmosphere. Pink candles are favored for weddings and entertaining because the color is linked to compassion and friendship.

Purple

Purple is a high-vibration color used in spiritual work, powerful healing, and meditation.

Blue

Blue is used along with purple to strengthen one's ability to perform complex healing and spiritual work. Blue also symbolizes tranquility, peace, increased visionary capacity, clairvoyance, and premonitions.

Green

Green represents the power and mystery of Mother Earth, including her ability to replenish, her fertility, her ability to aid growth, regeneration, and her ability to heal. Green is linked to all earthly concerns, especially financial dealings. Employment, securing a raise, attracting money, financial security, and even love magick are all connected with green candles.

Brown

Brown has varied readings according to the sources mentioned above. Many experts consider it an all-purpose candle. I subscribe to Scott Cunningham's belief, however, that brown is connected to animal spirit, therefore I use it to engage the power and ability of power animals, totem animals, and animal spirit allies. Brown can also be used for healing work involving animal companions or wild animals.

Black

Black is often connected to evil, curses, and hexes. I find these readings reflect cultural bias and internalized racism. For example, white is good, pure, positive, and spiritual, while black is dark, negative, dirty, and evil. As a painter and colorist, I understand from reading the works of Wassily Kandinsky and Henri Matisse that black contains all colors. From a purely scientific point of view, black absorbs light. For these reasons, once again I subscribe to Scott Cunningham's point of view that black can be used to absorb or banish negativity, and to fight off hexes and curses. Black contains all colors, thus it is a general, all-purpose candle.

Anointin' and Dressin' Candles

Anointing, or *dressing,* as it is more commonly called, is used in Hoodoo practice to add extra strength to candles by uniting them with your intent and energy. Dressing transforms the candle from being a mundane object to a magickally charged tool. Herbs and herb-infused oils are the best way of achieving a good dressing for jobs and tricks.

As an herbalist, I have noticed that many types of manufactured dressing and anointing oils have little herbal material in them. They are filled with synthetic ingredients and artificial colors. To achieve a proper charge powered by the great goddesses, create your own oils. It is simple and inexpensive. Rest assured that with the ingredients gathered from the earth and sea, coupled with your focused intentions, your candles will be fully charged and capable of getting the job done right, for they will contain ashe, the power of the universe! Place ingredients in a sterilized bottle with a cork or nonreactive cap. Shake or swirl before each use.

Basic Dressings

Banishing—To 3 ounces safflower oil, add 3 drops each of rose geranium, lilac, bergamot, and frankincense essential oils. Place a frankincense tear, a piece of amber, and a few dried rose petals inside the bottle.

Blessing—To 2 ounces sunflower and 1 ounce light olive oil, add 2 drops lavender essential oil and 2 drops vetiver essential oil. Place an amethyst stone and a cinnamon chip in the bottle.

Healing—To 2 ounces sunflower and 1 ounce light olive oil, add 4 drops jasmine essential oil, 3 drops attar of roses, 2 drops frankincense essential oil, and 3 drops myrrh essential oil. Place a few tears of frankincense and myrrh in the bottle.

Holy—To 2 ounces safflower and 1 ounce wheat germ oil, add 3 drops each of frankincense, myrrh, cedar, and hyssop essential oils. Drop in a few flakes of gold leaf (or a small gold necklace) and a piece of dried hyssop herb.

Love Draw—To 2½ ounces sweet almond and ½ ounce sesame seed oil, add 4 drops sandalwood essential oil, 4 drops attar of roses, and 3 drops patchouli essential oil. Place a turquoise stone and ¼ teaspoon magnetic sand in the bottle.

Luck Draw—To 3 ounces sweet almond oil, add 4 drops sandalwood essential oil and 4 drops bergamot essential oil. Drop a whole nutmeg, a piece of carnelian, and 2 whole allspice into the bottle.

Money Draw—To 3 ounces sunflower oil, add 2 drops each of basil, pine, lime, and peppermint essential oils. Drop in a dime, a nickel, and a quarter, and sprinkle in ½ teaspoon gold leaf flakes.

Protection from Evil Spirits—To 3 ounces sunflower oil, add 3 drops hyssop essential oil and 4 drops lavender essential oil. Drop a whole four-leaf clover (charm or real) into the bottle.

Van Van, or Opening the Way to Visions and Psychic Clarity—To 3 ounces sweet almond oil, add 4 drops lemon grass essential oil, 3 drops palmarosa essential oil, and 2 drops bitter almond essential oil. If available, add a pinch of magnetic sand for a power boost.

Application of Dressing

The candle color and dressing are important, but it is critical that the dressing is applied correctly. Put some dressing oil in your hands or on a paper towel. Wrap your hands or the paper towel around the candle. Begin in the center of the candle and stroke upwards first, then downwards. It is also popular to carve initials and appropriate symbols (dollar signs and male and female symbols, for example) into the candle. Some candles come encased in painted glass holders for luck, prosperity, or blessings, while others are covered with saints and prayers. For those who need a strong visual focus, try these specialty candles. Shaped candles are also formed into black cats, lovers, and so forth.

The Conjuring Altar

An obvious and useful place to utilize your charged candles is in your home on an altar. Most altars are created to accommodate one's personal needs. They are an area set aside as a personal space to generate and gather momentum; a place for focusing intent. Since the altar holds symbols and tools you hold sacred, it is an excellent gathering place for solitary magickal work and ceremonial healing. An altar also affords the opportunity for meditation, invocation, remembrance of ancestors, and deep reflection. It is a sacred space where you can take stock of your life and set priorities. Once you gain enough acuity for astral travel, it is a safe space for glimpsing the past and future.

Because of the humble origins of Hoodoo (rural, earth-based animism), there is no need for expensive materials or flashy tools. The suggestions below are influenced by African, Native American, and Asian folklore and magickal belief, which reflects the cultural milieu of early African American conjurers.

Disposal of Candle Wax

Before we get to the rituals, a few words need to be said about candle wax disposal. Wax from melted candles should be disposed of with careful consideration of the intent behind the burning. Most hoodoos wrap the wax remains in either paper or cloth. Several art supply shops sell beautiful handmade paper and different types of vegetable parchment that can be utilized for this purpose (see appendix B).

For most general purposes of a domestic nature, like love, home blessing, and protection, it is fine to bury the wrapped wax in the yard. For complex matters requiring spirit intervention, the wrapped wax can be buried in a graveyard. Wax burned for darker purposes is usually tossed into the center of a crossroad. For banishment, separation, and breaking hexes, the wrapped wax can be thrown over the left shoulder into a fierce storm. Retrieve after three days and bury at a crossroads. Quickly walk away without looking back.

In this last example, the combination of fire and water in ritual brings to mind the elegant Thai ritual called *Loy Krathong.* In early November, participants launch small boats filled with candles, incense, money, and fragrant gardenias on fresh, running water. If the candles stay lit until they flow out of sight, the wish will come true. I love this bringing together of the elements fire (candles), air (fragrance), water (river, stream, or lake), and earth (flowers).

Kinnikinnik

Kinnikinnik is an ancient Algonquin Indian word for the bearberry plant (*Arctostaphylos uva-ursi*) and the name of a special botanical mixture used in rituals. Kinnikinnik blends often contain the herb tobacco or other smoking ingredients, but are not always smoked. Sometimes they are added to medicine bundles to bring good health and to get rid of bad vibes, or they are burnt on their own to please the ancestors, for smudging, purification, or prayer. The following blend is derived from the Native American kinnikinnik.

KINNIKINNIK OFFERING

Use this blend as a special way to honor and remember your loved ones on their birthday or an anniversary, in a medicine bundle to attract good health and deter negative spirits, or before beginning ceremonial healing work.

¼ cup crushed red juniper berries
Handful of dried branches, bark,
    and shredded and dried leaves
    from a willow, oak, or birch tree
1 cup herbal blend of dried sage,
    rosemary, bearberry (uva ursi)
    leaves, and lavender buds

1 cup juniper, cedar, spruce, or
    pine needles
½ cup pure smoking tobacco
¼ teaspoon juniper essential oil
¼ teaspoon bergamot essential oil
¼ teaspoon white pine essential oil

Break the evergreen needles into ½" pieces and the tree branches and bark into 4–6" pieces.

To the evergreen needles add the crushed juniper berries. Mix in the tree branches, bark, and leaves, followed by the herbal blend and tobacco. Stir well.

Sprinkle the juniper, bergamot, and white pine essential oils onto the mixture and blend.

Store in a sterile glass or stainless-steel container with a tight-fitting lid and keep in a cool, dry place out of direct sunlight. Shake the container daily for 4 to 6 weeks, focusing on your intentions for the blend while you do so.

To honor your ancestors, place a charcoal block inside a chiminea or on top of your favorite flat rock or fossil outdoors or in a well-ventilated area. Light the charcoal and allow it to heat thoroughly. Put a pinch or two of the Kinnikinnik Offering onto the charcoal. Close your eyes, smell the aroma, and remember your ancestors with a special song, memory, or chant.

To make a small medicine bundle to carry on your person, wrap ½ cup of the matured Kinnikinnik Offering in muslin and secure it with a ribbon.

Yield: 20 ounces
Shelf life: 1 year

Fire

There is an active engagement between Chinese esoteric thought and Hoodoo. Incenses, powders, and washes fabricated in the U.S. that include a plethora of herbs grown in China (such as Chinese Wash) are essential to the hoodoo. There is also ample use of salt in rituals, a practice widely honored in feng shui.

Feng shui philosophy is incorporated into my altars. For example, I love candles and would love to cover my altar with their fragrant light. However, my enthusiasm is tempered by the ancient wisdom honored in feng shui. According to Simon Brown, author of *Practical Feng Shui*, fire is pure chi energy—the embodiment of passion, excitement, spontaneity, and brightness. The chi quality suggests that candlelight is good as a generator for energy, power, and inspiration. However, an excess of passion, too much excitement, or even uninformed spontaneity could weaken the efficacy of the job (spell), wishes, desires, or general environment. To balance the pure chi energy of candles, Brown suggests that the feng shui art of placement be utilized. Candles placed in an eastern or southeastern position of a room calms chi energy, while placing them in the northeast or southwest enhances chi energy.

Pure chi energy of candles can also be kept in check by placing objects that hold other types of energies near them on the altar. My favorites are fragrant flowers in clear water, especially since the ancestors also love fragrant floral bouquets. Jasmine, honeysuckle, roses, narcissus, and gardenia figure prominently in Hoodoo as flowers of choice. According to Joanna Trevelyan in *Holistic Home: Creating an Environment for Physical and Spiritual Well Being*, the water element calms the passionate energy of fire. Low, round, glass plates also symbolize water, so I set my altar candles on these. With the popularity of candles as decorative elements, glass plates can be found at discount chain stores like Wal-Mart or Target.

In *Holistic Home*, Trevelyan suggests flowers as representatives of a soil and tree element. To enhance the tree element, I include tall, thin greens during the winter months such as juniper, cedar, ferns, or eucalypti. Stones and fossils are also used as water and soil elements. Soil elements lend a sense of security, steadiness, and precaution to the events that take place at the altar.

Trevelyan also suggests careful consideration of candleholders. A metal-based holder, for example, such as wrought iron or silver, is connected to tree energy.

Metal brings an element of leadership, organization, depth, and solidity to your spiritual work. In accord with feng shui techniques, a low, flat, white bone china plate also serves as a tree element to balance the passionate energy of fire. I like to shop at antique shops, yard sales, and secondhand stores for silver, crystal, and bone china candleholders. Often these objects have an interesting strain of intrinsic good karma.

Water

Sadly, for a while our contact with our West African heritage dwindled significantly. The precious rituals of our people were either across the Atlantic or in relatively remote cultures such as the Gullah and Geechee of the South Carolina and Georgia Sea Islands. Now in the age of the Internet and affordable travel, with a fresh influx of African and African diasporic immigrants and the help of solid scholarship by Africanists, there is once again a great opportunity for meaningful interchange and direct contact with Africa. Yoruban, Vodoun, and animistic beliefs that our enslaved ancestors held dear have begun to be incorporated into our culture.

Within the Yoruban pantheon, seashells are revered for they contain the ashe of Yemoya-Olokun, earth mothers and queens of the sea. Ashe is the potentiality, power, mystery, and beauty of nature. Cowry shells represent the yoni, a divine image of female fecundity. Cowries also represent the fertility of Yemoya-Olokun, the creator deity. Conch shells play an especially prominent role in African diasporic traditions and are wonderful totemic additions to the altar. Seashells in their multiple shapes, textures, colors, and sizes play an important role in my altars because of their symbolic potency.

When full engagement of my ancestors or the person who I am working with is needed, I incorporate a bowl of Florida Water (see chapter 4) on the altar. If mourning, death, or remorse is involved, I use kananga water (see chapter 14). For banishment of evil, such as unhexing or uncrossing, I use either a bowl of kosher sea salt, sea water, and/or holy water.

Florida Water and kananga water are two sweet-smelling waters popularized in the mid-twentieth century that contain the essences of flowers, roots, and leaves. These special scented waters hold an esteemed place in Hoodoo. Florida

Water can still be found in many drugstores sold as a cologne. In addition to various African cultural linkages, sea salt and sea water are incorporated in Qabalistic ritual, European folklore, and Asian philosophy. Holy water is a Judeo-Christian element.

Earth

Another important element to the altar is earth. If you are brave or can get a hold of some, a glass or metal container filled with graveyard dirt should be a part of your altar. This is especially advisable if you can get the dirt from a family plot. The highest potency is derived from graveyard dirt taken from a grave at a crossroads (four corners). Graveyard dirt contains the spirit of the ancestors, the folk who look after us and mediate the spirit world. Some folks substitute graveyard dirt with mullein herb, topsoil, potting soil, or dirt from the garden. (For more on graveyard dirt and mullein herb, refer to chapter 6.)

Often fresh fruit or dried fruits are included as treats for the orishas. Fruit is included in Buddhist shrines and African altars to feed the ancestors. Dried limes are especially revered in Hoodoo for bringing luck, and as such, they are carried in mojo bags. I add dried limes, fresh lemons, and fresh oranges to my altars because I know my ancestors (especially my mother) love them.

I also keep the precious grains of wheat and cornmeal in a container on my altar. The grains are a symbol of fruitful harvest, fertility, and the continuity of life. Having corn on the altar invites the presence of numerous Native American goddesses into the home. Placed on the hearth it serves as a splendid tribute to Chicomecoatl, a Mexican hearth goddess who brings abundance. Chicomecoatl provides comfort, warmth, and security, while also assuring continued life through her generous promise of fertility.

Chicomecoatl wears the sun as a shield. Her warmth brings renewal, rebirth, energy, tonic, and inspiration. The following is a bathing ritual inspired by the warm, energizing qualities of this fire goddess.

CHICOMECOATL'S BATH

¼ cup pulverized dried marigold
  petals

¼ cup red rose petals

1 teaspoon orange peel

2½ cups Dead Sea salt

2½ cups coarse sea salt

3 cups Epsom salt

1 teaspoon rose geranium essential
  oil

¼ teaspoon petigrain essential oil

¼ teaspoon neroli essential oil

1 teaspoon peppermint essential oil

1 tablespoon sunflower oil

Mix together the marigold petals, rose petals, and orange peel and set aside.

Pour the Dead Sea salt, coarse sea salt, and Epsom salt in a large bowl and stir.

Put the rose geranium, petigrain, neroli, and peppermint essential oils and the sunflower oil in a small bowl and gently swirl together.

Pour the oil mixture over the salt mixture and stir. Add the botanical mixture and mix.

Store in an airtight plastic or stainless-steel container. To use, add 2 cups per bath.

Yield: 8 cups, or enough for 4 baths
Shelf life: 1 year

Family

I have several altars. Two are private, but the central one, where I gather energy, strength, and balance, is in my family room on top of the hearth. This altar contains dressed candles on top of fossils and rocks. Loose incense made up of fragrant leaves, juniper berries, frankincense and myrrh tears, and sandalwood and cedar chips are burned on top of charcoal inside of seashells. The readily apparent focus of the altar is numerous family photographs. My hearth altar has helped spark many creative projects while also helping to maintain unity, peace, balance, and positive spirits within the home. When my hearth altar is dusty, dirty, or dim, I take it as a direct reflection of a dim or confused spirit within my home or soul. I dust the altar lovingly with a feather duster sprayed lightly with Uplifting Dusting Blend. Earth, sea, air, fire, and family temper and anchor my life straight from the hearth.

UPLIFTING DUSTING BLEND

1 cup olive oil

½ teaspoon lavender essential oil

½ teaspoon lemon grass essential oil

¼ teaspoon neroli essential oil

Mix all ingredients together. Pour through a funnel into a spray bottle. Use on a feather duster or dust cloth.

chapter 6

The Elements of War

In traditional West African society, the main arbitrators between humans and spirits are hunters and warriors. For the most part, the hunters' and warriors' clothing easily identifies them. The ornate shirts worn by Mande, Asante, and a few other groups set them apart from normal citizens. These garments are laden with amulets, knotted cords, animal teeth, claws, horns, cowry shells, and bits of glass. The shirts are naturally dyed with tree bark teas, which leave an earthen tone. The bark is blessed with protective incantations during preparation. The sacred clothing, amulets, and animal substances help the warrior blend in spiritually and psychically with the wilderness. For the warrior, these are more than just shirts; they are shields that provide protection from weapons while also creating an air of invisibility.

In the book *In Sorcery's Shadow,* anthropologist Paul Stoller records his experiences with sorcerors and warriors. Stoller gives a rare glimpse into pre-Islamic African magick that has survived to the current day. Stoller and his wife, sociologist

Cheryl Olkes, tell the story of their apprenticeship to sorcerers from 1974 to 1986. They were taught by the Sohanci, descendants of the royal Songhay empire, which was at its height between 1493 and 1527. Many Sohanci, particularly from near the borders of Niger and Mali, are feared sorcerers called *zima*. Zima are people who shape and bend reality, effecting change. The Sohanci zima Stoller and Olkes studied under worked magick almost exclusively with powders made from wildcrafted mosses, grasses, barks, roots, and leaves. These powders are used medicinally among the villagers, but they are also used spiritually to appease the *tooru*. Tooru are the nobles of the spirit world who control the elements of the warrior: fire, lightning, thunder, and wind.

Cobras, vipers, boas, and pythons surround Tilliberi and Wanzerbe, the main villages of Stoller and Olkes's research. As the arbitrators between animals, spirits, and humans, zima coexist with these dangerous reptiles by harnessing their power. To harness the power of pythons, Stoller was instructed to kill a python and eat it as part of a power ritual. In a time structure similar to Hoodoo magickal practices, he cut it into seven pieces and ate one section daily for seven days. The consumption of the python imparted special magick to him, enabling him to transform the lessons of his apprenticeship into power.

In another striking account, Stoller shares his observations of the magickal use of powders at a crossroad in Wanzerbe. Shortly after this observation, he is transformed from a man of science to a believer in magick and a practicing zima:

> The morning of my departure I made coffee for the Sohanci, Moru, and myself. As I waited for the water to boil, I wondered how a simple rite like burning those powders at the crossroads could reunite an irreconcilably estranged couple. *What power,* I marveled. *What Power!**

As a White man from America, Stoller learned firsthand what African hunters and warriors have understood for centuries—that every plant and animal is full of *nyama.* Nyama is the unpredictable energy and action that flows through everything in the universe. Nyama is always present—it can be useful or dangerous. Hunters attempt

*Selection from *In Sorcery's Shadow* by Paul Stoller and Cheryl Olkes reprinted with permission by University of Chicago Press.

to understand and control the flow of nyama. The uses of snake venom in Hoodoo, for example, is a special art that requires mastery of nyama. Old-timers had this gift; they knew how to use venom to both harm and help people.

In Africa, this type of special knowledge is apparent for all to see. Hunter/warrior shirts reflect the experiences of the warrior or hunter, while also documenting his research of various medicines and tactics. The shirts contain knowledge required to extract venom from spiders and snakes among other risky ordeals. One warrior amulet called a *nyi-ji* captures the tears of prey.

Snake goddess with Erzulie veve

Examining the nyi-ji, or tears amulet, helps us understand the evolution of mojos in the United States. Nyi-ji grow out of a hunter's desire to take responsibility for taking life. It involves a secret ritual designed to redirect the nyama (life force) of the animal after it has been killed.

Roots of seven specific plants dug from seven separate footpaths are the main ingredients for the nyi-ji. Also included are a flower from the revered baobab tree, a large nicotiana blossom (from a tobacco plant), the staff or cane of a blind person, fiber from a hibiscus plant used to wash a medicine pot, and a woman's personal washcloth. Then all of these objects are burned down to white ash. The ashes are placed in the cavity of a horn. The stopper for the horn is pierced with a piece of iron and then the blood of a white rooster is poured over it.

This amulet is activated by pointing it at an animal. The concentrated power of the nyi-ji, combined with the strong intent of the hunter, makes the animal's eyes water. The tears obscure the animal's sight, making it easy to trap. Once the animal is killed, the hunter rushes up to it and waters an iron staff with the animal's tears.

This is but one of the powerful amulets that hunters wear on a ceremonial shirt. The numerous bulging pockets filled with amulets attest to the prowess and bravery of the wearer. The amulets announce that a spiritual force has been harnessed and is now working for the person wearing the shirt. Some of the pockets contain special blessings (magickal squares), a verse, or a prayer from the Koran. These magickal squares are folded the number of times that correspond to the deity being invoked and placed in some of the amulets.

The Asante wear these shirts for battle rather than for hunting. Traditional warriors feel a tremendous responsibility for their actions. They spend many years alone learning herbalism and the science of the trees (called *jiridon*) directly from the forest. Jiridon is used by hunters and warriors to honor the majestic qualities of their opponents or prey. (For more on jiridon, see chapter 2.)

The humble attitude of the fierce warriors and hunters is a reminder to hoodoos to be fair. Although far removed from the lifestyle of traditional warriors, we hunt, gather, and fight wars of a different type. It is critical that we don't become intoxicated by our own power.

Power of the Universe

Hoodoos are not only concerned with the earth, but are also concerned with the heavens as they are rich in myth. The astrological sign most closely aligned with fire is Scorpio. Scorpios are sensitive, aware, and full of intuitive potential. The emotional sensitivity of the Scorpio can cause miscommunications that lead to crisis. This is another important issue for hoodoo warriors to consider: a hot Scorpio head is irrational. Irrational thoughts may transform a perfectly innocent gesture into an enemy tactic in your mind. This could lead to an unjustified Hoodoo war, and trust me, this is something your world could do without.

The planetary ruler of fire is Mars. Mars is so hot that it cannot support life. The god Mars is linked with a hot and dry temperament. Mars Powder (which is easy to find commercially made) is a destructive powder when placed in the path of an enemy. Mars Powder will lead an enemy to trouble, but if the person is not your true enemy, it may well backfire in your direction.

Ogun, Orisha of the Warriors

The Yoruban brother of the Greek god Mars is Ogun. The two fire gods share various correspondences. Ogun is the warrior orisha, and not only is he associated with fire, he is also associated with metal as the god of iron. Linked with metalsmithing, Ogun holds a lofty position among the orisha of the Ifa, Lucumi, and Santeria paths.

Hoodoo warriors can benefit from the invocation of Ogun, for like Hoodoo itself, metallurgy and metalsmithing are dangerous and unpredictable. The Mande people in Africa see blacksmiths and spirits as being practically colleagues. The Mande credit blacksmiths with knowledge of healing, initiation, and sorcery. Blacksmiths are intermediaries between the wild, natural life and civil society. As manipulators of nature through their craft, blacksmiths shape wild nature into a useful form for the people.

Tools of the Hoodoo warrior incorporate iron and metal, thus they are imbued with the power of Ogun and the alchemy of the metalsmith. In the olden days, anvil dust was used for tricks and jobs. Today iron filings, magnetic sand, pyrite, rusted nails, ordinary nails from various significant sites, and coffin nails are still used by hoodoos.

Ogun's number is three. His colors are green and black. Images of warriors and hunters and their implements (such as swords, knives, and arrows) are associated with him. Iron or metal objects, including the prominent use of nails, correspond with Ogun. He enjoys rum or pineapple offerings, and his corresponding *ewe* (herbs) include parsley, hawthorn, and alfalfa. Spiritual baths in his honor should include eucalyptus and tobacco. Garlic is an important Ogun medicine.

Veve for Ogun with raspberry plant

Ogun's medicine is contained in the traditional Hoodoo formula Four Thieves Vinegar. Four Thieves Vinegar is used in protective magick by hoodoos, their families, and their clients who feel susceptible to tricks and jobs.

FOUR THIEVES VINEGAR

In 1772 during the height of the bubonic plague, four thieves conspired to rob the graves of the dead of precious possessions that were buried with them. They came from a family of perfumers who were knowledgeable of the health benefits of herbs and essential oils. The four thieves rubbed their bodies with a garlic-infused vinegar, and although the plague was highly contagious, they did not succumb to it. They were able to cheat death by using the ewe of Ogun.

16 ounces apple cider vinegar or   4 cloves garlic
    distilled white vinegar

Mince the garlic. Add a little of the vinegar to the garlic and macerate further until soft. Spoon this into a sterile jar and slowly pour in the rest of the vinegar. Let the bubbles subside and then cap.

Swirl gently daily for 3 to 4 weeks. Each time you do, chant the following:

Evil may come,
but it will not stay.
My Four Thieves Vinegar
will keep evil at bay.

For spiritual or physical immunity or protection, apply Four Thieves Vinegar to your body.

To build internal immunity, add ½ teaspoon Four Thieves Vinegar to 8 ounces water and drink.

Variation: In place of the garlic, use 4 herbs with antibacterial, antiseptic, and high spiritual vibrations such as lavender, hyssop, rosemary, sage, peppermint, or rue.

Yield: 16 ounces
Shelf life: 1 year

Oya, Orisha of the Wind

Oya is a fierce orisha. Her domain is the cemetery. She is responsible for swift actions, tornados, storms, quarrels, restlessness, change, and renewal. She is the essence of the winds of the four directions.

Oya is the color reddish-brown or rust (like rusty coffin nails); she is what are considered "earth" tones. Her number is nine. The parts of the body system she is affiliated with include the respiratory system: lungs, bronchial passages, and mucous membranes. Not coincidentally, these are the parts first affected by Hoodoo dusts and powders.

In order for your war magick to work, invoke Oya. Try some of the following suggestions at a crossroads or just outside a cemetery before or after a storm or on the ninth day of the month to invoke her spirit:

- Set out offerings of red wine, purple grapes, eggplant, plums, chickweed, or a bowl of rice and beans for her.

- Set out symbols she enjoys, such as tree branches felled from a storm, lightning water in a bowl or glass, or a found buffalo horn.

- Create a simple incense containing some of her favorite ewe (see below).

OYA INVOCATION

Burn this incense outdoors at a crossroad or just outside a cemetery.

Mud cloth, Nigerian-printed cloth, or other fabric the color of rust, burnt orange, or deep purple	Pinch of dried tobacco Pinch of dried comfrey Pinch of dried mullein

Blend together the tobacco, comfrey, and mullein.

Set out the cloth. Place a naturally fireproof surface on it, such as a piece of petrified wood, a fossil, stone, or large seashell. Place a charcoal block on the fireproof surface (a sulphur-containing type is okay since this is being burned outside).

Light the charcoal. When the charcoal is hot, put the incense blend on it and let it smolder as you contemplate the mystery and power of Oya.

Shango the Alchemist

Devotee to Shango

Shango is an alchemist orisha who protects us from evil. He possesses the fierceness and speed of lightning, thus he is often paired with Oya. Shango brings good *iwa-pele* (balance of character, yin-yang, male-female). Iw-pele is central to traditional African belief systems and has roots in ancient Khemet (ancient Black Egypt).

Shango is fiery and fierce, yet he is also cool, judicious, stately, and noble. He is associated with the numbers six and twelve and his color is red. Pay tribute to Shango before performing warrior tricks. Do this on the sixth or twelfth of the month by meditating on his power at the base of a tree holding a small basket containing okra, pebbles or rocks, a yam, red hibiscus flowers, and/or cayenne pepper.

Foot Track Magick

Confirmation concerning my grandma's involvement with Hoodoo and hoodoos came through Ma's repeated stories of "wars" with hants (ghosts) and with the neighbors in Montclair, New Jersey. "They'd throw the dust our way [toward the property boundaries], and then sure 'nough, Ma would spread some out so it would blow their way." She also sprinkled dust about to dispel the hants. "We were very afraid of hants living in our house," Ma relayed to me.

When I pinned my ma down for specifics about the dust, I found that it was mainly sulfur (brimstone), salt, cayenne, and black pepper—homemade Gopher's Dust (also known as *Goofer Dust*). In the arsenal of the hoodoo, Gopher's Dust is a chief weapon. It protects property, but it may also be used to blow bad intentions toward intruders with malicious plans. Gopher's Dust, which sometimes also incorporates snakeskin or a rattlesnake rattle, brings together the elements of earth and air, the two primary elements deployed for *foot track magick*. See appendix B for suppliers.

In *The Healing Wisdom of Africa,* Malidoma Patrice Some asserts the belief of his people, the Dagara of West Africa. Rather than supporting the concept asserted in Greek mythology and Judeo-Christian belief systems that the orisha exist high above us in the heavens, the Dagara (like many other indigenous groups) favor an animistic vision of the world. Animism places the ancestral spirits and creator beings among us on earth. The Dagara's spiritual framework supports my contention that we should tread lightly on the earth. Nevertheless, we should tread on her often to receive her powerful messages, memories, and magick through the soles of our feet.

Our feet hold incredible significance. Not only do our feet serve as our chief source of transportation, they are also the two things that bring us into daily contact with the spirit world. The soles of our feet function as receivers of divine messages and transmitters of our intentions to the spirit world.

In his landmark book *From Slavery to Freedom,* John Hope Franklin describes Africans as being primarily agrarian people. Land ownership was intimately connected to the richness and productivity of the soil. Important dignitaries were referred to as "grand priests/priestesses of the soil," "masters of the ground," and "administrators of the soil."

Family land holds a great deal of importance because it often holds family plots and the bones of our ancestors. The ancestral spirits are not seen as being dormant and buried; they continue to live through the trees, streams, and flowers. The animistic beliefs of West Africa are a product of a people with close affinities to the earth.

The hoodoo must always walk with purpose, fully cognizant of how she touches the earth. She knows the markers, texture, and scent of her daily path. A hoodoo with evil intentions seeks to capitalize on the purposeful hoodoo's knowledge of her path. Planting obstructions of a sensual, visual, or spiritual nature in her path is a sign that war plans are afoot.

Obstructions may consist of blueberries spread on a sidewalk or threshold. Blueberries leave a messy trace of your movements. They burst and splatter violently when you step on them. The plopping sounds and sight of purple-stained pavement are distracting and serve as a visual metaphor. Blueberries on your path are designed to cause confusion and fear.

Mustard seeds serve a similar purpose. The texture of the mustard seed is gritty and movement with them underfoot is noisy and annoying. Mustard seeds, especially when combined with mustard powder, is a sure-fire signal that you are under attack. The combined herbs are thought to lead you on a path to destruction. Mustard powder causes anxiety, stress, and personal difficulties.

Fruit and herbs are mild indicators of war compared to Hot Foot Powder or Stay Away Powder (see page 37). These powders are designed to keep unwanted folk away from your home, land, or office. Hot Foot Powder is full of the fire element. It is red, it smells acrid enough to burn the nostrils, and if stepped on with bare feet or handled improperly, it can cause irritation. This is due in large part to its high cayenne (*Capsicum frutescens* or *Capsicum* spp.) content. Cayenne has diaphoretic, rubefacient, and stimulant qualities. Ground cayenne (the form commonly used in Hoodoo dusts) is called *chili pepper* and it has the ability to energize the entire system. The tonic quality and fiery heat of chilis stimulate the flow of energy. In short, it is hard to ignore contact with cayenne.

The efficacy of Hot Foot Powder—or any other powder, for that matter—is not all in the fire element, however. The delivery system for powders is the air—a tool of Oya. For this reason, wear a dust mask when making and spreading these powders.

HOT FOOT POWDER

Use Hot Foot Powder on enemies, bullies, or abusers. It also works well for solicitors, door-to-door salespeople, the jilted lover who won't take the hint, and other everyday nuisances. Mix on a Tuesday, the day of Ogun and Mars. An evening of the waning moon is the best time for making this banishment dust.

2 cups pure cayenne (chili) powder   2 cups ground black pepper
2 cups sea salt

Drop the ingredients into a bowl as you charge them with your intentions:

Hot foot! Hot foot!
You have gotten too close for me,

[Drop in the cayenne powder]

Now is the time. I banish thee!

[Throw a pinch of the sea salt over your left shoulder, then add the rest to the cayenne]

Step here if you'd like
but it won't be for long.

[Add the pepper]

Examine your ways,
it's time to move on.

[Stir the powder clockwise 3 times]

Hot foot! Hot foot!
Burns through the sole.

[Stir powder counterclockwise 3 times]

Hot foot! Hot foot!
Cause you've been doin' me wrong.

[Stir powder clockwise 3 last times]

Hot foot, hot foot,
Move on! Move on!

Pour the mixture into a screw-top jar. Seal and store in a cool, dry place until ready to use.

To use on enemies, bullies, or abusers, repeat the chant listed above while spreading a generous amount of Hot Foot Powder into the wet footprints of the offender. If no wet prints are available, spread this on his or her usual path.

To fortify your home from everyday nuisances like solicitors, spread this powder on the perimeter of your property.

Yield: 6 cups
Shelf life: 6 months

Protection Rings

In addition to using Hot Foot Powder, you can magickally seal off your home from unwanted intruders using any of the following suggestions:

- Spread Gopher's Dust (see appendix B) around the perimeter of your home.

- Hang garlic on the doors.

- Burn a sage smudge stick or incense on your front and/or back stoop. For incense, use frankincense, myrrh, or a combination (2 to 1 ratio, respectively).

- Spread your urine around the perimeter of your property.

- Place protective flowers around your home (inside or out) to invite good spirits in, including daffodils, roses, jasmine, honeysuckle, lilac, violets, linden blossoms, or lavender.

WARRIOR'S PATH POWDER

When you need energy and rejuvenation after putting up the good fight (against enemies or hunting down a suitable job or home), try this treatment.

1 teaspoon chopped alkanet root	½ cup yellow cornmeal
2 tablespoons safflower oil	¼ cup arrowroot powder
⅛ teaspoon juniper berry essential oil	¼ cup ground marigold (calendula) blossoms
⅛ teaspoon neroli essential oil	¼ cup white clay (bentonite)

Steep the alkanet root in the safflower oil for 1 hour. Swirl it periodically to release the alkanet's rich red natural dye. Strain.

Use a dropper to add the juniper berry and neroli essential oils into the strained alkanet oil. Swirl or mix with a stirring wand.

In a separate bowl, mix together the cornmeal, arrowroot powder, marigold blossoms, and clay. Add the oil mixture and stir well.

Store in an airtight container. To use, place this mixture on the floor near the tub and powder your feet as you come out of the water.

Yield: 1¼ cups
Shelf life: 2 weeks

War Water Bottles

On her website and in her Lucky Mojo Curio Co. Catalogue, Hoodoo product designer and author Cat Yronwode discusses her personal recollections of the Hoodoo wars in Oakland, California, during the 1960s. Yronwode recalls hoodoos throwing and receiving bottles containing ominous visual messages in the form of various war waters. These bottles would break when hurled at an enemy's property, tree, or business, leaving a foul-smelling, dangerous mess to contend with. Yronwode sells War Water that contains Spanish moss, rusted nails, and coffin nails suspended in water.

I have also heard of hoodoos putting black feathers, blood, or blood substitutes (such as cherry juice, apple cider vinegar, tomato juice, beet juice, or pomegranate juice) into bottles. The real blood would most likely come from a freshly slaughtered black or white rooster. Black feathers from crows or ravens are also sometimes included in War Water bottles. These, combined with the emblematic coffin nail (an object strong enough to tie down wayward spirits) and the broken glass (which suggests the transparent spirit world), all come together to deliver the powerful, dark warning, "Watch your step! Tread lightly! Hoodoo is coming your way!"

Within a War Water bottle is a small, dark world—whether the hoodoo concocts a foul, swamp-inspired brew or a sweetly scented blood-red one. Broken glass is a metaphor for the glassy world of the spirits, but it has another place in African American tradition. Bottles are used as traps for wayward spirits on a property. The spirits are attracted to transparency.

The Kandu tradition of tying bottles to barren trees carried over to the United States and other strongholds of the African diaspora. The bottles are unnatural, cold, lifeless, and thus suggestive of death. From Virginia to Texas, bottles have been used in African American protective magick as charms (nkisi). Those who are steeped in the mysterious potency of bottles would take the tossing of or discovery of a War Water bottle on their property as being especially ominous. (For more on bottle trees, see chapter 14.)

WAR WATER

War Waters send a vividly threatening message. It is a study in contrasts: bright, blood-red color and strange, dark, floral scent. A glass bottle of War Water can be placed near the front door in such a way that opening the door causes the War Water to spill over, leak fake blood, or break altogether. Really angry hoodoos have been known to throw a bottle filled with War Water at a tree on their enemy's land, or even aim at the threshold or front door.

Handful of dried hibiscus flowers, or 2 hibiscus tea bags
½ cup distilled vinegar
½ cup lightning water
3 drops attar of roses
3 drops patchouli essential oil
3 drops vetiver essential oil
3 drops geranium essential oil
3 coffin nails (see note)
1 brown or black egg
Transparent tape

If using dried hibiscus flowers, decoct them in 2 cups very hot water for 20 to 30 minutes. If using tea bags, infuse them in 1 cup very hot water for the same time. Strain the decoction or squeeze out the tea bags and let cool.

Pour the hibiscus water into a large-mouthed jar. Add the vinegar, lightning water, attar of roses, and the essential oils. Swirl the contents of the jar to mix.

Carefully break the egg in half and clean out the eggshell. Place the coffin nails inside the two eggshell halves and tape shut. Place this in the jar and seal shut. Let steep outdoors for a full cycle of the moon.

Note: Coffin nails can be obtained from a Hoodoo supplier. See appendix B.

Graveyard Dirt

A central component in the hoodoo's bag of tricks is graveyard dirt. Some say it is all for evil, but how could that be with all of the sweet, innocent people that have passed on to the spirit realm buried there? In the old days, folk collected dirt from specific types of graves to perform certain jobs, a tradition that is still prevalent in Santeria. For example, the dirt from a young child's grave is imbued with sweetness. The grave of an elder who lived a long, happy, generous life is a site for gathering dirt imbued with wisdom and compassion. Dirt is also taken from specific locations, like a racetrack for gambling luck or the grounds of a court for a favorable outcome in a court case. Before we talk about collecting graveyard dirt, however, we need to understand the implications of it and the angelic beings that guard the cemeteries.

Elegba

Elegba (also known as Eshu-Elegba) is the orisha of gateways, woods, and cross-roads. Most cemeteries have an impressive iron gateway that guards it; it is here that you may leave your offering to the gatekeeper Elegba. Cemeteries are also partially wooded (for more on trees and cemeteries, see chapter 14). Many cemeteries take up a large amount of space and they are at or near a crossroads. Pay homage to Elegba, along with Oya and Shango, when you collect or use your graveyard dirt, or make or use powders containing it.

ELEGBA SPIRIT ALTAR AND BATH

Before or after visiting the cemetery, create an altar and be sure to take a bath. Elegba is judicious or punitive and he is known as a trickster. It is best to pay homage and remove his influence when it is not desired.

2 cups sugar
1 orange
Handful of dried lemon verbena
Sea salt
Red cloth
1 fresh coconut, halved
Almonds, sliced or whole
Small plate of cooked yams or
    roasted corn
1 black-and-white candle
Tobacco
Large flat stone or marble tile

Place the sugar in a bowl. Squeeze the juice of the entire orange over the sugar and stir. (Orange sizes vary, but the mixture should be a thick paste, so add more sugar if needed.) Crumble in the lemon verbena and mix. Set aside.

Clean the tub by placing the sea salt on a sponge and scrubbing. Rinse well.

Place the candle on the cloth. Set out the coconut and almonds in a bowl, the plate of yams or roasted corn, and the bowl containing the sugar-orange-lemon verbena mixture.

Set out the stone or marble tile on a table. Light a charcoal block on it. When the charcoal gets hot, place the tobacco on it.

Draw your bath. Get in, relax, and reflect on the energy of Elegba and the work at hand.

OYA'S HERBAL GRAVEYARD DIRT

Mullein is associated with Oya. Those who cannot or choose not to gather dirt from a burial ground can use it as a substitute for graveyard dirt.

To create an herbal graveyard dirt substitute, crumble 1 cup dried mullein into a bowl (double or triple according to portion desired). Use this in place of graveyard dirt. For additional richness, add ¼ cup each of Oya's other ewe: dried, crumbled chickweed, comfrey, and pure tobacco.

The Crossroads

There is mystique surrounding singer Robert Johnson. This is due in part to the belief that he sold his soul to the devil at the crossroads to become a better musician. Judeo-Christian interpretations of crossroads led us to believe that the devil resides there. Countless stories and songs speak about meetings with the devil at the crossroads.

Cross Road Blues (take 2)
by Robert Johnson

I went to the crossroad
fell down on my knees

I went to the crossroad
fell down on my knees

Asked the Lord above "Have mercy, now
save poor Bob, if you please"

Mmmmm, standin' at the crossroad
I tried to flag a ride

Standin' at the crossroad
I tried to flag a ride

Didn't nobody seem to know me
everybody pass me by

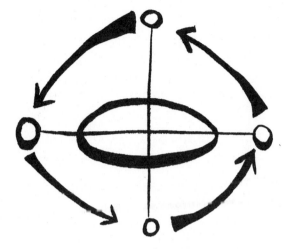

Figure 5: Yowa Cross.

Mmm, the sun goin' down, boy
dark gon' catch me here
oooo ooee eeee

boy, dark gon' catch me here
I haven't got no lovin' sweet woman that
love and feel my care

You can run, you can run
tell my friend-boy Willie Brown

You can run, you can run
tell my friend-boy Willie Brown
Lord, that I'm standin' at the crossroad, babe
I believe I'm sinkin' down

To understand the feelings of early African Americans toward a fork in the road or crossroads, it is useful to look back to the Kongo cosmology. In this cosmology, there is a great deal of reverence for the crossroads. The crossroads is the center of the four winds. It is sacred ground suitable for oath-taking or making agreements.

The Yowa Cross (Figure 5) can be interpreted as a type of crossroads. The vertical line can be visualized as a path and the horizontal line as a boundary (to a cemetery, for example). The center links the two worlds: the one of the living with that of the dead. The center of the crossroads is not entirely in our mundane world, nor is it completely in the realm of the spirits either. This center is a sacred ground, a place where folk make agreements and arrangements.

Historically, blues performers would go to a crossroads at midnight with their guitar or harmonica and try to bargain with Eshu-Elegba to be able to play better. Gamblers would bring their dice, drummers brought their drums, sculptors brought their carving tools, and so forth. Manual dexterity is an important tool and the belief that a special orisha resided in this sacred location sparked many visits to the crossroads by creative people and other seekers.

Surely there are times when even the most patient hoodoo will want to retaliate against the ill will thrown her way. Fire-fueled emotion knows no boundaries. Through the brilliant blaze of anger and the haze of smoldering resentment, we lose track of the purpose behind our actions. With rationality and clarity lost, how can we purposefully practice our craft? When or if you arrive at this crossroad, it is a good time to turn to the Egyptian sun god, Sun Ra. Use the invocation below.

SUN RA INVOCATION

The Egyptian sun god Ra can be useful when trying to defeat an enemy, and this enemy could well be your own personal issues (e.g., self-loathing, low self-esteem, lack of courage or conviction). Sit outside on a day and at a time when the sun is bright.

Hold a topaz necklace with gold clasps in your left hand and say the following:

> Sun Ra, Sun Ra
> Come into my life
> Help me gain the strength and the courage
> To overcome personal strife.
>
> Sun Ra, Sun Ra
> The pressure cannot win
> As I look to your bright warming rays
> Let the healing begin.

After this invocation, embrace another tool of the hoodoo: the renewing possibilities of peace using water. This is explored fully in the next chapter.

chapter 7

Keepin' the Peace

Peace comes through the waters of pure spirit. Water is the elixir of life and as such it is important to all of us. Hoodoo developed within rural agrarian cultures, particularly through the meaningful interchange between African Americans and Native Americans. As former Africans, the new Black Americans retained the reverence for water that dominates traditional West African belief systems. Oshun, Yemoya-Olokun, Mami Wata, Oya, Oba, Hara Ke, Mujaji, and Ichar-Tsirew are all West African goddesses and orishas who live in bodies of water or who are embodied in rain—and there are hundreds more. These and other goddesses and orishas are celebrated during the West African New Year, which falls in mid-March, during harvests and other seasonal observances. African lore and water mythology have a sisterhood of beliefs residing in the New World. As African Americans mixed socially and intermarried with various American tribes, they began to apply their beliefs and magickal systems to plants and animals indigenous to the Americas.

The development of blending scent with water to create sweet waters began in Egypt and took root in West Africa in the form of orange blossom water. Sweet waters, imbued with herbal medicines and magickal incantations, were embraced by hoodoos and conjurers for their tight fit with the purpose at hand.

Waters of Peace

As we saw in previous chapters, careful attention is paid to the cleansing of pathways in Hoodoo, especially the home. Hoodoos are leery of intent being tracked into a private space by the feet of those who might harbor ill will. For a thoroughly cleansed path, a simulated river or stream is recommended using *blued* water (with Mrs. Stuart's bluing or similar products). This invites the presence of the water orisha Yemoya-Olokun, mothers of the oceans and rivers. The presence of the creator beings lends especially potent juju to the task of clearing, since Yemoya is an angelic Yoruban deity whose power and promise is often likened to the attributes of the Virgin Mary in Christianity. Yemoya-Olokun are loved by many for their capacity for understanding, depth, and generosity. (An extensive cross-cultural examination of the manifestations and evolution of the Virgin Mary is contained in Barbara G. Walker's *The Woman's Encyclopedia of Myths and Secrets*. Barbara Walker and Robert Farris Thompson, author of *Flash of the Spirit*, both illustrate the direct correlation between Mary and Yemoya-Olokun.)

Yemoya-Olokun with jasmine

The orisha aligned with water are Great Mother Yemoya-Olokun and Oshun. The water orisha sit on the opposite end of the color wheel from Oya and Shango. Yemoya-Olokun and Oshun are embodied by blue, green, and white, while Oya and Shango are burnt orange, red, and black.

Another deity connected to water is Erinlé. Erinlé, the great hunter orisha, is neither fully male or female. This quality is common in many

Yoruban orisha, but this hermaphrodite reigns above ground *and* in the water—a most unusual ability. On land, Erinlé resides in the forest and on farms with relatives. In the sea, Erinlé lives with Yemoya-Olokun. The androgynous deity Erinlé is honored as the orisha of herbalism. Erinlé is also linked to the fertility of humans, and is the companion to animals, while being responsible for the abundance of life in the oceans and rivers.

Water orisha bring a calming, steady influence—a presence that can help us return to equilibrium. To engage them, incorporate the colors white, silver, green, or blue into your rituals. Oshun resides in the lakes and rivers, so utilizing river rocks, pebbles, and the color brown is inviting to her. Yemoya-Olokun is the foam of the ocean, so wear charged aquamarine, topaz, or sapphire earrings to keep her coolness near your head.

To protect yourself from evil, wear jewelry containing turquoise. Turquoise is a very stable, sacred stone, especially when combined with silver, a metal known for its ability to protect while also bringing good fortune. I would also suggest fortifying your home against dust and powder attacks by using the cool, blue water mentioned previously. This procedure is described fully in chapter 4.

I have lovely ways of keeping the calming, steady, loving influences of the water orishas in my life. I mulch my flower garden with river rocks. Anyone coming into my home must first pass through my flowers and protective rocks. Whenever possible, I also have a small, portable, slate water fountain bubbling nearby.

I like starting and ending my days near the warm fire of my portable Yemoya-Olokun/Oshun altar. This simple altar is a handmade earthenware plate of about fourteen inches in diameter. On top of the plate are seashells containing water, and seven candles in blue, white, and purple. Occasionally I dress the candles with oils associated with the water orisha.

> *I've known rivers:*
> *I've known rivers ancient as the world and older than the flow of human blood in human veins.*
> *My soul has grown deep like the rivers.*
> *I bathed in the Euphrates when dawns were young.*
> *I built my hut near the Congo and it lulled me to sleep.*
> *I looked upon the Nile and raised the pyramids above it.*
> *I heard the singing of the Mississippi when Abe Lincoln went down to New Orleans, and I've seen its muddy bosom turn all golden in the sunset.*
> *I've known rivers:*
> *Ancient, dusky rivers.*
> *My soul has grown deep like the rivers.*
>
> —Langston Hughes,
> "The Negro Speaks of Rivers"

Some folks borrow from Catholicism and Qabalistic practices and sprinkle holy water around the perimeter of their home or space. Others who prefer to leave out the Judeo-Christian religiosity sprinkle natural waters used prominently in West Africa such as rain, lightning, river, or seawater. Still others incorporate Florida Water, rose water, lavender water, or orange blossom water into their tricks, rituals, and jobs. These are all defensive, peaceful, protective measures.

Of the group of waters I prefer lavender water and rose water. Lavender water is uplifting, calming, and quietly sensual. It brings into the room the wisdom of the crone. I also keep rose water chilled in my refrigerator. Each day when I experience tension and stress, I spray my head, temples, face, and neck. I repeat this process before going to bed. Many people know roses as being beautiful on a decorative level, but the rose is one of the most ancient herbs that works on the entire nervous system to calm, soothe, and protect.

Bathing is another way to cool ourselves down, temper and all.

WATER ORISHA'S SWEET WATER WASH

With Yemoya-Olokun and Erinlé in mind, try this hair and body wash and conditioner. This sweet water wash combines sea kelp and Irish moss—two gifts from Yemoya-Olokun—with wholesome nutrients from Erinlé, and is perfumed with the green scent of the banks of river goddess Oshun.

1 cup distilled water	¼ cup orange blossom water
½ cup soapwort root	¼ cup powdered sea kelp
½ cup powdered Irish moss	½ teaspoon ocean-scented perfume
¼ cup coconut milk	or fragrance oil (see note)

Bring the distilled water to a boil. Add the soapwort root and reduce heat to low. Simmer for 30 minutes.

After 30 minutes, turn off heat. Allow to steep an additional 15 minutes. Then strain the soapwort through a sieve.

Return the infusion to the pot and bring to a boil. Add the Irish moss one tablespoon at a time, stirring vigorously with each addition. When all the Irish moss is added, reduce heat to low. Cover and allow to thicken for 30 minutes. After 30 minutes, strain.

Using a freestanding mixer or a whisk, mix together the coconut milk and orange blossom water until blended. Stir in the soapwort mixture. Add the sea kelp one tablespoon at a time and blend until smooth. Finally, mix in the perfume.

Store in a sterile, capped bottle in the refrigerator.

Note: May substitute with 3 drops juniper essential oil, 4 drops bergamot essential oil, 2 drops vetiver essential oil, and 2 drops pine essential oil.

Yield: Approximately 10 ounces
Shelf life: 1 month

SACRED SPACE RITUAL

If you feel that Yemoya-Olokun or Erinlé is close to your spirit, or if you would like to bring the feelings of the ocean, river, and forests into your home, try this spirited bathroom ritual.

Feather or feather duster
White satin or silk cloth
Cowry and conch shells
1 river rock, fish fossil, or beach pebble
Glass of vodka, brandy, or rum
4 coins
1 charged crystal
A few loose greens from a tropical, leafy plant or a fern

Incense or tobacco
1 blue candle
1 green candle
1 white candle
Peace Oil (recipe follows)
Sea salt
Rose water, diluted flower essences, holy water, or rainwater
Water Orisha's Sweet Water Wash (recipe page 122)

Dress the candles with the Peace Oil.

Clean a table or window ledge in your bathroom by lightly brushing it with the feather or feather duster. Lay down the white cloth.

Arrange the shells on the cloth. Put the river rock, fish fossil, or beach pebble in the center. Next to it put the glass of spirits.

Arrange the four coins around the river rock and glass of spirits. Put one in each of the four directions: north, south, east, and west.

Dip the crystal in the glass of spirits and then set it on the central rock. Set out the greens. Put the incense or tobacco and the candles on a fireproof plate or tile and light them.

Sanctify the bathtub by wetting the surface with a sea sponge. Sprinkle the sea salt in and around the tub and scrub until clean. Rinse the scrubbed areas and then spritz with the rose water, diluted flower essences, holy water, or rainwater.

Run a steaming-hot bath. When the bath is drawn, grab the crystal, get in, and lay back. Take slow, deep, cleansing breaths.

Close your eyes and focus on clearing your mind. See where your thoughts take you as you gaze at the candles, smell the aromas, and soak in the power of your sacred space.

Set the crystal on the side of the tub. Wet your hair and then pour on the Sweet Water Wash. Visualize your troubles being washed away as you rinse the suds from your hair. As the bubbles trail down your body, let your worries and anxieties drain away and into the waters beneath you.

Grab a natural sponge and lather up. This is your time to be quiet and still within yourself. Allow the spirits to move you.

When you are done, pull the plug and visualize your troubles draining out with the water.

Variation: For deep cleansing, think about what you want lifted from you as you wet your hair and pour on the Sweet Water Wash. What would make you feel lighter, clearer, or more at ease? Make a plea for your desire three times. Finish by saying "Blessed Be," or "Thank you for listening to me."

PEACE OIL

8 ounces olive oil
3 tablespoons crumbled dried
   hyssop
2 tablespoons sandalwood chips
½ teaspoon myrrh essential oil

1 teaspoon frankincense essential
   oil
1 8-ounce decorative crystal or other
   clear bottle with a cork or
   nonmetallic screw top

Pour the olive oil into the bottle. Add the hyssop and sandalwood.

Seal the bottle and store in a place away from direct sunlight. Let the herbs steep for a complete moon cycle.

Myrrh, Frankincense, and Peaceful Goddesses

When handling myrrh, you are engaging the power of Binah. Binah is discerning, highly spiritual, loving, stable, and possesses acute awareness. Qabalists link this angelic spirit with the spirit of myrrh. In the Tree of Life, Binah is the third sephirah. She is a divine mother and her name means "The Understanding."

Both myrrh and frankincense are mildly sedating and uplifting to the spirit. Many people know of these incenses' importance in Christianity, but they are also two natural resins sacred to the Khemetians (ancient Black Egyptians). Their rich scent and thick cloying quality is related to Anubis, Osiris, and Ra. When the resins are used as an essential oil, however, they take on the feminine form, suggestive of Isis.

Isis incense is a popular incense and powder used by Hoodoos. Since Isis's attributes center around her protective abilities, she is thanked for security and abundance. To invoke the goddesses, create a sacred invitation using frankincense and myrrh blended with sandalwood or copal.

On a Monday evening of a waxing moon, strain out the herbs using a fine sieve. Recite the following as you finish making the oil:

Wholesome herbs of hyssop and sandalwood
Release your ashe
For it contains all that is pure and good

[*Gently swirl the essential oils into the strained olive oil*]

Fragrant nuggets so rich and so warm
Imbue this Peace Oil with your magick

[*Swirl the blend again and begin pouring it
through a funnel into the decorative bottle*]

No more harm,
No more harm!
Herbs, leaves, and stones work like a charm.

Libations

Various groups of Africans and Africans in the Americas use libations to salute the spirits and to feed the Great Mother. The following are simple ways to integrate the concept of using libations or the water spirit in your life and ritual work:

1. Place a special crystal bowl or a reflective metal dish on your altar, mantle, shelf, or dresser. Pour in a saline solution made from ⅔ cup tap water mixed with 1 tablespoon sea salt. Replenish once the solution is absorbed back into the spirit realm; you will notice this has happened when the bowl is empty.

2. Substitute the saltwater in #1 with Florida Water (a sweet water enjoyed by ancestor spirits) or kananga water (a water that helps ease mourning).

3. Substitute vodka, gin, or rum for the saltwater in #1 (spirits enjoyed by your ancestors).

After setting out your libation, say the following incantation:

> May the ashe of the universe imbue life
> with the cleansing spray of Yemoya-Olokun.
> Praise be to the ancestors.
> So it is said, and so it is done. Ase!

Dirt and Minerals

Because the earth is our mother, we can go to her for comfort, contemplation, and peace of mind. One of my favorite ways to do this is putzing around in the garden. I love to play in dirt and I get my fill of this activity weeding, mulching, and, most of all, planting seeds deep in the depths of the Great Mother. Starting a Hoodoo herb garden is a great way to stay in touch with the earth. Easy-to-grow plants needed for Hoodoo tricks include marigolds (calendula), peppermint, catnip, lemon trees, antique fragrant roses, sunflowers, lavender, rosemary, thyme, basil, garlic, hyssop, and artemisia.

Mud Play

Another accessible way to become engaged with the coolness of the Earth Mother is through playing in sand or dirt. If you have a little one, grandchild, or are a childcare provider, get down and dirty. Play with the children in their sandboxes. Bring water and mix it with the dirt to make mounds. Mounds represent the breasts and belly of the Great Mother. Even making sand castles is relaxing. Through building them we mix water with the earth, thus we are re-establishing much-needed contact with our origins.

MUD PLAY EXERCISE

Do this peaceful exercise when you are consumed with stress, anxiety, or thoughts of war.

Fill a plastic bucket partway with dirt. Add just enough water to make a clay-like substance and mix well.

Invert the bucket and remove the mud. Pat it gently into a mound, just as you would stroke a pregnant belly. For further calming, place your cheek against the belly form. You could also add two smaller mounds to represent breasts for further reflection.

SIMULATED DEATH AND REBIRTH EXERCISE

Another great way to absorb the stability and assurance of contact with the Earth Mother is through burial. Yes, you heard me right! The next time you are at the beach, let someone you trust bury you (but not your head). Lay absolutely still and stay that way as long as possible. When you are still, meditate, focus on healing, and relax. When you are ready, break free and plunge yourself into the crisp depths of the nearby lake or ocean.

Mud Bath

Africans and African Americans have a long history of using clay and mud for cleansing. Now there are many products on the market that contain Rhassoul mud. Rhassoul mud comes from the Atlas Mountains of Morocco. The mud is believed to be an excellent cleanser and detoxifier for the hair and skin. Covering yourself in mud sounds like the last way to get clean, but it really does work by pulling impurities out of us. This is also another way to have intimate contact with the Earth Mother.

RHASSOUL BODY AND SOUL CLEANSING MUD

Follow this recipe for a stimulating bath. The orange blossom water is moisturizing and has a heavenly scent. The ylang ylang–frankincense blend is uplifting to the spirit, will encourage stability and spiritual balance, and is excellent for the skin and hair. Plus, the aroma accentuates the peace-inducing quality of the mud.

1 cup Rhassoul mud (see note)
¼ teaspoon frankincense essential oil

½ teaspoon ylang ylang essential oil
½ cup orange blossom water

Draw a bath. Add the Rhassoul mud to the bath water and swirl to mix well. Stir the ylang ylang and frankincense oils into the orange blossom water. Add this to bath. Get in the tub and relax.

When you get out of the tub, *do not* pull the plug. Instead, let the mud settle on the bottom of the tub for a few minutes. Scrape out as much of it as possible, put it into a bucket, and bury it, if possible. Otherwise, discard in the trash.

When the tub is as clear as possible, pull the plug to drain the water. Clean the tub with salt, if necessary. You can shower afterwards to remove traces of the mud from your hair and skin.

Note: Rhassoul mud is also called Moroccan red clay. It is available through many herbal supply shops. See appendix B for resources.

Dirt Bowl

An important reminder of our connection with the Earth Mother is to keep a crystal or metal bowl full of earth in the home. You can set this bowl on your personal altar, perhaps on top of a piece of beautiful mud cloth.

chapter 8

Prosperity

After reading this book up to this point, one thing is clear: Hoodoo is eclectic. African belief systems do not honor hard boundaries. Hoodoo is fluid; elements, herbs, and practices used for one type of job or trick might easily be transferred to another.

So is the fluidity within drawin' power. We may at any given time need to draw love, luck, or prosperity to us, and some of the significant colors, stones, and roots used are interchangeable. For example, the color green may be a new association when it comes to the arena of love, while most of us have already established a connection between green and money.

A few useful things to remember as you attempt to draw luck and prosperity include:

· Clear thoughts, good intentions, and an impeccable lifestyle will greatly enhance the possibility of realizing your goals.

> Nature teaches us how to suckle the great Mother Earth. Born out of her continuously fertile womb, the plants and trees are proud to show to us what the natural juice of our mother tastes like and how invigorating and empowering it is to rely on what she gives. Every person with a little spiritual awareness will recognize that Earth is our mother.
>
> —Malidoma Patrice Some
> *The Healing Wisdom of Africa*

- The support of love—whether it be from friends, family, or yourself—is prosperity and you are lucky if you have any one of these.

- Honor the spirit of the Earth Mother; she is the most passionate provider of all.

Growin' Green

To fully unite the concept of honoring the Great Mother with prosperity or luck, growin' greens is the most helpful. There is a rich and lengthy history of using gardens, plants, berries, grasses, roots, leaves, and fruit to draw money, wealth, or the general well-being that is a result of prosperity. For example, the bromeliad (*Crypanthus* spp.), a lovely blooming houseplant, is said to attract wealth. Also, in Irish folklore, folks plant money in pots along with a new plant. The plant is watered regularly, and a year or so later there should be more.

In certain areas of Mexico, potted marigolds are placed at the entryway to homes and businesses. Their bright golden color is thought of as a magnet for good spirits as it represents the life force: the sun. The spirits (who are often one's own ancestors) bring fortune and prosperity to your door along with them while they visit the flowers at your door. Planting calendula at the doorway of one's business also invites good fortune.

Hoodoos have their own unique recipes, formulas, spells, and rituals dedicated to generating cash, prosperity, luck, and wealth. Herbs and other natural ingredients are given specific attributes based on their shape, color, smell, and taste. The attributes are selected to closely match the needs and tastes of the spirit helpers. The use of herbs is often combined with incantations, prayers, talismans, and charms.

Good spirits love heavily scented, sweet-smelling flowers. (You will recognize some of these in the next chapter.) Among their favorites are the following:

- camellia (*Camellia japonica*)

- bergamot (*Mentha citrata*)

- honeysuckle (*Lonicera caprifolium*)

- Roman chamomile (*Anthemis nobilis*)

- Jasmine (*Jasminum officinale* or *J. odoratissimum*)

It is best to attempt to grow these fragrant gifts very close to your home on a balcony, deck, or in pots. Honeysuckle and jasmine are particularly fragrant at night, thus they cater to spirits that lurk about in the evenings. Bergamot and camellia are attractive to spirits of the air. Roman chamomile is an easy-to-grow ground cover, and it makes a handy place for helpful spirits to live right in your yard.

Money-drawing spirits are attracted to leafy green herbs, such as the following:

- fenugreek (*Trigonella foenum graecum*)

- cinquefoil (five-finger grass) (*Potentilla reptans*)

- alfalfa (*Medicago sativa*)

- basil (*Ocimum basilicum*)

- marjoram (*Origanum majorana*)

- vervain (*Verbena officinalis*)

- bay (*Laurus nobilis*)

Money-bringing spirits gravitate toward musky plants that bear the earthy aroma of the Great Mother, such as the following:

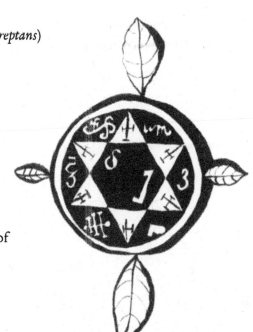

Bay leaf for eloquence talisman

- sandalwood (*Santalum album*)

- vetiver (*Vetiveria zizanioides*)

- nutmeg (*Myristica fragrans*)

- black tea (*Camellia sinensis*)

- John the Conqueror (salep) (*Ipomoea jalapa*)

- Little John chew (galangal) (*Alpinia galanga*)

- ginger (*Zingiber officinalis*)

- cinnamon (*Cinnamomum zeylanicum*)

- allspice (*Pimenta officinalis*)

- horse chestnuts (buckeye) (*Aesculus hippocastanum*)

- cloves (*Syzygium aromaticum*)

Ancestral spirits enjoy offerings of food, money, and drink. If you provide for them, they do what they can to bring you the money, prosperity, and luck you desire. Typical offerings include the following:

- honey or molasses

- red wine, gin, vodka, or rum

- blackberries

- wild or cultivated grapes

- oats

- corn

- wheat

- oranges

- coconuts

- pineapples

- coins and paper money

Prosperity and riches talisman with basil

Lodestones, magnetic sand, and fool's gold (pyrite) attract money, love, and luck. The attraction qualities of the magnetic stones and sand can be enhanced by matching the color and the oils they are soaked in with the purpose at hand. Oils, root powders, and charged magnetic sand are sprinkled on mojos to recharge or feed their drawing powers.

I would urge you to use your own creativity and means to create a magickal household that is welcoming to money-drawing spirits. What comes from your heart usually works best. The following are a few ideas to get you going. Remember that money-drawing magick works best when started during a waxing moon on the day of Jupiter (Thursday).

CLOVER CHARM

Press a five-leaf (or four-leaf) clover (*Trifolium* spp.) between two heavy books. After a few days, take the clover out and laminate it. I suggest taking two pieces of waxed paper of about 2" square and sandwiching the clover between the waxed paper. Iron the paper with an iron set on low. Once it cools off, place the pressed clover in a locket and wear it every day, carry it in your wallet pressed between your paper money, or put it under a candle-holder.

HIGH JOHN CHARM

John the Conqueror root (also called High John*) embodies the spirit of a heroic, coura-geous, fearless survivor of slavery. Carrying this magickal root on your person by itself or in a mojo is thought to bring good fortune. The sunflower oil inspires positive energy and the attar of roses is a high-vibrational oil.*

John the Conqueror root
4 ounces sunflower oil

¼ teaspoon attar of roses (see note)

Blend together the sunflower oil and attar of roses. Soak the root in this mixture for one week, swirling daily.

After one week, remove the root and gently blot away any excess oil. Carry it in your wallet or purse.

Note: May substitute with palmarosa or rose geranium essential oil or rose fragrance oil.

Variation: To make a mojo, place the root inside a green flannel along with one whole nutmeg, several whole cloves, and a 3-inch-long cinnamon stick. Sprinkle this with sandalwood and vetiver essential oils. Dip a sewing needle in the sunflower-rose oil blend and sew the flannel together with green cotton thread.

HIGH JOHN POWDER

Sprinkle this powder on your High John Charm or your money to bring good fortune.

⅓ cup John the Conqueror root
   chips
½ cup dried rose petals

¼ cup magnetic sand
⅛ teaspoon attar of roses (see note)

Grind the John the Conqueror root and rose petals into a powder. Add the magnetic sand and stir. Mix in the attar of roses.

    Seal in an airtight container and let mature for 4 to 6 weeks. Shake contents periodically to keep mixture light and airy.

    Store in an airtight, stainless-steel container.

Note: May substitute with palmarosa or rose geranium essential oil or rose fragrance oil.

Yield: ¾ cup
Shelf life: 1 year

Amulets from Ancient Egypt

If we don't allow greed to overwhelm us, it is easy to identify with the wisdom of the ancient Egyptians. Quite simply, luck is to have a long, healthy, and vigorous life. There are several amulets still widely available that can be of assistance in this pursuit.

    Scarabs are small carved sculptures (sometimes made into jewelry) that absorb evil. They are based on the *Scarabaeus sacer,* an Egyptian dung-eating beetle. I would advise against wearing scarabs because they constantly absorb evil—evil that you could reabsorb if you are wearing one. Carrying one safely in a mojo bag, or, better yet, having them in your home is a much more practical option.

    Tet (or *Thet;* pronounced "tit") *of Isis* is an emblem of Isis, the Great Mother. Typically it is either made from red stones, like carnelian or jasper, although sometimes it is made from a red faience. The red symbolizes the power of our blood, especially as women. The Tet looks vaguely like female reproductive organs, thus it embodies the power of a woman's fertility in all of its different forms. You might find this amulet listed as *Knot of Isis, Belt of Isis,* or *Buckle of Isis.*

Nephthys, Nut, and Isis (Egyptian trinity) with ankh

The amulet that most people readily identify with Egypt is the *ankh*. The ankh is a symbolic representation of life, both in its spiritual manifestation and its physical one. The ankh was believed to resurrect the dead by emanating so much power that anyone in close proximity to it would feel a surge of energy. Its loop is thought by some scholars to represent a womb, while the elongated area is symbolic of a penis. The ankh unifies the male and female powers and the dualities of life and death. In these days when so many of us are "dead tired" and "dead to the world," perhaps carrying a powerful energy source like an ankh is more appropriate than ever.

Charming Gifts of the Sea

As humans, we were first nurtured in the sea of our mother's belly. The sea as mother has many manifestations in many cultures. She represents the cosmic womb. The Ifa goddess of life Yemoya-Olokun and the Fon/Ewe serpentine goddess Mami Wata are powerful sea goddesses. Isis, the great Egyptian Earth Mother, is also a goddess of the sea, as is Inanna, an earlier incarnation of Isis hailing from Assyria. The Virgin Mary is closely associated with the sea, and her colors, like Isis and Yemoya-Olokun, are silver, blue, and white. Aphrodite and

The Seven Powers of Africa Incense

The Seven Powers of Africa is a popular incense blend used by people of various faiths and paths, particularly within the African diaspora. Seven powerful orishas' essences come together to make the Seven Powers of Africa. This incense draws its strength from a host of Ifa orisha from Yorubaland and the lucky number seven.

- *Shango:* popularity, eloquence, male, fire, lightning, stones, and war.
- *Elegba:* trickster, gatekeeper, guardian of the crossroads, and messenger.
- *Obatala:* wisdom of the elders, keeper of knowledge, and peacemaker.
- *Oshun:* goddess of rivers, creativity, sensuality, and the arts.
- *Ogun:* warrior god of metals, protection, and shields.
- *Orunmilla:* prophet, teacher, father of mysteries, and esoteric one.
- *Yemoya-Olokun:* Great Mothers and goddesses of the sea and life.

Venus, goddesses of love and compassion, sprang forth from the seafoam of the ocean—their home.

The sea is the place of origin; the genesis of life itself. Using elements from the sea brings compassion, care, friendship, love, luck, and prosperity. Below are great ways to use elements of the sea in money-drawing magick. These blends are designed to help encourage prosperity to flow your way.

Irish Moss

Irish moss (*Chondrus crispus*) is a natural seaweed that can be carried on the person, placed in a dream pillow, or powdered and spread under rugs to attract good fortune. To infuse, pour water that has been boiled (and cooled for a few minutes) over it. Cover. Steep 20 to 30 minutes. Strain. You can use this in your hair; it is a great styling gel, yet it also brings the spiritual aspects of the sea close to your head for meditation and inspiration.

GODDESS SEA SCRUB FOR PROSPERITY, LUCK, AND COMPASSION

Wash down your door and threshold with this blend. A blue wash of your doorway and even the pathway to your home imbues your entryway with the grace of the sea goddesses. Some hoodoos strengthen their blue wash water with vinegar, urine, ammonia, baking soda, or saltpeter.

3 anil balls	¾ bucket rainwater, lightning water,
¼ cup coarse sea salt	spring water, or tap water
1 cup Bulgarian rose water	(see note)

Add the anil balls to an empty bucket. Pour in the sea salt. Add in the water and rose water. Let sit for 30 minutes or more, stirring periodically until the balls and salt dissolve.

Scrub your front stairs, entryway, and sidewalk with this mixture as desired. You can double or triple the recipe, depending on how large an area you are working.

Note: When trying to decide what water to choose, consider that rainwater represents the gods' and goddesses' compassionate tears for humanity. For when you need to effect a brisk change in your circumstances, use lightning water, which symbolizes Oya, the goddess of changes. Use spring water for power. Tap water is okay too, but it lacks the spiritual charge of the other choices.

MONEY BATHING RITUAL

Epsom salt helps you relax and receive your blessings. Vervain is a formidable herb; its name is derived from the Celtic ferfan, *meaning "to drive away." The herb is a sacred one with many purposes, including protection and money and luck drawing. Basil is linked to money and vitality spells, while pine is a harbinger of health, prosperity, and good fortune. Eucalyptus and tea tree oil have penetrating scents that open the way to great receptivity. Elder flowers are linked to general well-being and prosperity.*

2 cups coarse sea salt

2 cups Epsom salt

Handful of combined dried vervain
   leaves or flowers, peppermint,
   and elder flowers

½ cup sea kelp

⅛ teaspoon pine essential oil

⅛ teaspoon eucalyptus essential oil

⅛ teaspoon tea tree oil

¼ cup fool's gold (pyrite) chips

2 handfuls of fresh pine needles

1 cup dried vervain

1 cup dried basil

1 green candle

Ground allspice

Ground cinnamon

Olive oil

Put the Epsom and sea salts in a large bowl. Crumble the elder blossoms, vervain, and peppermint over the salts. Stir in the sea kelp.

In a separate, nonreactive bowl, swirl together the oils. Then using a dropper, sprinkle this over the salts and herbs. Stir, and add the fool's gold.

Let this mixture sit in a closed container away from heat and light for 2 weeks, shaking it daily to blend.

When ready, mix a little bit of the olive oil with the ground allspice and cinnamon. Rub this on the green candle while focusing on your desires. Light the candle.

Next, tear the pine needles into small pieces and crumble the vervain and basil in your hands. Strew these on the floor and window ledge in your bathroom.

Draw a warm bath. Add 2 cups of the matured salt blend to the water. Get in, enjoy, and relax. When you are finished, be sure to extinguish the candle.

Yield: 4 cups, or enough for 2 baths
Shelf life: 3 months

LAVISH YOUR MONEY
WITH LOVE TO ATTRACT MORE

1. Rub dollar bills, your wallet, or your cash register (if you have a business) with fresh dill, basil, or mint, or ground allspice, cinnamon, or nutmeg.

2. Sprinkle powdered ginger or calamus root in the corners of the room where your hearth is (stove or fireplace). You can also keep powdered ginger in a bowl on your altar, under your bed, or any other strategic location.

3. Wrap a horse chestnut (buckeye) with a dollar bill and bind it with hemp string. Carry this money-drawing charm in your pocket.

Use the Element of Fire

As I discussed in depth in chapter 6, the reverence for the prestige of metalsmiths and the metal god Ogun have spilled over into Hoodoo. Fire is an element that is essential to our survival and well-being. Those special folk like metalsmiths and hoodoos who can use fire for transformation reap the benefits of prosperity.

MONEY-DRAWING FIRES

1. Make a simple loose incense by first crumbling any combination of the following dried herbs into a bowl: vervain, peppermint leaves, bay, cloves, orange peel, sandalwood, or cinnamon sticks or chips. Then sprinkle your incense mixture with black tea leaves and a few drops of lavender, lime, and clary sage essential oils. Mix well, and let sit for 3 days before burning a pinch or two on a hot charcoal.

2. Put saltwater in a large crystal or glass fruit bowl. Drop multicolored coins into the bottom, along with a few seashells. Float 3 lotus flower-shaped scented candles in the water. Light them as you focus on your desires for prosperity. Concentrate on what you need as you focus on the candles.

3. Carve dollar signs in a green pillar candle. Rub the candle with bay laurel essential oil and place it in a fireproof holder. Place seven money-plant seed pods around the candleholder. Trim back the wick to ¼" and light. Let it burn 2 minutes, then blow it out. Add a few drops of bay laurel oil to the wax puddle near the wick. Relight the candle and focus on your wealth and financial security becoming a reality. Open a window or the door to let your good fortune flow in.

Horseshoes and Nails

As mentioned earlier, metals and metalsmithing play important roles in traditional West African society, culture, and spirituality. The idea of transforming a mundane, stiff material into something useful is an act of alchemy that is treasured. The admiration for the transformative aspect of metalsmithing and its ephemera lead to a wealth of traditions within Hoodoo. Two of the objects that are the subjects of the most lore are horseshoes and nails.

In chapter 3, I discussed the etiquette, symbolism, and uses of the broom. There is also a significant amount of documentation recorded by folklorists concerning horseshoes. For example, in order for a horseshoe to be lucky, the finder must pick it up and carry it prong upwards. It should also be hung like a U shape: the curved part at the bottom and the prongs at the top. This manner of hanging allows the horseshoe to become a symbolic vessel that attracts and contains luck. In the past, horseshoes were hung outdoors—either on trees or fences.

When the horse was a primary form of transportation, you could walk around and find horseshoes. Horseshoes with the nails still intact were thought to be especially lucky. Some practitioners would work with the nails themselves to draw good fortune, but for the most part it was considered unlucky to remove the nails.

Nails were also important binders in a practical way for carpentry and in a metaphysical sense. It was believed that you could drive nails into someone's tracks at the heel to make them stay close to you. To keep a lover close by, his or her shoes were buried under the front step or porch and a simple pine plank was nailed on top. In short, nails are binding tools that can lock in your intentions. Their ability to do so is a result of the magickal way in which they were formed.

Lucky Hand Washes

For the most part, luck was not a generic entity in African belief systems or in its manifestations in Hoodoo. Luck was intimately tied to a specific desire: getting a job, finding a lover, having a healthy child, or finding decent housing. A great deal of lucklore hinges on manual dexterity. With manual dexterity, a person could get and hold a good job as a blues musician or draw money through games of chance (cards and dice, to be specific). Lucky Hand Washes are popular within Hoodoo for they ensure manual dexterity, which makes their wearer lucky.

The primary ingredient in Lucky Hand Washes is chamomile. Chamomile has a reputation as being a magickal lure for luck. For example, when playing cards, throwing dice, or playing games at the casino, a calm, cool head enables one to concentrate, focus, and call on intuition. Chamomile is a gentle nervine herb, so it calms the nervous system and induces a feeling of well-being. Even folks who don't gamble can still depend on the medicinal quality of chamomile flowers to keep a level head in competitions, studies, and athletic events.

LUCKY HAND WASH

2 cups fresh chamomile flowers, 2 chamomile tea bags, or 2 tablespoons dried chamomile flowers
3 cups tap water

2 tablespoons 100-proof vodka or gin
8 drops German chamomile essential oil

Bring the water to a boil. Let sit for 3 minutes, then pour over the chamomile flowers. Cover. Steep for 15 minutes.

Strain the chamomile brew over a bowl. Stir in the vodka or gin. Add the essential oil one drop at a time, and pour through a funnel into a bottle.

When needed, pour a small amount of the wash into a bowl and soak your hands. You can also put some of this in a spritzer bottle and spray your hands (privately) when you take a break from playing your games.

Yield: 12 ounces
Shelf life: 1 year

LUCKY HAND RUB

Folks in New Orleans have sworn by this formula to bring specific types of luck.

3–5 lucky hand roots
1¼ cup sweet almond oil
½ cup sunflower oil

¼ cup rose fragrance oil
2 vitamin E capsules, or 1 teaspoon
   wheat germ oil

Place the ingredients in a sterile, screw-top jar in the order listed. Swirl contents and cap. Store in a cool, dark place for 6 weeks. Swirl daily to help the lucky hand roots release their magickal qualities into the oil.

After 6 weeks, rub the oil on your hands or feet before games, gambling, job-hunting, and so on, or use it to charge lucky candles. There are many ways to use the soaked lucky hand roots also. Put them in mojo bags designed for luck, money, or love draw. Add them to a spice necklace, or wear one over your heart for love. Put one in your wallet for money, or in your shoe to bring you in good directions (to find things like opportunities, jobs, an apartment, etc.).

Variation: To make an all-purpose luck-drawing oil, replace the lucky hand roots with tiny lodestones.

Yield: 8 ounces
Shelf life: 1 year

DEVIL'S SHOESTRING RUB

Devil's shoestring (Viburnum alnifolium) *is a stringy, barked stick that is used to help get you out of trouble. When you need help finding a job, housing, or are having trouble with bill collectors, this rub may help. For a potent blend, begin this work on the waxing or full moon.*

3 dried devil's shoestrings
1 cup bourbon

1 cup 100-proof vodka
1 tablespoon camphor essential oil

Using your dominant hand, pound the devil's shoestrings with a mallet until they are broken down into small pieces. (You can also pulsate them in a food processor if you are so inclined, but I recommend the mallet because that way you can more easily imbue it with your intent.) Put all of it in a jar.

Add the bourbon and vodka and swish around to mix. Add the essential oil and swirl together. Let the mixture steep for 4 to 6 weeks, swirling daily, before using.

Yield: 2 cups
Shelf life: 1 year

MONEY-DRAWING FLOOR WASH

3–5 teaspoons "green"-scented essential oil (one or a combination), such as pine, bay, marjoram, or holy basil

Bucket of very hot water
Handful of fresh basil leaves

Add the basil leaves to the bucket of hot water. Cover and allow to infuse 20 minutes.

After 20 minutes, remove the basil leaves. Add the essential oil(s). Use immediately.

Use to wash floors and walls, sponge off a mailbox, telephone, fax machine, computer, or whatever other equipment helps bring word of new income opportunities or paychecks.

Money Jars

There are many different types of money jars. One is made using fenugreek seeds.

To make a money jar with fenugreek seeds, begin by thinking of your fenugreek seeds as money seeds. While focusing on this thought, fill a glass jar halfway with fenugreek seeds. Every day add two more seeds while visualizing your wealth growing. Do this until the jar is full. Then bury the seeds while praying that your wishes will come true. Repeat until your wishes are realized.

Another type of money jar is a bit more common, but no less effective. For this money jar, deposit your change in a beautiful bottle or jar. Sprinkle in potpourri from time to time. When the jar is full, start another one and you most certainly will be growing your money.

MONEY EGG

Eggs hold the promise of new beginnings and surprises. Using eggs magickally helps us obtain our wishes.

1 organic white egg
1 silver dollar or 50-cent piece
Invisible tape

1 jasmine flower, or 3 drops jasmine
   absolute

Crack the egg exactly in half. Wash the interior carefully and pat dry.

Put the silver dollar or 50-cent piece in the bottom of the egg. Tape it shut. Rub the egg delicately with the jasmine flower or oil while requesting that it hatch some money for you. Hold the money egg to your chest and speak to it softly as you caress it.

Bury the egg in your garden or in a plant holder if you live in an apartment or dormitory. Visit the site often, and pour sweet libations of orange blossom water or rose water on the site. During each visit, concentrate on the promise held within your money egg.

chapter 9

Gettin' Some Love & Keepin' It Close

Hoodoo is concerned with the practical areas of everyday life. One of the most important concerns is love—gettin' some (using attraction magick) and then keepin' it close. We respectfully incorporate all of the magickal tools available for love magick courtesy of Mother Nature.

Making and Maintaining a Love Mojo

My little he and she are nestled inside a red flannel. They rest there with a pair of roots that create a male-female dynamic: pungent angelica root, which is the powerful protectress of women and children, and the formidable John the Conqueror root. A delicate white seashell mounted on silver provides the aura of the Great Mother of the sea, Yemoya-Olokun. A smattering of dried patchouli and violet leaves bring further protection and powerful emanations.

My *helping hand* (mojo) has been gently spritzed with two of the most spiritual flowers on earth—rose water and lavender water—then left to dry. After my mojo dried, I dressed it again with Lodestone Oil and a bit of Van Van Oil. The Lodestone Oil bottle holds a tiny pair of the magnetic stones inside and it has a musky earth scent, courtesy of patchouli. Lodestone Oil reinforces my intent for the helping hand, for its duty is to draw goodness, prosperity, and protective forces. The Van Van Oil contains magnetic sand (another attraction substance), and it is scented with a combination of lemon grass and citronella essential oils. A few cuttings of actual lemon grass constantly imbue the oil with their positive vibrations and uplifting nature.

Of course, this great accumulation of sweet floral water, oils, and stone is a bit messy. To carry it safely on my person, I sprinkled the contents with magnetic sand and tied it off with a purple ribbon. Purple, as you will recall from reading chapter 5, is the color of high spirituality and healing work.

Next my helping hand was submitted to fire. I smudged it with a handmade incense blend called Hand Smudging Incense (see below). The smudged mojo was then placed inside a sock. A sock contains the intent carried from the soles of the feet.

Finally, the helping hand was ready for its own carrying pouch. In my case, I used a splendid hand-crocheted pouch from Jamaica. This way it can always be on my person. When this is not possible, of course, I put it in my purse. You can also put it in your pocket, backpack, or briefcase. At night as I drift off to sleep, my mojo is placed either under my pillow or under my mattress near a bowl of scented water. The bowl contains eucalyptus, white pine, and tea tree essential oils. These are great oils for opening the way, as they inspire clarity. The combination of camphor-type oils is inviting to positive spirits and personal improvement.

Success comes not through just the ingredients alone. The important thing to remember, as is discussed in detail in chapter 2, is to imbue the helping hand with ashe and fortify it as often as possible with the message of your intent.

HAND SMUDGING INCENSE

The smoke of this incense is a powerful cleanser. Smudge a helping hand with it under the light of a waxing moon.

1 dried orange slice (see page 156)
½ teaspoon dried lavender buds
2 dried rosebuds
3–5 dried olive leaves
Pinch of dried patchouli leaves

4–5 copal resin balls
5 frankincense tears
Pinch of dried sunflower petals
Pinch of dried calendula buds

Perfume
5 drops clary sage essential oil
5 drops ylang ylang essential oil

5 drops vetiver essential oil
5 drops lime essential oil

Combine all ingredients and grind to form a coarse powder. To make the perfume, combine all oils in a separate bowl. Then sprinkle over the incense powder. Cast a pinch of this exquisite earth incense on a white-hot charcoal block.

To smudge your mojo, hold it in your dominant hand as you recite the following:

[*Exhale*]

All that is harmless, negative, and full of greed,

[*Inhale*]

Healing, positivity, enlightening directions to help with real needs.

[*Exhale*]

Waste, vanity, and the unjust,

[*Inhale*]

Life force, freedom, energy—a must!

[*Exhale*]

The deadening spiral of destruction and mistrust,

[*Inhale*]

Power of the universe from the goddesses I trust.

History and Traditions of Hoodoo Love Magick

Now, you may be wondering what is the history of this type of drawin' magick. Hoodoos use drawing magick for a variety of practical needs, primarily love, luck, and prosperity. The lodestones used in this type of magick are magnetic stones made from magnetite. The use of lodestone is traced back to European alchemist Albertus Magnus, who lived in the thirteenth century. Alchemists at this time sought to turn ordinary ingredients into extraordinarily valuable materials like gold, creating elaborate formulas and recipes in the process. Albertus Magnus wrote during the Middle Ages, but his work or the works attributed to him remain in circulation to this day.

The works of Magnus gripped the African American community from the earliest days of Hoodoo and continue to be widely read in the Black magickal community. Two works by Magnus still in commercial distribution are *Egyptian Secrets, or White and Black Art for Man and Beast: Revealing the Forbidden Knowledge and Mysteries of Ancient Philosophers* and *The Book of Secrets of Albertus Magnus: Of the Virtues of Herbs, Stones & Certain Beasts.* Of these two, I find the latter the most intriguing. Many of the magickal attributes ascribed to lodestone (spelled *loadstone* in his text) are still respected. It is useful to consider when delving into the Magnus texts that they were a small part of the popular literature of the day; the first printings of the book were in 1559 and then 1637.

Magnes or *loadstone* (magnetite; magnetic iron oxide) was described in 1600 by William Gilbert as being in the act of coitus, and this terminology is deeply embedded in the magickal uses of the stone by hoodoos. A male stone and a female stone are so attracted to each other, they seem to be constantly locked together in a state of climactic intercourse. A hoodoo seeks to capitalize off of their draw to one another in a mojo bag. It is believed that the matched pair of stones can draw to their owners love, luck, and prosperity.

Animal magnetism behavior is also mimicked or incorporated into Hoodoo love tricks. This type of mimicry is done in several ways. The following trick was reported to folklorist Ruth Bass by conjurer Menthy. It concerns Hoodoo practices in the Bayou Pierre swamplands in Mississippi.

> *Take a woman's (or a man's) foot track dirt, mix it with your own. Mix the two with red onion juice. Tie it in a red flannel. Carry flannel (mojo) in left breast-pocket and it will draw the person to you.*
>
> —Ruth Bass, "Mojo" from interview with hoodoo Old Divinity

Devil's shoestring mixed with snail-water, the tracks from woman's or (man's) right foot, gun powder and blue [lode] stone will keep her [him] faithful. Devil's shoestring a power wielding, lucky charm is mixed with snail-water—we all know how slowly snails move (an optimal metaphor for a lover staying in a fixed place [fidelity]). Mix with the woman's foot track dirt (her spiritual essence) put some fear into her, with gun powder and a drawing stone (blue stone) and you have a recipe for keeping a loved one close.*

Other traditional Hoodoo love and fidelity tricks that incorporate animals or mimic animal behavior include carrying a raccoon penis as a symbol of masculine virility. Marking one's territory is also used. Urine has been widely used in traditional love formulas. It is used to wash a doorway or bedroom floor to keep a lover faithful. Some informants have even resorted to boiling their loved one's hair in their urine to bind them. The first urine of the morning, which is highly concentrated with hormones, is reputedly the preferred substance for washing.

Besides urine, other human substances are used in Hoodoo love magick. The essential bodily fluids from the person performing the trick are sometimes added to the potential lover's drink, food (especially tomato-based stews), and even breakfast coffee. Others hoodoo through a mojo bag and put the bodily fluids within or on the exterior of the bag. These fluids include vaginal fluid, saliva, blood, menstrual blood, or semen.

Hair and knots are also used in Hoodoo love magick. Hair, as we know now, contains significant portions of DNA. It is on top of our seat of thought (brain) and it is always around to observe vibrations. A lock of hair was often plucked and entwined in the melange of a mojo charm.

There are folks completely opposed to using these methods. Instead, they draw from the plant kingdom to utilize musky scents. Sandalwood (*Santalum album*) is a superb substitute for using human or animal body fluids. Sandalwood is the only herb that chemically replicates the structure of sexual scents, or pheromones. Sandalwood can be burned on a hot charcoal alone or in combination with copal and rose petals. Other musky herbs that smell like the moistness of the earth include oakmoss (smoky), angelica (peppery), vetiver (deep and mellow), ambrette (deer musk), and patchouli (depths of the forest).

*Ruth Bass, "Mojo," in *From My People: 400 Years of African American Folklore,* ed. Daryl Cumber Dance, 591 (New York: Norton Books, 2002).

Certain herbs are also named for animals because they embody some of their qualities. Deer's tongue (*Frasera speciosa* or *Liatris odoratissima*) has a scent similar to vanilla, or what we might imagine an innocent deer's breath to smell like. Deer's tongue can be worn in a mojo bag, purse, briefcase, backpack, shoes, or pockets. It is thought of as an aphrodisiac, and for this reason it is also sprinkled under and on top of the bed. Goose leeks, which are more commonly called daffodils, are love, luck, and fertility charms. Daffodils look like a goose, but they also bear a remarkable resemblance to the male sex organs: the bulbs are the testicles, the stem is the penis, and the flower is the ejaculating penis. Wearing a daffodil or putting a bouquet of them in the bedroom is thought to inspire intense passion. A particularly enchanting version of the daffodil, which you can find available during the spring (high time for mating rituals) is poet's narcissus (*Narcissus poeticus*).

As mentioned above, the first urine of the morning is highly concentrated with hormones. It also smells a bit acrid. To simulate the strength of this liquid, some folks use apple cider vinegar, ammonia, Red Devil lye (which I would strongly discourage because of toxic fumes), and brimstone (sulphur).

Photographs have been used for several different types of love magick as well. To attract a lover, a photograph is charmed by its owner. A wish is written to the ancestors and spirits and this wish is placed underneath the photograph of the potential lover. A red or pink candle is burned on top of the photo, and sometimes this candle is anointed with Follow Me Boy Oil, or Lover Come to Me Oil, or oils named after love goddesses such as Cleopatra, Queen of Sheba, Venus, or Aphrodite. As the anointed candle is burned, the conjurer focuses on envisioning a union with his or her lover, the type of life they'll lead together, and so forth.

Often though, a third-party hoodoo is called in to help release the grip of love that is not mutually agreeable. For this type of trick, a photograph is also used. The photograph is submerged in a liquid substance: turpentine (derived from the powerful pine tree), liquor, or even plain water. The hoodoo focuses on rubbing the annoying person out of the client's life as he or she swirls the photograph about in the vat of liquid. The annoying person does not die, but he or she has been known to find love elsewhere after this trick has been done.

I don't know about you, but these uses of personal body fluids, hair, and photographs bring an important point to my mind: keep your eyes open, stay aware, stay on top of your game, and watch your stuff so no one can hoodoo you in this way!

Aromatherapy for Hoodoo Love Draw

A great deal of Hoodoo love magick draws upon aromatherapy and herbalism. Long before aromatherapy was in vogue in the U.S., hoodoos and conjurers used the allure of scent to attract and bind love. Today the tradition continues to flourish and develop along with the aromatherapy movement. Fragrant oils, hair pomades, and incense in a surprising array of scents are always available in the Black community within Afrocentric gift stores.

Lavender (*Lavandula officinalis*)

Lavender is the great yin-yang plant—or in West Africa it would be considered a *fadenya* (father-child)-*badenya* (mother-child)–balanced plant. Its shape is slightly phallic, upright, and pointed toward the sky. Its smell is pleasing, relaxing, and somewhat androgynous. Lavender is favored in Hoodoo formulas for those who want to attract same-sex love. The buds can be carried on the person in the pocket, purse, wallet, or a mojo bag. Lavender water can be added to baths, spiritual wash waters (for cleaning the floors), used to rinse underwear, and used as an ironing spritz for bedclothes and other linens. The oil can be diluted with a scentless oil such as safflower or sunflower oil and placed within the parts of the hair. Pure lavender essential oil can also be dabbed on the pulse points and worn as a love-drawing perfume. The smell varies widely with different species. I prefer the 40/42 essential oil from France or Oregon.

Lotus (*Nelumbo nucifera*)

Lotus oil is sometimes used in Hoodoo love formulas. Pure lotus oil of the type favored by our African ancestors is extinct, but the current version is still very lovely. Lotus flowers were revered in ancient Khemet and worn as hair ornaments, on necklaces, or on top of the head. *Nymphaea caerulea* (blue lotus) is the genus most frequently depicted in Egyptian art.

The scent and physical structure of the lotus flower is likened to hyacinth and also to the sexuality of women. The white lotus, *Nymphaea lotus* L., only blooms at night, which is another sexual metaphor to the Egyptians who thrived on symbolism. For the Egyptians, the lotus was synonymous with love, and became the focus for the mythic tales of creation (after all, it grows in water). The lotus was the primary accompaniment to women from the Old Kingdom until the decline of Egyptian civilization. The plant is slightly narcotic, causing sedation and deep relaxation. An excellent source for lotus oil is Scents of Earth (listed in appendix B). The genus currently available is *Nymphaea lotus.*

> *I wish I were her Nubian slave*
> *Surely, she would make me bring*
> *a bowl of mandrake fruits,*
> *And when she holds it in her hand,*
> *she would breathe from it,*
> *Thus offering me the colour*
> *of her entire body*
>
> —translated from
> ancient Egyptian papyrus,
> in *Sacred Luxuries* by Lise Manniche

Mandrake Root (*Mandragora officinarum* L.)

One of the favorite herbal roots for drawing men is mandrake. Shaped like a man, mandrake roots are sometimes formed into poppets (dolls) to represent the desired individual. The poppet is inscribed with the desired person's initials, talked to, dreamed upon, and spritzed with the personal perfume of the person desiring love.

Mandrake has a very ancient history that goes back to the New Kingdom of ancient Khemet (Egpyt) when it was called *reremt.* The intoxicating effects derived from inhaling mandrake root was used to ensure a deep, hypnotic sleep. Mandrake is actually a poisonous hallucinogenic and can induce a zombielike state close to death if ingested or inhaled. I would advise adding only a smidgen of this potent aphrodisiac to your dream pillow or mojo bag.

Myrtle (*Myrtus communis*)

Myrtle is an herb thought to lead to a wonderful life. It is reminiscent of orange blossom—spicy and a little sweet. Wearing or carrying the leaves inspires beauty and fidelity. Intimately linked with marriage, myrtle has been worn by brides from various cultures for hundreds of years.

Vanilla (*Vanilla planifolia*)

Vanilla is widely available in raw form and as candles or soaps. It is also sold as an absolute. Vanilla is sweet and creamy, soothing, romantic, quiet, and gentle.

Violet (*Viola odorata*)

Violet is quite popular in powders, incenses, and foot track magick. This is a very feminine herb associated with chastity, innocence, and calming anxiety that may arise around sexual encounters.

Willow (*Salix* spp.)

Willow is the conjurer's gift. When the leaves are carried in a mojo bag, they draw love. They also ensure good luck, as they protect against evil hexing and ill health. Willow is associated with a staggering host of goddesses, including Artemis, Ceres, Hecate, and Hera. To conjure them and enlist their help, light a charcoal block, place it in a seashell, sprinkle willow bark and sandalwood on the charcoal, and do your bidding. Pussy willows are also suggestive of male and female sexuality, new love, and the renewal of spring. Wreaths, broom handles, and wands can be fashioned from willow.

> *Chewing heart root in the presence of a person, will soften that person's heart toward you.*
>
> —Ruth Bass, "Mojo"
> from interview with hoodoo Old Divinity

Pomanders

Orange pomanders have a heartwarming, uplifting fragrance that creates a positive environment suitable for love to take root. I place them in any room where loving, friendly, warm vibrations are desired. A recipe follows on page 155, but first a few notes on the ingredients for pomanders.

Cinnamon (*Cinnamomum zeylanicum*)

Cinnamon ensures fidelity, it opens our dimensions so that a higher realm of consciousness is revealed, and it is stimulating and energizing. Cinnamon is especially attractive to men.

Cloves (*Syzygium aromaticum* or *Caryophyllus aromaticus*)

Cloves draw love and encourage harmony in the home.

Nutmeg (*Myristica fragrans*)

Narcotic in large quantities, nutmeg is a preferred spice used by hoodoos for its drawing powers. It is also an intoxicating aphrodisiac.

Orange (*Citrus sinesis*)

The folk name for the orange, *love fruit*, indicates why it is so favored by hoodoos for love work. The blossoms are thought to guarantee faithfulness and a happy marriage. Added to the bath, it helps the bather become more attractive. There are several different ways you can use the orange for attraction and love.

Queen Elizabeth (Orris) Root (*Iris florentina*)

Inviting, tempting, and attractive Queen Elizabeth root binds love formulas. In ancient Khemet, the scent and power of the iris (Queen Elizabeth) was considered to be strong enough to transform any other plant it came into contact with. In Hoodoo, Queen Elizabeth root is believed to enhance the power of individual herbs and to generally strengthen any mojo or potion to which it is added. The powder of this root is sprinkled on the bed (under the fitted sheet).

QUEEN ELIZABETH'S LOVE DUST

This recipe makes a very lightly scented powder with a gentle, spiritual nature. Using the violets will intensify the scent, making it sweeter and a bit more alluring. In case of allergies, create a more dilute, yet still fragrant formula consisting of equal parts lavender and arrowroot powders. Use this dust as a personal sachet or add it to love-draw mojos.

4 ounces Queen Elizabeth root powder
4 ounces arrowroot powder

4 ounces powdered lavender buds
3–4 fresh fragrant violets, optional

Mix the Queen Elizabeth root, arrowroot, and lavender together in a bowl. Put them in a dusting powder container or powder shaker.

If using the violets, gently remove the petals from the flowers. (Make sure the flowers are dry, without any dew or rainwater on them.) Add the petals to the powder, cover, and shake to cover the petals. Leave for 4 to 5 days, until the powder has the scent you prefer.

When ready, with clean, dry hands remove and discard the flower petals. Put blend in a dusting powder container or powder shaker.

Yield: 12 ounces
Shelf life: 6 months to 1 year

LOVE FRUIT POMANDER

5–7 medium oranges
1 cup whole cloves, approximately
¼ cup ground cinnamon
¼ cup ground cloves

¼ cup ground Queen Elizabeth root
¼ cup ground nutmeg
Large needle

Prick an orange 3 or 4 times with the needle while saying:

Awaken, mouthwatering juices of joy.

Insert the cloves into the holes and say:

Attract and preserve the magickal power of love.
May my home be showered with orange-scented warmth,
Drenched in golden tenderness, shrouded with care.

Continue this process until the orange is completely covered with cloves. Repeat with the rest of the oranges.

Mix the ground cinnamon, cloves, Queen Elizabeth root, and nutmeg in a paper bag. Repeat the above chant while putting 1 orange in the bag. Shake to cover it with the powder. Repeat this process until all the oranges are covered in the powder.

Poke a few holes in a large, clean, brown paper shopping bag. Place all of the oranges in the bag. Sprinkle them with freshly ground cinnamon and cloves and close. Let the bag sit in a cool, dark place for 4 weeks, shaking it periodically.

After 4 weeks, place the oranges out in an earthenware or glass bowl. Delicate, uplifting messages from the energizing scent will waft through the room, lending a feeling of well-being. If you celebrate Christmas, you can tie a ribbon around the pomander and use it as a Christmas tree ornament. This inspires a loving holiday warmth during family get-togethers.

Yield: 5–7 pomanders
Shelf life: infinite

LOVE-DRAWING INCENSE

This incense is perfect to burn while focusing on attracting love. Burn it when you are alone or during a date or social occasion.

2 cups dried orange slices (see note)
1 cup mixture of cinnamon bark and chips
1 cracked nutmeg
½ cup crumbled fragrant rosebuds
¼ cup whole cloves
1 tablespoon dragon's blood

5–7 drops cassia essential oil
5–7 drops neroli essential oil
5–7 drops sweet orange essential oil
½ cup blend of powdered Queen Elizabeth root, ground orange peel, ground cinnamon, ground nutmeg, and ground bay leaves

Grind the first six ingredients separately. Mix together in the order given and stir well. Add the spices and essential oils. Burn on a white (hot) charcoal block placed inside a large seashell. Store in a metal or plastic container capped tightly.

Note: To make dried orange slices, preheat the oven to 185 degrees. Slice 3 to 4 oranges to about ¼". Place the slices in the oven on foil. Bake for 6 to 8 hours, turning periodically.

Yield: Approximately 3 cups
Shelf life: 1 year

Sunkissed Love Draw Tips

Neroli (*Citrus aurantium* or *C. bigaradia*) is an expensive, intense orange scent derived from orange blossoms (don't despair, a little goes a very long way). Neroli is known to alleviate anxiety that may arise during sexual encounters, and it alleviates stress. The following are a few tips for using neroli (orange blossom) essential oil:

· Add a few drops of neroli essential oil to your bath for an intoxicating, aphrodisiac bath.

· Try adding 3 drops of neroli essential oil to your unscented shampoo or conditioner.

- Add 3 to 4 drops of neroli essential oil to ½ cup safflower, sweet almond, grapeseed, or sunflower oil. Use this on your scalp for a tantalizing scent before a date. During a date, you can use this same oil as a stimulating massage oil.

- Put some orange blossom oil diluted with distilled water in a spritz bottle. Spritz your bedroom before or after lovemaking, or spritz yourself after bathing.

Neroli

SPIRIT OF LOVE FLOOR WASH

1 bucket of rain or mountain spring water
5 drops neroli essential oil
4 drops valencia orange (sweet orange) essential oil

2 drops cassia essential oil
½ cup orange blossom water
⅛ cup concentrated lemon-scented dish detergent

Mix together all ingredients in the order given.

Before a hot date, use this blend to cleanse the areas where you will be together. Wear plastic gloves as you do.

The Rose

No other plant is as intimately linked to love as the rose (*Rosa* spp.). When working with roses, seek out the old-fashioned scented types, such as those listed below, rather than the more neutral tea roses. Roses are beautiful, and like the lotus, they suggest female genitalia in the height of passion. The blush of the rose is often likened to the blush of a bride or a sexual partner during orgasm. In parts of Africa and the Middle East, holy temples are spiritually cleansed entirely with highly potent Bulgarian rose water. Rose water enhances the sacred environment.

A little-known fact is that roses are a systemic nervine (*translation:* they calm and soothe your nerves). Only your imagination sets the limits when it comes to using roses in love-drawing potions and tricks.

Old-Fashioned Shrub Roses for the Hoodoo's Garden

Apothecary's Rose—This is a richly fragrant, medicinal rose with a spicy scent. It has been used since medieval times to treat a variety of health disorders. Rose water can be created from this species, although Bulgarian and damask roses are used most.

Belle de Crecy—This is considered the purest rose scent.

Bulgarian Rose and Damask—The sweet, fragrant roses from which quality rose water and attar of roses is made.

Celestial—This contains the aroma of clean skin.

Kazanlik—In Bulgaria, rose oil (attar of roses) is made from this rose.

Madame Isaac Pereire, Guinee, and Souvenir de la Malmaison—These are stunning and fragrant.

Maiden's Blush—This is considered to be refined.

ROMANTIC ROSE PROJECTS

- Buy fragrant red or pink roses. Peel the petals away from the core and stem. Float them in a bath for two. Light vanilla-scented candles for a pleasant accent.

- Sprinkle rose petals on your mattress, under your bed, on your bed, in your closets, in your purse, or any place else where the compassionate spirit of the rose is desired.

- Add ¼ cup rose water to 1 cup milk. Stir in 1 teaspoon of rose hip oil. Add this blend to your bathwater for a soothing, romantic bath.

- Put a fragrant rose in your hair before going out to a party or on a date.

- Spritz your wet body after a bath or shower with fragrant rose water.

- Spritz your face and hair with rose water before leaving home, especially if inhibitions and tension are coming between you and finding love.

- Before company arrives, set out 7 to 9 lit candles scented with a relaxing essential oil such as neroli, sandalwood, chamomile, or lavender in the room where you will be entertaining. Spread rose petals around the base of the candleholders.

LOVE BEADS

This project is a blast from our past. It combines the love-drawing power of roses with rose quartz, the stone of friendship and love, and Isis's (the moon's) love metal, silver. Love Beads are a rich blend of herbs, aromatherapy, folklore, myth, and the hoodoo's magick.

4 dozen fragrant organic pink or red roses, approximately
1¼ cups spring water
1 cup rose water (see note)
1½ cup powdered Queen Elizabeth root
¼–½ cup powdered benzoin
¼–½ cup powdered gum arabic
Bamboo skewers
Dram of attar of roses (may substitute palmarosa or rose geranium essential oil)
Fine sandpaper
36" piece of waxed linen string
Chamois cloth, optional
Rose quartz beads, optional
Silver beads, optional
Sandalwood beads, optional

Go to the garden after the dew has evaporated (near noon on a Friday of the first quarter of the new moon). Harvest the roses respectfully and put them in a shopping bag. Bring them inside and separate the petals from the heads. Remove the white heel. Do this gently while focusing on the healing power of roses, loving memories, and warm thoughts.

Using a mortar and pestle or food processor, pulverize the roses in small batches. (To add some of your personal ashe, prick your finger with a rose thorn and squeeze a few drops of blood into the roses.) Then, if rich and dark-colored, add the roses to a Dutch oven. If they are a more natural pink or red color, use an enamel or stainless-steel pot. Add 1 cup of the spring water and ½ cup of the rose water. Simmer on low for 1 hour. After 1 hour, remove from heat. Cover, and let sit for 24 hours.

The next day, stir and add another ¼ cup spring water and ¼ cup rose water. Simmer again on low for 1 hour. After 1 hour, remove from heat. Cover, and let sit for 24 hours.

On the third day, add ⅛ cup rose water. Simmer on low for 1 hour. After 1 hour, remove from heat. Cover, and let sit for 24 hours.

On the fourth day, stir the blend and scrape it into a nonreactive bowl.

In a separate bowl, mix together 1 cup of the Queen Elizabeth root, ¼ cup of the benzoin, and ¼ cup of the gum arabic. Stir this into the water-roses mixture. It should form a firm, doughlike consistency. If there is still too much liquid, add a second portion of the powders. Knead until blended.

Make a ball out of some of the dough. Roll it into a snake shape, and then cut it into ½" pieces.

Place the bamboo skewers over an empty bowl. Lightly oil your fingertips and palms with the attar of roses (or substitute). Roll a piece of the dough into a bead, and then push it onto a skewer. Repeat this process until the dough is gone. Then gently twirl the beads so they don't stick.

Shakespeare's rose

The beads will take 3 to 7 days to dry. Do not expose them to extreme temperatures or conditions.

When dry, remove the beads from the skewers. Sand them gently with the sandpaper and wipe clean with the chamois cloth, if using.

Tie a double knot in the waxed linen about 2" from the end. Decide on an arrangement if using additional types of beads. String the beads on the waxed linen, leaving 2" on the other end. Double-knot to hold the beads. Finish by tying both ends together and double-knot again.

Do not varnish the beads. They will eventually take on a natural patina, as well as your unique scent, with age.

Note: Add more rose water if the rose pulp becomes too dry. Be careful not to add too much or the batch might be too watery to make beads. While cooking the pulp, watch it carefully to avoid sticking.

Variation: If you are not feeling crafty enough to make genuine rose Love Beads, there are some alternatives. Numerous precious and semiprecious stones attract and express love. To make a personalized statement that exudes love, choose from the following: agate, amber, beryl, calcite, chrysocolla, emerald, jade, lapis lazuli, moonstone, rhodochrosite, sapphire, tourmaline, topaz, turquoise. Finish in silver and don't forget the rose quartz. Any one of these stones can also be charged and carried in a pouch around your neck or added to a mojo bag.

PASSION GARLAND

Hoodoos have been fond of using peppers to motivate folks for a very long time. You can utilize the sizzling hot quality of red peppers in a garland for your bed or bedroom window. Stringing the red peppers with dried orange slices draws even more positive love vibrations to your boudoir!

Bright red cayenne peppers	Hemp string
Dried orange slices (see page 156)	Needle

Pierce holes through the peppers and dried orange slices with the needle. String them on the hemp. For binding action, feel free to tie knots between each pepper and orange added. Hang where desired.

LOVE POTION

Gently heat 2 cups red wine and 2 cracked cardamom pods (do not boil). At the end, add 3–4 orange slices. Remove from heat and pour into 2 glasses. Drink with your lover. (Stick your finger with a needle and add a few droplets of your blood if you dare.)

MIDNIGHT SUMMER DREAM POTPOURRI

This recipe incorporates the spirit of summer love. The sunflowers are for the brightness of the sun, the rosebuds for romantic impressions, the juniper berries for hope for a great future and fertile dreams, neroli for passion, patchouli and Queen Elizabeth root for musk, and much more.

1 cup dried red and pink rosebuds

1 cup dried red and pink rose petals

2 cups dried sunflower petals

1 cup dried lavender buds

1½ cups dried orange slices (see page 156)

1 cup juniper berries

½ cup bay leaves

¼ cup cinnamon chips

1 cup cellulose fiber

½ cup Queen Elizabeth root

2 teaspoons fresh-cut grass fragrance oil

1 teaspoon neroli essential oil

1 teaspoon carnation essential oil

2 teaspoons attar of roses or rose fragrance oil

½ teaspoon patchouli essential oil

2 teaspoons laurel berry essential oil

2 teaspoons sweet orange essential oil

Stir together the rosebuds, rose petals, sunflower petals, lavender buds, 1 cup of the orange slices, and ½ cup of the juniper berries in a large, nonreactive bowl.

In a medium-sized bowl, grind the remaining juniper berries along with the bay leaves, the remainder of the orange slices, and the cinnamon chips. Grind until everything is a fine powder. Add the cellulose and Queen Elizabeth root.

In a separate small bowl, mix together the grass, neroli, carnation, rose, patchouli, laurel berry, and sweet orange oils.

Slowly stir in the oil mixture to the powdered mixture in the medium bowl. When blended, add this to the botanicals in the large bowl and stir to mix.

Put blend in a large canister, seal, and store away from sunlight for 4 to 6 weeks. Shake the mixture daily.

To prepare for love rituals, dates, or friendly gatherings, set the mixture out in bowls. You may also place a bowl of this next to the bedside table or under the bed. It can be used sparingly in love letters. Place some of the potpourri inside a muslin bag and place it in your purse or briefcase. Carrying the love potpourri around with you inspires security, confidence, and love.

Yield: Approximately 10 cups
Shelf life: 6 months

LOVE MOJO BAG

Do this work during a waxing moon on a Friday (day of Venus). The nutmeg is for fidelity, the balm of Gilead is to attract love, and the chili pepper is for sizzling, passionate love.

Red flannel	3 dried rosebuds
1 whole nutmeg	1 dried chili pepper
Pinch of dried balm of Gilead buds	Magnetic sand
1 pair of male and female lodestones	3 drops attar of roses

Using your dominant hand, add the nutmeg, balm of Gilead, lodestones, rosebuds, and chili pepper to the flannel. Sprinkle with the magnetic sand and seal the bag. Feed the bag immediately with the attar of roses and repeat bimonthly on Fridays or as needed.

LOVE BUD LIP SMACKER

1 teaspoon cocoa butter	1 vitamin E capsule, or ⅛ teaspoon
1 teaspoon shea butter	wheat germ oil
½ teaspoon beeswax pastilles	⅛ teaspoon watermelon, peach,
1 tablespoon safflower or grapeseed oil	strawberry, or other fragrance oil

Preheat the oven to 350 degrees.

Place the cocoa butter, shea butter, safflower or grapeseed oil, and beeswax in a stainless-steel or Pyrex container. Put in the oven for 5 minutes or until melted. (Keep your eyes on this; do not overheat.) Let the mixture cool 5 to 7 minutes, but do not allow it to congeal.

Add the wheat germ oil or vitamin E (prick the capsule with a pin), and drop in the fruit-flavored oil. Swirl to mix well.

Pour into a metal or plastic lip balm tin. Do not disturb until it is set. When set, cover. Store in a cool, dry place.

Yield: Approximately 1 ounce
Shelf life: 6 months

PASSION OIL

1¼ cup sweet almond oil   1 vitamin E capsule
¼ cup sesame oil   1 essential oil set (see note)
½ cup apricot or peach kernel oil

Mix together the first four ingredients. Then add the set of essential oils into the carrier oil mixture using a dropper and swirl. Pour through a funnel into a bottle.

To use, rub on the body after a bath or use as a romantic rub before lovemaking.

Note: Choose your favorite scent family:

Earthy musk scent: patchouli, lavender, sandalwood, vanilla (absolute or fragrance oil)

Sweet floral scent: ylang ylang, palmarosa, neroli, vetiver

Green citrus scent: lime, rosemary, clary sage, lavender

1 set is 4 drops of each essential oil in a family mixed together.

Yield: 2 cups
Shelf life: 6 months

chapter 10

Fertility

While weddings should be a completely joyous occasion, the sentiment of joy is often buried by anxiety, stress, and tension. Within several groups in West Africa, impending weddings are times to celebrate a new, productive stage in a woman's life. During this time she is elevated to the position of royalty; she is queen for a few weeks. Similar to our bridal showers, the young "queens" are lavished with gifts and they are also feted with indulgent natural beautification recipes.

As I have mentioned previously, the West African traditional lifestyle and cultural framework observes a strict separation of wilderness and village. A woman about to be married is caught between the two worlds, because she rests mentally in a state of unpredictability. Some of the women's organizations paint the bride-to-be ceremoniously with either red camwood to symbolize the bloody ordeal of childbirth ahead, or with white kaolin to denote her close affiliation with the spirit world.

Rightly considered a fragile time in a woman's life, betrothal is likened to the limbo between death and life. There is an impending dread of what the woman may suffer in her new family and in childbirth. She is also encouraged to gain weight so that she will represent herself as being fertile and capable of having many children.

Now I know not many Americans will be into the idea of gaining weight before their nuptials, but the idea of taking a little time out should be required medicine. Take time out for rituals that salute and enhance both your spirit and your appearance to keep your wedding plans in the right spirit.

The following recipes are combined with ritual and invocation. Prenuptial Shampoo conjures the most beautiful Lakota goddess, Wohpe. Wohpe is the symbol of the meteor, and her stories and songs concern her relationship to the air and sky.

Wohpe enjoys smoking the peace pipe and the sweet scent of sweetgrass. A sweetgrass ritual is at the beginning of this recipe. Wohpe is the goddess of pleasure (something we need a little more of), wishes, cycles, beauty, rituals, and time.

This recipe takes lots of time, but Wohpe's element of time is given as a gift to distract you from prenuptial nervousness and stress. Engagement with ancient goddesses, ingredients, rituals, and with nature invigorates, calms, and soothes the soul.

PRENUPTIAL SHAMPOO

This recipe makes an ample amount of shampoo, can serve as an herbal hair and body wash, or a delightful bath for two.

4 cups lightning water or spring water

1 sweetgrass braid

½ cup dried yucca root, or 1 cup chopped fresh

Handful of fresh corn silk, or ½ cup dried

1 tablespoon slippery elm bark

2 tablespoons dried elder flowers

Handful of fresh columbine flowers, optional

1 tablespoon maple syrup

1 teaspoon sunflower oil

¼ teaspoon white pine essential oil

¼ teaspoon cedar essential oil

¼ teaspoon juniper berry essential oil

1 tablespoon 100-proof vodka

Step 1: Drawin' the Spirits of the Fire

Set a large stockpot on a campfire grill or stove on medium. Add the lightning or spring water.

Light the sweetgrass braid or incense. (This is a traditional Native American practice for beginning sacred ceremonies.) Blow out the flame and slowly wave the smoking sweetgrass over your head(s). Inhale the wild vanilla scent of the smoldering grass. This is the spirit of the prairie—a spirit with such openness and exquisite beauty that she alone can pull you through most ordeals.

Concentrate on building positive thoughts to replace your anxiety. Breathe in through your mouth and exhale through your nose on counts of 6. Circle the smoking braid around the pot. (If you are outdoors, circle the campfire.) Focus on the image of your positive thoughts filling the pot. Visualize your positive energy bringing the pot to a boil. Breathe deeply until you have reached a state of calm.

Step 2: Invitation to the Water and Earth

Place the yucca in a sturdy plastic bag. Pound it 50 times with a mallet, each time releasing any remaining tension into the root. Then hold your head over the pot of simmering water, inhale, and let your sweat drip into the pot.

Pour the pulverized yucca root chunks into the pot. Add the corn silk, slippery elm bark, elder flowers, and, if available, columbine flowers. Heat the herbs over medium heat until they are near the boiling point.

Add the syrup and stir. Reduce heat to low, cover, and simmer 20 minutes. During that time, take the cover off periodically and steam your face and hair.

Each of these ingredients has a time-honored place in Native American beauty medicine. Corn silk is a softener/detangling hair conditioner, and slippery elm bark contains a mucilage useful in managing flyaway hair and defining naturally curly hair. Columbine flowers give off a slightly oily fluid when infused that adds sheen, and maple syrup is a humectant, an especially useful attribute when working with dry or curly hair.

Run a bath and set your favorite candles around the bathtub. Leave them unlit for the time being. Bless the bath water and the bathroom with smoking sweetgrass.

Step 3: Invocation of the Air

Strain the brew. In a separate small bowl, mix the sunflower oil and white pine needle, cedar, and juniper essential oils. Add the vodka and swirl to mix. Inhale the gentle fragrances as you drop them using a dropper into the strained brew.

Pour the Prenuptial Shampoo into a pitcher. Light the candles around the bathtub. Enjoy the evocative powers of the herbs, roots, aromas, and incense of the Native Americans in the magickal space you have created while you visualize a positive future together. Store any unused shampoo in the refrigerator.

Yield: 22 ounces
Shelf life: 30 days

Goddesses of Fertility

Corn has been an important staple food used to nourish both animals and people since the beginning of time. Tied to growth, life, and death, corn is a symbol of fertility and prosperity. Hang dried corn on your front door, place a bowl of corn-meal on your altar, and hang more still by your hearth (stove) in the kitchen. As you gaze upon the dried corn or pass a bit of cornmeal from hand to hand, seek fertility—whether it be in a physical or spiritual sense—and contemplate the god-desses of corn:

- *Memu* is the Ugandan creator being whose symbols are corn and beer. Memu, like most goddesses of the harvest, brings love, compassion, and nourish-ment into our lives.

- *Odudua* is the creator goddess of the Ifa pantheon of the Yoruba people of Nigeria. Shrouded in blackness (her favorite color), her presence invites fertility, love, and community. Odudua's spirituality is connected to the African American winter holiday Kwanza. Kwanza is a celebration of the har-vest that features corn prominently. It also seeks continued fertility within Black culture.

- In North America, Corn Ma is simply called *Corn Mother* by various indigenous groups. She is conjured through fertility dances, special songs, and sacred foods. *Selu* is an American corn mother of the Southwest.

In addition to conjuring up these corn goddesses, you can also draw fertility from the corn plant (*Dracaena fragrans*), an easy-to-grow, common houseplant. The corn plant is one of the sacred plants of Candomble and is called *peregun* in

Brazil. The sacred leaves are placed on the walls of sacred spaces in the form of a crossroads (an X) or placed in a vase. Corn plant is used as a ghost repellent.

PLANTING DREAMS AND WISHES RITUAL

Dip your fingers into a bowl of soil on your altar or soil from a houseplant. Let your touch plant seeds of ideas and dreams of the future. Conjure the African Earth Mothers as you work:

- *Asase Yaa* is the old woman of the earth. Her charge is controlling the fertility of the soil, ensuring a bountiful harvest, and acting as the womb of the earth. Chanting her name softly and then gradually more loudly in an undulating crescendo instills a feeling of well-being and balance: "Asase Yaa, Asase Yaa, Asase Yaa, ASASE YAA!"

- *Ala* of Ghana is a complete African earth goddess figure. She controls fertility, natural phenomena, abundance, outcomes of harvest, animals, plants, humans, and represents the womb of the earth. When communities build her special house it is called a *mbari*, which means "to crown her." Mbari House is a seat of knowledge for the community.

For those of you finished with childbearing (or if you aren't interested in becoming pregnant), Ala is the one to look to, as she nurses her people with knowledge rather than mother's milk. Metaphysical Ala, elder mother of the village of life, is associated with the fertility of ideas and human growth potential. This is a Great Mother who came to the height of her powers after menopause. The awesome crone power of Ala the wisewoman is revered, feared, and respected. Ala is the conjurer of luck, happiness, harvest, fertility, cleansing (spiritual and physical), birth, and death.

Makela, Queen of Sheba

Makela, queen of Sheba (or Shabu), has many a fanciful tale woven around her in Arabian folklore, which include magickal flying carpets and talking to birds. Hoodoos have been fascinated with her since Hoodoo began. She epitomizes the powerful, independent woman of knowledge.

Makela began her reign at the age of fifteen, gaining enormous wealth, respect, and wisdom. She is remembered as being very attractive with a melodic public-speaking voice. The boundaries of her empire are blurred; some historians believe she was queen of territories that expand across present-day Yemen, lower Egypt, Ethiopia, and northern India.

The mythic essences of the queen of Sheba and her husband King Solomon are condensed into several different types of incenses, oils, and powders by contemporary hoodoos. Most often, the couple are conjured regarding matters of the heart, quests for knowledge, or power.

With Makela's mystique in mind, I created a hair frappe fit for a modern-day queen of Sheba. Included are ingredients she loved, which are also nurturing for curly hair: frankincense, myrrh, aloe vera, and roses. Also included are a couple of the gifts presented to her by King Solomon when they wed: coconut, avocado, wine, and honey—all natural indulgences.

QUEEN OF SHEBA'S
ROYAL CONDITIONING FRAPPE

3 tablespoons aloe vera gel	1 teaspoon avocado oil
⅛ teaspoon frankincense essential oil	½ cup coconut water
	½ cup coconut milk
⅛ teaspoon myrrh essential oil	1 tablespoon raw clover blossom
⅛ teaspoon sandalwood essential oil	honey, warmed
⅛ teaspoon attar of roses (see note)	2 tablespoons red wine

Put the aloe vera gel, frankincense oil, myrrh oil, sandalwood oil, attar of roses, and avocado oil in a blender or food processor and pulse for 30 seconds. Add the coconut water, coconut milk, honey, and wine, and blend for 1 minute.

To use, pour blend over hair and massage in. Rinse well with cool water.

Note: Can also substitute palmarosa or rose geranium essential oil.

Yield: Approximately 8 ounces
Shelf life: Use immediately

Mawu

Hoodoos are known for drawing down the power of the moon. African moon goddess Mawu embodies the creative energy of spring. Therefore, she is a goddess to invoke for productivity and fertile imagination. Mawu's liquidity and mystical fluidity has been known to benefit couples as well, especially when one or both partners get fixed ideas that cause arguments. Mawu likes to be thanked by passionate lovemaking that rejoices in her gifts as giver of life.

Mawu's Lather, then, is an aphrodisiac preparation. The ritual that goes with it enables you to tap into the mystical energy of the night and use it at will. The scent is designed to stimulate eroticism and aid in the art of love draw. Make it one night; make out the next. The shampoo lasts for a full lunar cycle, so watch it!

The combinations of herbs in Mawu's Lather lend themselves to the deep cleansing necessary to clarify hair that has been exposed to toxic vibrations. It is also helpful for limp, oily hair as it gives volume. Sage, burdock, and southernwood have been noted by herbalists for centuries as hair strengtheners. Yucca also is widely used in Mexico and in the southwestern United States by various groups for their cleansing and strengthening properties. The luster of the moon will reflect well once your hair has been kissed by the magick of Mawu.

MAWU'S LATHER

A treatment with this lather is a revitalizing first step to embarking on fertility rites and love rituals—especially if embarked upon under the new moon.

1 cup fresh yucca leaves and/or roots, or ½ cup dried

½ cup soapbark

1 cup fresh bouncin' Bet (soapwort) leaves and/or roots, or ½ cup dried

1 cup fresh burdock leaves, or ⅓ cup dried

1 cup fresh lad's love (southernwood) leaves, or ⅓ cup dried

Handful of fresh sage leaves, or ⅛ cup dried

4 cups spring water

1 cup Irish moss

½ cup ground Queen Elizabeth root

⅛ teaspoon sandalwood essential oil

⅛ teaspoon frankincense essential oil

⅛ teaspoon ylang ylang essential oil

⅛ teaspoon vetiver essential oil

2 tablespoons 100-proof vodka

Put the yucca, soapbark, and dried soapwort in a food processor and pulsate for 90 seconds. If using fresh soapwort leaves, add them as a second step and pulsate for 60 seconds. If working by hand, put the yucca, soapbark, and soapwort in a plastic bag and pound 50 times with a mallet until pulpy.

Heat the blend in a stockpot until it comes to a boil. Add the burdock, lad's love, and sage and simmer 3 minutes. Remove from heat and let cool.

When the brew is cool, pour it into a sun tea jar or other clear container with a screw top. Set out under Mawu (the moon). (If the weather is too cold, set the container on a window ledge indoors.) Let steep overnight.

The next day, place the brew in a blender in small batches. Blend each batch on medium for 1 minute, then strain.

Put the Irish moss in a small pot and pour enough of the brew in to cover the moss. Heat gently for 20 minutes. Whisk the Queen Elizabeth root into remaining brew and beat until creamy. Strain moss after it has rehydrated (about 20 minutes). Add to brew as a thickener.

In a separate small bowl, mix together the vodka with the essential oils. Add this to the shampoo and blend. Funnel into a bottle.

Store in the refrigerator. Shake well before each use. Use as a shampoo and body cleanser.

Yield: 40 ounces, or 8 shampoos
Shelf life: 28–30 days

Nefertiti

Nefertiti, queen of Amarna, Egypt, was acclaimed for a luminous beauty that was as vibrant inside as out. She was an active leader and radiant companion to King Amenhotep IV. The two had a unique vision previously unheard of in Egypt—they wanted their kingdom to worship one almighty god, Amen. They designed the city of Amarna to shine artistically and led by example.

As an uncommonly attractive woman in both intellect and beauty, Queen Nefertiti had formidable enemies. Her enemies tried to destroy all record of her, but in the end we are left to meditate on Nefertiti's legendary sculptural image, an image of refined divinity that survived physical assaults and the ravages of time.

Queen Nefertiti is a wisewoman to contemplate when we are overwhelmed by life.

In northern Africa and the Middle East, queens of Nefertiti's day often took milk baths to moisturize and heal their sun-dried skin. If you want to feel like a queen, lie back and enjoy the sensual, moisturizing treat of the bath of the ancients.

Befitting a queen, Nefertiti's Milk Bath contains choice ingredients gathered from around the world. South African aloe vera soothes and encourages new skin growth. Aloe vera gel is great for sensitive skin and acts as a humectant, keeping skin moist in the harshest conditions. Roses were—and still are—revered for their hypnotic fragrance. Fresh rose petals and rose oil, along with sensual orange blossom water, lend an

Nefertiti

air of romance to Nefertiti's Bath. Myrrh has been mentioned throughout history and featured prominently in the Bible as one of the three kings' gifts to baby Jesus. Myrrh was sought the world over as a precious preservative, healer of infections, tooth polish, heady scent for incense and perfumes, as well as for its ability to nurture the skin. Kaolin is the substance of the spirit realm. Adding this to your bath will draw anxiety away from you, as you'll be caressed by water with a silky density.

NEFERTITI'S MILK BATH

Try this bath with someone special for a romantic getaway right in your own home.

1 cup whole milk or cream
1 cup orange blossom water
¼ cup aloe vera gel
⅛ teaspoon attar of roses (see note)
¼ teaspoon myrrh essential oil

½ cup white kaolin
1 cup fresh scented organic rose or
   other organic flower petals,
   optional

Plug tub and run water. Add the milk.

Put the orange blossom water in a bowl. Whisk in the aloe vera gel, followed by the attar of roses and myrrh oil. Pour this mixture under the running tap.

Once the tub is half full, turn off the water and add the scented rose petals, if available. Set fragrant candles and incense around the tub.

Get in, sit back, and relax. Soak in the ancient skin nourishment of legendary queens for as long as you please.

Note: May substitute palmarosa or rose geranium essential oil.

APRES DE BAIN FOREPLAY OIL

Head and foot rubs are wonderful traditions enjoyed by our ancestors that help us care for, comfort, and caress one another. The following sensual oil massage is a recipe for love.

1 cup sweet almond oil
½ cup apricot kernel oil, rose hip
   seed oil, or peach kernel oil (see
   note)

1 vitamin E capsule
⅛ teaspoon white lotus essential oil
⅛ teaspoon neroli essential oil
⅛ teaspoon sandalwood essential oil

Mix ingredients in the order given. Swirl to mix and decant to a squirt-top plastic bottle. Store away from heat and direct sunlight.

To use, warm a little oil in your hands and get busy!

Note: If unavailable, substitute sweet almond oil.

chapter 11

Sacred Rites of Commitment

In Suriname, *lobi singi* express moralizing tales and proverbs—a form of communication revered in Africa and the African diaspora. Below are three lobi singi. The first is the voice of an overlooked woman suffering from unrequited love. The second is a public confession. The third is the lament of a rejected woman who comments on the lackluster appeal of her rival. All were collected by Harold Courlander in *A Treasury of Afro-American Folklore*. These lobi singi use flowers and plants as central metaphors, which tie them into the global tradition called the *language of flowers*.

The overlooked woman:

> Wanton, how can you say I am not beautiful?
> Two beautiful flowers bore me.

A rose-bud was my mother.
A bachelor-button was my father.
How can you say I am not beautiful?
Two beautiful flowers bore me.

The guilty man:

If I were a rich man
I would buy a large farm.
And what would I plant in it?
And what would I plant in it?
I would plant experience in it
So that when I went forth
Experience would be a perfume for my body.

The rejected woman speaks of her rival:

A passionate love without anything
Is wearying.
It comes to resemble a rose
with no fragrance.

The Language of Flowers

In Victorian England there was a form of expression called the "language of flowers." In this language, flowers are hieroglyphs. This language was understood by many—the giver of flowers could communicate with his or her loved one through the selection of flowers. This language filtered down and into the vivid folkloric imagination of the Americas, and blended well with the highly structured ancient plant lore already understood for thousands of years by the ancestors of the newly enslaved Africans.

If you are a bride-to-be, insist that your floral bouquet contain a few of these symbolic flowers. If you are a close friend to a newly married couple, give them a bouquet of these flowers after the honeymoon or on their anniversary.

Balm of Gilead (prefer *Commiphora opobalsamum* but may use *Cedronella canariensis*): "I'm ready for love."

Bergamot (*Citrus aurantium* var. *bergamia*): Bergamot inspires confidence; gives energy.

Carnation, red (*Dianthus caryophyllus*): "This love is really hot!"

Daisy (*Chrysanthemum leucanthemum* or *Bellis perennis*): Although not strongly scented, the daisy speaks of true love unfettered by appearances. "You are my real first love."

Forget-me-not (*Myosotis sylvatica*): "Well, you won't, will you?"

Gardenia (*Gardenia augusta*): One of the only perfectly balanced scents around—the gardenia contains a top note as well as a middle and base note. Can be worn in the hair, placed near the bed, or carried in a bouquet.

Honeysuckle (*Lonicera caprifolium*): "This is it—let's get hitched."

Hollyhock (*Ilex aquifolium* and *I. opaca*): "I am fertile. How about you?"

Jasmine (*Jasminum officinale*): Jasmine eases anxieties. It is romantic and narcotic. In parts of Asia, jasmine flowers are floated in tea; the brew is meant to be deeply relaxing. Jasmine also says, "I saw you in my dreams."

Lemon verbena (*Lippia citriodora*): "I am excited and mesmerized by you."

Meadowsweet (*Spiraea filipendula*): Meadowsweet, also called brideswort, is a traditional flower given to brides to wish them luck and calm their nerves.

> *I offer flowers. I sow flower seeds. I plant flowers. I assemble flowers. I pick flowers. I pick different flowers. I remove flowers. I seek flowers. I offer flowers. I arrange flowers. I thread a flower. I string flowers. I make flowers. I form them to be extending, uneven, rounded, round bouquets of flowers.*
>
> *I make a flower necklace, a flower garland, a paper of flowers, a bouquet, a flower shield, hand flowers. I thread them. I string them. I provide them with grass. I provide them with leaves. I make a pendant of them. I smell something. I smell them. I cause one to smell something. I cause him to smell. I offer flowers to one. I offer him flowers. I provide him with flowers. I provide one with flowers. I provide one with a flower necklace. I provide him with a flower necklace. I place a garland on one. I provide him with a garland. I clothe one in flowers. I cover him in flowers. I love him in flowers.*
>
> —Aztec song

Orange blossom (*Citrus sinesis*): "I'm ready for a real commitment."

Myrtle (*Myrtus communis*): Myrtle is considered the top love herb. It helps assure fidelity and joyful relationships. It can be worn by the bride with a veil or carried as part of the bridal bouquet.

Rose (*Rosa* spp.; any of the species mentioned in chapter 10): "My soul belongs to you."

Tulip, red (*Tulipa* spp.): "I love you."

More Floral Ideas

Love Boxes

Growing honeysuckle, sweet myrtle, jasmine, fragrant roses, gardenias, balm of Gilead, and meadowsweet in window boxes is an excellent way of assuring that your love will continue to stay fresh and alive. Jasmine and gardenia make attractive, relatively easy-to-grow indoor plants—perfect for the boudoir. As you tend to these plants daily, contemplate the growth of your love.

As you invite flowers into your love life, knowledgeable of their voices, don't leave out the lovely magnolia (*Magnolia grandiflora*). Since magnolias grow so well in the southern United States, they are intimately entwined in the love lore of Hoodoo. Magnolias are trees of the love goddess and planet Venus. Plant one on your new property, if possible, to have a good supply of the leaves and flowers. Putting a few magnolia leaves under the bed, mattress, or pillows is thought to ensure fidelity.

Love symbols for Erzulie

Botanical Necklaces

Wearing a necklace of flowers—especially the flowers listed above—will help calm the nerves of the bride and bridesmaids during the wedding ceremony, while also inviting positive spirits to bring their blessings. A necklace of flowers (also called a *lei* in Hawaii) can be made by a florist, or you can simply string a selection of flowers on fishing line (nylon thread).

Spice necklaces work the same magick on the groom and groomsmen. See below.

THE HOODOO'S BOTANICAL NECKLACE

This is a multipurpose, magickal Hoodoo necklace designed to attract good influences and positive spirits into the life of the wearer. Many aspects of the necklace are flexible: it is unisex, it can be worn inside or outside the shirt (depending on its purpose and the wearer's skin sensitivities), and you can adjust the recipe and use ingredients you have on hand. Begin this project at dusk on a Sunday of the waxing moon.

½ cup whole allspice
¼ cup whole star anise
¼ cup black cardamom pods
¼ tablespoon musk seed
   (*Abelmoschus moschatus*)
1 accent root (see note)
¼ cup fresh cranberries

¼ cup Florida Water
½ cup rose water
½ cup orange blossom water
½ cup lavender water
Awl, or large needle
36" waxed linen string

Begin by focusing on your special intentions. Combine the sweet waters, and add the allspice, anise, cardamom, musk seed, and accent root. Let soak overnight, outdoors if possible. Write a note on regular paper that states your intentions and place it next to the soaking ingredients (hold it down with a river rock or pebble if necessary).

The next day, blot the soaked spices and root with a towel as you continue to focus on your intentions. Arrange the spices, root, and the cranberries on a beading tray (or similar) in a pleasing, balanced arrangement. The accent root should be in the center in order to hang low on the chest like a pendant. Place the small, smooth seeds and spices near the closure at the neck.

Hold both of your hands over the necklace design and visualize positive energy flowing out through your hands. Close your eyes; breathe deeply as you cast a positive charge over the necklace. Make a double knot on one end of the string; make sure at least 2" are free behind the knot.

Thread the awl with the string. Pierce the softened spices, root, and cranberries one at a time and slide them onto the string. When done, tie another double knot at the opposite end in the same manner. Bring both sides together and double-knot it again to make a permanent closure for the necklace.

Hold the necklace in your two hands and breathe your healing energy over it while you close your eyes and focus on your intentions. Use your dominant hand to hang the necklace up on a nail to dry. Let dry 2 weeks.

Note: You might need to drill a hole through the root with a small drill bit. Also, when selecting an accent root, consider using the following: Adam and Eve root (to attract love), angelica root (protective shield specifically helpful to mothers and children, and also for health and divination), devil's shoestring (protective shield from evil influences and a luck magnet), John the Conqueror root (protection and strength for multiple purposes), or lucky hand root (multiple purposes, including love, luck, prosperity, and protection).

Scented Stationery

Treat a cotton ball with attar of roses, lavender, lilac, orange, patchouli, or sandalwood essential oil and add it to a box of stationery. Let it sit for 3 to 4 days, then remove. The sheets of paper will be scented and ready to use for a love letter, thank-yous, and what-not.

Handmade Botanical Paper

Handmade botanical paper is widely available. The touch of the artisan's hand makes your wedding thank-you cards, or shower, wedding, and reception invitations special. The botanicals listed below may be inserted into the paper or, as in the case of mango leaf, glued or stamped on. Consider the symbolism of the plants embedded in handmade paper when making your selections. See appendix B for fine handmade paper sources.

Algae: Good fortune, prosperity

Banana leaf: Fertility, vitality, health

Calendula: Brightness, success, well wishes

Coconut: A tree of love; has myriad symbols in African belief systems: cleansing, purity, greetings to the gods, goddesses, and ancestral spirits

Fig bark (amato paper): Fidelity, chastity

Iris: Strength

Lily: Purity

Mango leaf: Fertility, community, family

Pineapple: Friendly greetings, warmth

Rose: Sensuality, beauty, joy

Seaweed: Same as algae

Tamarind: A tree of love (Venus, Oshun, Erzulie); sensuality, sharing, community

Tobacco leaf (*Nicotiana*): Salutations to the ancestors, family, community

Cards and Envelopes—Your cards and envelopes can also be made simply from *parchment*, a paperlike material that has been highly valued for hundreds of years in Ethiopia as the choice material for magick scrolls. Parchment in Ethiopia is usually made from goats or other animals, however, beautiful and durable parchments can also be made from vegetables and printed using vegetable inks (see appendix B for suppliers).

Muslim cultures put sacred scriptures, poems, and notes on parchment and fold it in a unique way to make a square. These squares were found and preserved on the Sea Coast Islands of Georgia. The practice has been borrowed by Hoodoo and other magickal paths.

Papyrus is another paperlike substance from ancient Khemet that would make a striking announcement card. It would also reflect heritage and history in honor of the ancestors.

Inks

Of course, if you are going to involve the magickal symbolism of herbs and flowers into your wedding ceremony, the ink that is used (perhaps for filling in the details or on the envelopes) should also play an important role.

Dragon's Blood—Dragon's blood is associated with passion, strength, vitality, and motivation. Some people buy a regular red ink and add a few small chunks of dragon's blood to it to imbue the ink with the mythology of the magickal ingredient. Dragon's blood is also sold ready-made.

Dove's Blood—Dove's blood is a sweet-smelling herbal substitute for real blood (at least in most cases). It is an emblem of peace.

Floral—Add 2 drops of attar of roses, lavender essential oil, orange essential oil, patchouli essential oil, lotus essential oil, jasmine fragrance oil, hyacinth fragrance oil, or honeysuckle fragrance oil to a bottle of dragon's blood ink.

Indigo—The tranquil blue color of indigo evokes the sky, air, and water goddesses. Indigo is an important plant around the world; its production and processing is largely "women's work." The plant is highly valued as a dye material in West African cloth production. You could possibly have indigo tablecloths at the reception coordinated with indigo ink and stationery.

Sepia—Sepia is a sumptuous, semiglossy, natural ink derived from cuttlefish in the Mediterranean.

Walnut—Walnut is readily available as an ink. Walnuts are trees of the sun; the ink is a warm brown and sensual, and speaks of the Earth Mother's presence. This would bring a very positive vibration to your correspondences. Walnuts also have an important history in magickal herbalism; all nuts are symbolic of wombs and are thought to inspire fertility.

Strewing

In *Sacred Leaves of Candomble*, Professor Robert Voeks shares his comprehensive research on the magickal and medicinal uses of plants by Afro-Brazilians. He describes how the *barracao* (meeting places) are prepared with *folhas de pisar* (sacred leaves). *Mariuo* are placed on the tops of the windows. Mariuo are akin to our notion of garlands; they are sacred leaves from the eye of liturgical palms that are shredded and woven together. The floors are covered in folhas de pisar, which is designed to absorb negative energy and dispel evil held in the tracks of the visitors to the barracao.

This ancient custom is called *strewing* in Anglo-America and parts of Europe. Strewing was once widely used in temples and churches and continues to be used during weddings. It is employed for the same purpose as the folhas de pisar of Brazil: to dispel evil influences.

Handmade herbal confetti makes an alluring blend for your flower girl to strew. When the bridal party walks on the path, the aromatic scent is released for the benefit of all.

CONFETTI

Confetti can be tossed, placed on guests' tables, and inserted into invitations and thank-you cards to give them a unique scent. Ideal confetti should vary widely in texture, fragrance, and color.

Suggested Botanicals

angelica

rosemary

peppermint

cedar

pine needles

juniper berries

rose hips

hibiscus

lavender

rose petals

rosebuds

violet leaves and flowers

bay leaves

lemon verbena leaves

linden leaves

cosmos

pansies

saffron

sunflower petals

forget-me-nots

glitter

silk threads

Preservative

3 whole dried vanilla beans

4–5 crumbled bay leaves

¼ cup blue juniper berries

¼ cup dried orange rind ribbons

⅛ cup cinnamon chips or sticks

2 teaspoons ground cloves

2 teaspoons ground nutmeg

2 teaspoons ground allspice

½ cup orris root powder

Perfume

⅛ teaspoon rose geranium
  essential oil

⅛ teaspoon lime essential oil

⅛ teaspoon vetiver essential oil

3 drops neroli essential oil

3 drops attar of roses, or rose
  fragrance oil

Shred a variety of materials from the botanicals list—enough to make about 4 to 6 cups. Put mixture in a large bowl and set aside.

To make the preservative, chop the vanilla beans into ½" pieces. Place in a medium-sized bowl.

Separately pulverize the bay leaves, juniper berries, orange rind, and cinnamon into a fine powder. Add this to the bowl with the vanilla beans.

Stir in the cloves, nutmeg, and allspice to the vanilla blend. Then add the orris root powder. Pour this preservative into the large bowl of botanicals.

To make the perfume, combine the rose geranium, lime, and vetiver essential oils. Add the neroli and attar of roses and swirl to mix. Pour this perfume over the botanical mixture.

Seal the confetti container and store away from heat and direct sunlight. Shake daily for 4 to 6 weeks before using.

Hoodoo in Shower Gifts, Wedding Accents, and Home Decor

Talisman

Adam and Eve root (*Orchid* spp.) as a pair are known to aid with fidelity and draw love. This makes a great gift for newlyweds. The groom should keep the male-shaped one, while the bride should keep the female one. Both the male and female can also be carried in a mojo flannel alone or combined with a small pair of matched lodestones.

Cloth

For an Egyptian or North African influence, use white linen or undyed hemp. For a West African influence, use kente cloth, indigo, or mud cloth accents. Kuba raffia cloth is a highly refined ceremonial cloth that would enhance the idea of jumping over the broom (perhaps you could jump the broom on a piece of Kuba cloth?). Symbolically this would bring together the idea of the wilderness (before marriage) and civility (domesticity of marriage), which is the intent of jumping the broom.

Crown

Although not fully embraced by mainstream society, herbal and floral crowns or head wreaths can imbue your ceremony with very positive juju. Plants that hoodoos use to attract positive spirits include sweet myrtle, jasmine, gardenia, lilies, tuberose, fern, baby's breath, mimosa, daisy, iris, narcissus, pine needles, and moss. A sprig of rue should also be added to dispel evil spirits.

Coconut Candles

Coconut candles that are created using the coconut hull as a holder are available in many shops. Coconuts are an important food in West Africa; they are used both in sweet and savory dishes as well as drinks. Nourishing, soothing, and cleansing, coconuts are also signs of fertility and the fecundity of the earth. With its shape and internal fluid, coconuts symbolize the womb.

Cowry Shells

The word *cowry* is derived from the Sanskrit *Kauri,* and is the same as Kali-Cunti, the yoni (female genitalia) of the universe. In ancient cultures, the cowry shell represented the divine vulva and the idea of rebirth. There is some speculation also that it may symbolize the Eye of Horus, an ancient protection amulet for the evil eye. Skeletons as far back as 20,000 BC have been found lavishly decorated with cowry shells, and cowries used to encourage rebirth decorated Egyptian sarcophagi. The Romans knew the cowry as *Matriculus,* and this is where we get the word *matriculate.* Cowries were the Roman symbol of the *Alma Mater,* which translates to "Soul Mother."*

In the past, cowries were important symbols in Khemet, Greece, Rome, Polynesia, and the Middle East where they were associated with the goddess Astarte. Today, cowries are revered in West African culture. They have been (and still are) used for currency, divination, ornamentation, and in rites of passage. Today the cowry shell is a symbol of Black people around the globe, indicating our connection to the earth, sea, and to the motherland.

Cowry shells are also symbols of purity, cleansing, and new beginnings, so they would be quite relevant in an ancestor-inspired wedding. Cowry shells could be placed on napkin holders, used in jewelry for the bride and groom, or used as hair ornamentation for the entire bridal party.

Palm Leaves

As I discussed in chapter 3, palm leaves are as important as broom corn in ceremonial rites of passage in West Africa. Potted palm trees can be used as accents, or palm leaves can be placed on the ground to consecrate the area for the bridal party with the ashe of the ancestors and blessings from the motherland.

Animals

Use depictions of an animal, such as the zebra to represent quickness and grace. The leopard or tiger, which symbolize tenacity and the spirit of survival, would

*Barbara Walker, *The Woman's Encyclopedia of Myths and Secrets* (Edison, NJ: Castle Books, 1991), 182.

serve well as a fabric pattern for reception tablecloths. Symbolic representation of animals lends some of their mojo and ashe to your special ceremony, so choose the one that suits your personality.

Incense

Either smudging the wedding ground first with sage, or discreetly burning a sacred incense blend including ground frankincense, myrrh, rose petals, and lavender would invite high spiritual vibrations to the ceremony.

Lotus

Lotus oil inspires erotic interludes as does sandalwood and neroli essential oils. Consider giving a high-quality erotic oil as a shower gift. Lotus wallpaper is popular and is believed to inspire a happy home.

Sistrum

The sistrum, a rattle-type hand instrument, is a symbol of Isis and Hathor. With the renewed interest in Egypt and Khemet and the continued adoration of Isis, sistrums continue to be made and marketed. The sistrum/rattle is useful in shaking up sedentary behaviors and spicing up the love life. Hathor likes women to always be beautiful and to enjoy themselves, so she responds to sensual erotic dances while shaking the sistrum. Sistrums make good conversation pieces at bridal showers, and if you are the bride-to-be, perhaps your sisters can show you some good dance moves inspired by the sound.

The Book of Days

The new moon is the best time for initiating lovemaking, love tricks, and wedding ceremonies. Mid- to late spring is also the height of fertility in the Northern Hemisphere, thus it is considered a good time for weddings.

June 2 is the day attributed to the Roman goddess Juno, goddess of marriage. Juno looks out for the safety of children and women. Therefore, June 2 is a good day for a wedding.

Saturday, the day many people select for their weddings, is actually a day for endings, unhexing, and break-ups. Sunday is a day for successful ventures. Friday is the day of the planet Venus, so it is linked with love.

After the Ceremony

For better or worse (excuse the pun), rice is an important part of African American history. It is used in our soul food recipes, for good luck, and a New Year's Day would be loathed to pass without it. Contrary to urban folklore, throwing rice at a wedding does not cause birds to explode, but it is slippery and messy to clean up. Still, throwing rice after a ceremony is an interesting confluence of Hoodoo (magickal lore), American tradition, and African American history. Not only does rice symbolically attempt to assure our fertile new life, but it also speaks of our freedom from enslavement.

Rice came into prevalence as a strewing grain when times were bad economically. After all, this custom grew out of agrarian harvest rites. The preferred grains were barley and wheat, also emblems of the fertility of the Earth Mother, which were known to be great protective shields.

Ever wonder why all the bridesmaids and groomsmen are dressed the same? This is a pagan tradition that grew out of the superstition that evil spirits would show up at the wedding or reception and make trouble for the bride or groom, perhaps even killing them. Dressing everyone similarly was believed to act as a foil to these devilish attempts. The noisemakers tied at the back of the car and/or beeping were also designed to annoy and dispel evil spirits from playing pranks (or worse) on the new couple.

Reception

The reception is an important time to incorporate magickal and historical elements into the ceremony. After the ceremony, many folks traditionally begin to concentrate on fertility—hence the honeymoon and large feast. Life doesn't always work in this linear fashion anymore; there are same-sex marriages, marriages that blend pre-existing families, and couples who vow to remain childless. Still, for those who seek to have children, there are numerous ways to engage the spirits and use Hoodoo to help out.

One of the first ways is through the envelopes given to the couple. It is customary to give money along with cards. Rubbing the money with cornmeal, lotus oil, sandalwood oil, or rose oil inspires romance. Cinnamon is an energy-drawing herb, so placing a few chips of cinnamon in the envelope would help. A few poppy seeds or black mustard seeds would be a fertility blessing as well.

At the reception, the bridal party should be surrounded by fruit and flowers as they draw luck, fertility, and good fortune. If the couple is to stand under an arbor or bough, it should be covered with grapevines and grapes or raspberry and strawberry brambles—both are attractive to fertility-granting spirits.

A banquet that includes ample fruit such as mangos, papayas, pineapples, peaches, cherries, and watermelon draws fertility. Black-eyed peas combined with rice and stewed tomatoes (also called Hoppin' John) with corn bread and peach cobbler would make a down-home addition. Hoppin' John is a traditional fixture used during New Year's Day to bring good luck. Peach cobbler is another traditional soul food that also invites fertility. In Jamaica, couples have a rich rum cake that is baked with pennies inside. This is thought to bring good luck as well.

Last but not least, always consider the ancestor spirits. Leave a few empty chairs and place settings for them to partake in the festivities or make a small altar in their honor. See chapter 5 for more specific altar ideas.

The Honey Moon

Because weddings grew out of a necessity for barter and trade (through dowries), they were more about business than pleasure in the beginning. Still, often the family of the bride would prepare a month's worth of honey beer or other sweet honey drink to get the marriage started on a good foot.

Honey is such a wonderful and valuable treat. It was on the wedding wish list of the queen of Sheba. The ancients of Africa, the Middle East, and Europe knew of the versatility of honey. If you would like to include honey in your honeymoon plans, here are a few tips:

- Used sparingly, honey is a great hair conditioner, ingredient in facials, lip balm, sore-throat soother, and liniment of love.

- Honey also takes on the flavors of flowers and herbs famously, which turns it into an even more sensual treat. For herbal-infused honey, see page 242.

- Honey infused with herbs and flowers is an excellent sweetener for cakes and drinks, such as ginger beer, orange blossom water, rose water, or herbal tea.

- Warmed honey makes an edible body butter.

Hoodoo Child

In the last few chapters we have discussed love, fidelity, marriage, and fertility. While hardly any aspect of life follows this sort of linear progression, for some folks love and marriage lead to pregnancy, childbirth, and childrearing. For others, love leads to the acceptance of the self, and to some, fertility is the force that brings great ideas to fruition.

This chapter is designed to help the woman who is trying to imbue her pregnancy and childbirth with the earth magick and nurturing implicit in Hoodoo. There is also information provided for the inception of life of the Hoodoo child, as well as guidance for the rites of passage into adulthood. For the elder crone finished with childrearing, rituals and helpful hints are provided as well.

Hopefully this chapter will be useful to all, regardless of gender. Whether you need strength to nurture ideas, are pregnant with hope, are expecting a child, or if you are acting as the support person to a pregnant woman, pregnancy and expectation are important elements of the human condition. Pairing expectation with Hoodoo, pregnancy—whether actual or conceptual—becomes all the more mystical.

Pregnancy

Water

By now you are familiar with water as it relates to both your mundane and magickal lives. I have introduced you to rain goddesses, water spirits, spiritual baths, and washes. As the essence of life and bay of the fetus, water is of vital importance in pregnancy and childbirth. I have four children, and all were brought into the world by natural means—primarily in the primal squatting position and using water as an aid. Water is essential in helping maintain balance, creating harmony, finding peace, and offering comfort during the turbulent periods of pregnancy, postpartum, nursing, and beyond.

In many different parts of the world, women in the third trimester wade into water to allow the current to rock their wombs. They let the water cradle and caress their bellies, and then rhythmically sway back and forth to the movement of the tides. This simple ritual brings comfort to both mother and child.

During pregnancy we begin to feel impossibly heavy; for many of us this is the heaviest weight we have ever been. Water offers a bit of respite from the heaviness as it affords an opportunity to be temporarily weightless. Simply floating in a cool pond, lake, or even a swimming pool creates a striking counterpoint to our everyday experience.

At home, bathing also offers comfort—if it is permitted by your physician or midwife. My favorite pregnancy baths include ones made as follows:

- Add 2 cups milk to a warm bath.

- Add ½ cup kaolin or Rhassoul mud for a silky bath that draws impurities from within.

- Add ½ cup orange blossom water, rose water, lavender water, or sandalwood water to your regular bath.

- For a relaxing herbal bath, add 2 cups water infused with chamomile, lavender, oat straw, and calendula, and then strained.

- For dry skin, add 2 cups water infused with marshmallow, burdock root, or St. John's wort and then strained.

- Add oils dispersed in 1 cup aloe vera gel or milk, such as 1 tablespoon avocado oil, pumpkin seed oil, rose hip seed oil, hemp oil, kukui nut oil, sweet almond oil, or olive oil.

- Uplifting scented oils can also be added to the above aloe vera gel/milk and oil solution, such as neroli, sandalwood, lotus, clary sage, bergamot, attar of roses, or geranium (try 5 drops in any combination).

- Add scented oils for protection such as myrrh, narcissus, or angelica to the above-mentioned aloe vera gel/milk and oil solution (again, try 5 drops in any combination).

Use oil in a bath carefully and, if at all possible, have someone assist you getting out of the tub to avoid slipping.

Staying hydrated is also important. The following are a few suggestions:

- Add sliced cucumber to a pitcher of water for a cooling way to strike equilibrium while also quenching your thirst.

- Try peppermint tea (iced or hot) with honey. Peppermint is one of the ewe of the Great Mother and the goddess of fertility Yemoya.

- Red is the color of vitality, energy, sensuality, and blood. Rose hips are a rich source of vitamin C and when brewed, they create a delightful red tea. Sip rose hip tea as you visualize yourself becoming increasingly healthy and strong. Hibiscus tea made from dried red hibiscus flowers is also a vivid red color and makes a refreshingly tart tea.

- Eat watery foods (such as watermelon, honeydew, and cantaloupe) for a nourishing and good way to stay hydrated. The seeds of the rotund fruits are also visual reminders of the mystery of fertility.

Earth

Staying in touch with the earth is as important as getting adequate water; both types of contact are related to spirit. In Uttar Pradesh, India, an incredible substance is made called Baked Earth Attar. The earth comes from Kannuj, India. It is soaked in sandalwood oil and contains the delicate aroma of monsoonal rains.

Mother and child making offerings

Wearing Baked Earth Attar, a natural perfume, is believed to inspire confidence, relaxation, and escape from fear, just as if you were being embraced by Earth Mama herself. Pregnant women in northern India rub this attar on their bellies and bodies months before the birth of their child, believing that it assures the baby's soul a smooth passage into this world.

Another way to stay in touch with the earth is to tread on it. Ample walking outdoors is good exercise for mom and at the same time helps rock and comfort the baby.

As mentioned above, mud baths are relaxing and they help clear up pimples that may arise during pregnancy as a result of hormonal fluctuations. Ran Knishinsky, author of *The Clay Cure*, takes this one step further and touts the numerous benefits of eating clay, an activity that Africans and African Americans have engaged in for centuries. Knishinsky shares scientific findings on the benefits of eating earth. Pure clay regulates the bowels, reduces headaches, fights acne and pimples, while also ridding the body of all sorts of toxins. Knishinsky recommends eating a refined, pure clay called *montmorillonite* (sometimes referred to as *bentonite*). See *The Clay Cure* for more information.

Plants

Berries—Berries such as strawberries, raspberries, and blueberries are high in vitamins and contain trace minerals, which makes them an excellent choice for pregnant women. Black folks often say babies "draw the goodness away from the mother's teeth," meaning pregnancy robs the pregnant mother's body of calcium and other minerals important to maintain good dental hygiene. Plants helpful with counteracting this phenomenon include strawberries (*Fragaria vesca*). Mashing a strawberry (the smaller, wild types are best) and rubbing it on the teeth serves as a whitener.

Myrrh (Commiphora myrrha; C. molmol)—Myrrh powder can be sprinkled on top of a wet toothbrush and used as a tooth-cleansing polish that deters infection.

Sage (Salvia officinalis)—Sage is also called nature's toothbrush. Sage contains chemicals and enzymes that help fight tooth and gum decay. To use, prepare a tisane and rinse the mouth with it several times a day. Adding tea tree oil gives a further boost to the natural mouthwash. Also, simply rubbing a fresh sage leaf over the gums and teeth is effective. Potted sage can be grown quite easily in the kitchen.

Raspberry Leaf (Rubus idaeus)—The most prominent and sought-after plant during pregnancy (as well as other important stages in a woman's development) is raspberry leaf. Raspberry leaf contains *fragrine*, an alkaloid that helps strengthen the uterus, produce effective contractions during labor, tone the womb, and expel the afterbirth. In the case of miscarriage or abortion, raspberry leaf tea is used to restore regular menstrual cycles, control the flow of blood, and rebuild strength. When a young woman is embarking upon menarche, she should begin her lifetime of raspberry-tea drinking since in addition to the other aspects mentioned, it also helps reduce menstrual pain by toning the uterine muscles.

Burdock Root (Artium lappa)—Fresh burdock root is a filling, nutritious, wholesome herb that offers spiritual benefits as well. Try chopping ¼ cup of fresh root and adding tasty spices such as cinnamon, nutmeg, cardamom, or anise, along with molasses or honey as a sweetener. For those women who have trouble keeping anything in their stomach as a result of morning sickness, burdock root can help you maintain some nutrients. Carry burdock root as a protective charm.

Nettle (Urtica dioica)—Nettle is a mineral-rich herb that is thought to increase the supply of breast milk in animals and humans. Nettle tea makes a good hair tonic for dull, lifeless hair and is touted as a hair-growth tonic—a useful herb to try if you experience hair loss after pregnancy or during menopause. The replenishing ability of nettle is also used to offset the imbalance caused by surgery, C-section, abortion, and miscarriage.

Dandelion (**Taraxacum officinale**)—Sometimes there can seem to be an infinite array of ills suffered by the pregnant and postpartum woman. Thankfully, we have the simple, abundant weed dandelion. Dandelion contains calcium and vitamins C and B complex so it helps strengthen and invigorate the sluggish system. Dandelion root tea is also helpful in equalizing hormonal imbalance, PMS, menstrual irregularity, and easing the passage into menopause.

I enjoy dandelion leaves prepared just like collard or mustard greens. To begin, saute a couple of cloves of minced garlic and a small minced onion in a stockpot. Add a dash of fresh cayenne pepper, a pinch of black pepper, and a pinch of sea salt. When the onion begins to brown, add enough broth and water to deglaze the pot. Fill the pot loosely with cleaned, chopped dandelion greens and top off with a splash of vinegar. Cook until tender. Eat a bowl of these bitter greens on their own or as a nutrition-packed side dish.

Dandelion leaves can be cooked until tender without spices and used as an herbal poultice to soothe swollen breasts and tender nipples. You can also soak a cotton washcloth in dandelion tea and apply them to the breasts. Dandelion root dried and chopped makes an excellent coffee substitute.

Roses (**Rosa *spp.***)—Roses are great soothers of the heart. Spritzing your clothing, face, and hair with rose water is calming to the nerves. You can also add rose honey to various herbal teas and other beverages.

Violet (**Viola odorata**)—Violet is another kind, old-fashioned aid for the pregnant woman. Try soaking dried violet leaves in grapeseed, moringa, or sweet almond oil for 4 to 6 weeks. Strain and add a few drops of attar of roses. Rub the violet/rose oil on sore breasts for relief.

Oats (**Avena sativa**)—Oats are gentle on the digestive system, irritated nerves, or itchy skin. Taking a sitz bath (shallow soak) with oat straw tea is an energy booster that combats stress, insomnia, and bodyache. Oat tea helps control hot flashes, headache, nervousness, depression, and mood swings. A pillow stuffed with oat straw (4" x 6" suggested size) helps fight irrational thoughts, insomnia, mood swings, and has been used by people who experience the trauma of miscarriage or forced abortion. Oat straw tea also strengthens bones and teeth.

Lavender (Lavandula officinalis)—Apart from raspberry leaf, lavender is one of the most highly touted women's herbs. As you will see later in the chapter, it is almost a panacea, it has so many helpful qualities to women. Lavender buds can be sipped as a tea or steeped in honey for several weeks to create a soul-warming sweetener. Lavender water spritzed on the face, hair, or body lifts depression and equalizes mood. A lavender hand or foot bath has the same effect.

Mugwort (Artemisia vulgaris)—Fumigation, also called *perfumo* in ancient Khemet or *smudging* by Native Americans, has been used for thousands of years by Black women for healing. Uterine difficulties were treated by fumigation. Smoldering herbs were held close to a woman's open vagina to introduce healing medicine into her body.

One of the herbs most useful for transmitting its medicine through heat is mugwort, also called *crone wort*. I do not advise administering heat to the vaginal area unless done by a trained professional, however, heating the back with a crone wort smudge stick offers relief for back spasms and pains that arise from carrying excess weight. To apply, light a crone wort smudge stick. Blow out the flame. Have someone hold the stick a few inches from your spine while you stand. Let the heated herb penetrate your body along with the ancient wisdom of the healer Crone Ma contained within it.

Another useful way of receiving Crone Ma's comfort is by infusing her feathery leaves in oil to create a pain-relieving body oil. To begin, loosely fill a jar with fresh mugwort leaves and then pour in a gentle oil such as sweet almond oil or grapeseed oil. Add ½ teaspoon wheat germ oil or 1 vitamin E capsule as a preservative. Swirl daily to release the green earth medicine for a full cycle of the moon. When ready, remove the leaves. Rub on body where needed.

Oils

Moringa oil (*Moringa oleifera; M. pterygosperma*), also called *bak* in Khemet, was used by ancient Egyptians and Nubians specifically as a belly rub for pregnant women. Other silky oils that can be used for this purpose include sweet almond oil, grapeseed oil, and hemp seed oil.

Cod liver oil, an old standby in the Black community, is a useful vitamin/mineral tonic with the essential fatty acids that are robbed from the mother during pregnancy. Evening primrose oil is used to counteract mood swings and ease difficult rites of passage such as menopause. Rose hip seed oil is good also to take orally. Both evening primrose and rose hip seed are thought to benefit skin tone, clarity, and vibrant appearance. Try taking 1 teaspoon of cod liver oil, rose hip seed oil, or evening primrose oil 2 to 3 times per day.

Nesting

In previous chapters I have spoken about the priority given to the separation of wilderness and village society in West Africa. Pregnancy is a state that is likened to the wilderness because it is fraught with incalculable unpredictability and irrationality. Sometimes nesting—that is, preparing your home for the coming of a child—is the only thing under your control. As pregnant women we, like many other types of animals, become obsessed with creating a suitable environment to comfort ourselves and welcome our young ones. Using roots, feathers, sweet waters, and plants assists significantly with nesting rituals for the Hoodoo child.

Just as a bird creates her nest with feathers, so, too, can the mother-to-be. Feather down comforters are plush and relaxing, especially when paired with a feather pillow. Satin, brushed cotton, or silk sheets are also delightful natural fabrics that create an aura of tranquility. Being that our hair can become a bit brittle and fragile during pregnancy, try silk or satin sheets and pillowcases. Silk and satin provide an added benefit beyond mere comfort, as they deter the tangling or snaring of hair, thereby limiting hair breakage and loss.

Essential Oils

Essential oils are essences of plants, usually created by steam distillation or cold pressing. They offer a quick and relatively easy way of using aroma to create healing environments. There are a wide array of oils available and many are recommended for pregnancy and childbirth. You need to do the work; experiment and test scents to decide which scent families you prefer.

Neroli and ylang ylang are highly recommended, but for those with a quiet temperament or who prefer subtlety, these oils are probably too loud.

Lemon grass has been around for thousands of years. It was called *camel grass* in ancient times, and it was so revered by the Nubians that it was named *Kushite grass* after the great empire of Kush, an ancient Black kingdom. Lemon grass is a high-vibrational herb/oil and it is prominent in Vodoun and Hoodoo as a reception herb—that is, it is useful for those who want to open the way for spiritual messages. Like neroli and ylang ylang, it has a high-frequency, soprano note, yet it is more citrus and earthy than floral.

The citrus essential oils (such as orange, lime, lemon, and grapefruit) are sharp, bright, upward, yet fleeting. Citrus oils are nearly ephemeral and need to be grounded by a base note and a middle tone so that they can function in a perfume blend.

Lavender, rosemary, tea tree, hyssop, and eucalyptus essential oils are great disinfectants and create a spiritually and physically clean environment. Yet, they may be too medicinal smelling and overwhelmingly green for some.

Clary sage is a green scent that is recommended as well. Clary sage has a smell that reminds me of a grandfatherly cologne. When you want the cuddle of grandfather or another male elder, this is the scent for you. However, if you lean more toward the floral, fleeting scents, clary sage is a scent to avoid.

Geranium (rose geranium), *rose de boise,* and bergamot are scents that I feel belong in the middle. They are slightly floral, but not overwhelmingly sweet or chatty.

Patchouli, vetiver, angelica root, myrrh, and frankincense are deeply earthy base tones. They give off a dark, moist vibration and they are effective scent preservatives.

To clear the home environment, add ½ teaspoon each of lavender, orange, and pine essential oils to a soapy bucket of water. This makes a floor wash that is not only an effective antibacterial agent, but each scent also alleviates depression and adds bright spirituality to the home. If you prefer, you can limit the wash to one scent. Use 2 teaspoons of one of the essential oils per bucket of water.

For morning sickness, a sharper, minty aroma that is clean and refreshing is helpful. I suggest an oil mixture containing eucalyptus, camphor, lemon grass, and orange for an air freshener.

Pillows

Dream pillows can help deter disturbing dreams, nightmares, and restless evenings. Choose your stuffing from the following ingredients: rose petals, lavender, chamomile, hops, mullein, or moss. Cover with soft flannel and use alone, or place a miniature pillow inside your regular pillow.

Eye pillows are great after a crying spell or exhaustion. Stuff a tea bag with ground flax seeds. Chill, then apply to the eyes. Cucumber or potato slices work by the same principle; the three ingredients each reduce puffiness and swelling.

Pregnancy Charms

Having a magickally charged charm bag offers spiritual strength and protection. Choose from the following:

- Place an angelica root, burdock root, charged red agate, and malachite stone in a yellow, purple, blue, or red flannel.

- Soak 1 John the Conqueror root in rose oil for 4 to 6 weeks. Place in a red flannel and add a charged brown jasper and jade stone. Hold this as you drift off to sleep or wear it close to the heart.

- Wear lapis lazuli, sapphire, jade, carnelian, or aquamarine jewelry.

Childbirth

During childbirth, being in control, comforted, and natural are the three primary elements of survival. As a hoodoo, sticking to the principle of utilizing these elements during childbirth is as essential as ever.

If you can bring nothing else with you when giving birth, bring a hot water bottle. Have someone fill it with very hot, but not boiling, water. Wrap it in a piece of flannel and place on the areas where you feel the most pain.

Also, prepare small sachets of lavender buds and leaves to squeeze hard and smell during labor. Yes, once again this kindly comforter to women is key.

Water from a lake, spring, or river can be applied to the forehead with a cloth. Rose water, orange blossom water, or lavender water can be used similarly.

Smoldering Herbs of Childbirth

Frankincense and myrrh bring the protection and wisdom of the ancients. Have some of the incense ready to burn as your contractions pick up.

In ancient Mesopotamia and Egypt, the childbirthing incense of choice was a mixture of anise seed and Low John powder (*Trillium grandiflorum*) tossed onto a white-hot charcoal. Ambrette, a natural seed with a musky aroma, was used in the same way. Ambrette, or *musk seed* as it is sometimes called, is easy to find in Middle Eastern grocery stores. In several Native American groups, juniper and uva ursi (bearberry) are burned as a childbirthing incense.

Amber is the stone of the shaman/healer. It is essential to the hoodoo, as it symbolizes the healing energy of the sun. Almost since the beginning of time, amber chips have been ground and placed on hot charcoal or wood to be used as a birthing incense.

BIG MAMA'S HEALING BALM

During pregnancy, this healing balm keeps the vaginal and perineal region pliable, thus lessening the possibility of tears or an episiotomy. It can also be rubbed on areas prone to stretch marks, like thighs, breasts, and the belly.

Dried burdock root	8 ounces sweet almond, canola,
Dried chickweed leaves	corn, sunflower, or grapeseed oil
Dried calendula flowers	1 ounce shea butter
Dried nettle leaves	1 ounce cocoa butter
10-ounce jar	1 ounce beeswax pastilles

Add enough of the burdock, chickweed, calendula, and nettles to loosely fill the jar. Add the oil and cap. Let infuse for 4 to 6 weeks.

After 4 to 6 weeks, strain the infusion. Add 5 ounces of it to a saucepan, along with the shea butter, cocoa butter, and beeswax pastilles. Heat on low until the wax and butters melt. Stir periodically to mix ingredients.

Pour into a sturdy plastic jar with a screw top or a stainless-steel balm jar. Allow the balm to cool before sealing.

To use, warm about a teaspoon in your hands. Apply to areas in need of conditioning and strengthening. Increase the frequency of applications toward the end of the third trimester. Bring this to the hospital for use prior to crowning.

Yield: 8 ounces
Shelf life: 1 year

Natural Single-Ingredient Body Butters

If you don't have time or energy to make a healing balm and no one can do it for you, try a simple one-ingredient body butter. Ever since I can remember, Black folks have sworn by cocoa butter as a skin conditioner. Now there are many other butters imported from Africa and South America that we can use as well. Ready-made single-ingredient body butters include mango, shea, and aloe. Body butters have venerable histories; people from Egypt through South Africa and throughout the Americas have utilized their natural medicine to pamper women whose skin is in transition.

Yemoya-Olokun

Yemoya-Olokun is the Great Mother orisha who guides birthing and nurturing. Sipping teas made from her herbs (such as mints, passion flower, or lemon verbena) help out early in the birthing process. (Each herb is uplifting and with a perfect balance of comfort and energy.) Sucking ice cubes made from these teas brings Yemoya-Olokun's sweet protective medicine to your birth experience.

Yemoya-Olokun's sacred ewe are seaweed, kelp, aloe vera, bay, mint, and lemon verbena. They can be used for spiritual washes, but do not sit in a brew of these herbs. Instead, pour them over your head as you stand outdoors, or in the tub if necessary, to receive her precious gifts.

Focus

Focus is a tremendously important tool that helps our ability to endure. Sard, a type of quartz crystal, has been useful to birthing women for thousands of years. Pumice stone was also given to women to hold during birth. (I'd suggest putting this inside a flannel to protect the hands from the gritty surface.) Crystal balls are excellent focusing and divination tools that may help you scry the state and disposition of your child. Cowry and other shells are smooth to the touch and, as they symbolize the process of creation, they make excellent focusing tools. If permissible, a white, purple, blue, red, orange, or green candle can also provide excellent focus and spiritual strength. (See chapter 5 for qualities of each colored candle.)

Sound

Bring a CD with the tranquil sounds of nature to your birthing room. Whether it be of the rainforest, rain, thunder, ocean waves, African drumming, Australian didgeridoo, Lakota flute, ancient Egyptian sistrum, or even the humble tambourine beloved in Black churches, each type of sound or instrument calms the agitated spirit. If at all possible, have someone play an instrument live for you, or if you have the strength, try shaking a sistrum or tambourine during various parts of your labor. This is not only calming to you, but it helps assist your baby, who is undergoing significant trauma.

The single most important thing to do when in labor (unless you are having a water labor) is to try to maintain contact with the earth. Walking places keeps us in touch with the ancestors and it also rocks the baby. Walk as long as possible and try to give birth squatting. This primal position, along with primal screams and a naked body, are natural and conducive to a healthful birth in accord with the ancestors and creative beings.

The Blessed Event

When finally your labor of love is complete, you will probably be drained physically and emotionally. This is the time for support. Try to have your mother, sisterfriends, cousins, or neighbors lend the support by helping with housework, cooking, chores, and other children if you have any. Many of the things in this book may sound simple in today's world of complexity, but the simplicity inherent to Hoodoo is an integral part of its magick.

It is critical to walk during labor, use the elements for comfort, and have a village—however eclectic—around you during and after birth. Once you have assembled your circle of support, ask them to look at the baby with you and see what names come to mind. Naming a child beforehand is convenient but ill advised in terms of the African sensibility. Many times an ancestor returns to a village in the form of a child, and naming this "old spirit being" wisely is crucial to his or her happiness.

Another essential element of Hoodoo is intuition—or seeing the *signs*, as we call it. Knowing the signs in terms of naming a child is important. This is why having people around to laugh, tell stories, and share is vital. It allows a chance for wisewomen in the group to observe the child for reactions, signs, or the special glimmer in his or her eye that expresses the child's innermost personality. In Africa, naming ceremonies are a rite of passage and often take place many months after birth. In our fast-moving culture of the West, this long period is more difficult to ascertain, but bringing people around and having a more casual name-finding ceremony shared over potluck meals and drink makes a good substitute.

Some simple signs to look for are what types of flowers and plants you receive as gifts, particular colors or fragrances your child is drawn to, or the day, month, or time of day of birth. Perhaps you can name the child for his or her month or birthstone? Animals, birds, or reptiles that come to you during those first few days may also be messengers in terms of what the goddesses, ancestors, or nature spirits desire in terms of a name for the child. Use your creativity and intuition as a hoodoo during this time. Just as your body has opened impossibly wide, so, too, has your perception and intuitive abilities. Strive to maintain balance, wait, watch, listen, and be patient when selecting a name for your child.

If the birth took you by surprise, you might have to instruct a sisterfriend on how you want the child's room and your home prepared. Have someone bless the home with a highly spiritual incense blend.

WELCOME LITTLE SPIRIT INCENSE BLEND

Choose what is most pleasing to you from the following and grind each ingredient: rosemary, rose petals, juniper berries, hyssop, angelica root, sage, lavender, frankincense, lemon grass, myrrh, cinnamon, or copal. Burn on a few hot bamboo charcoal blocks. You could even just burn one of these ingredients to purify the air. Be sure to open the windows and doors and let the dank spirits that may have been lurking escape.

SPIRIT WASH

I recommend the following welcoming, cleansing wash for the nursery or family bedroom. You could also use Chinese Wash (see page 58) or "Lift Me Up" Pine Floor Wash (see page 238).

4 cups very hot water	½ teaspoon rosemary essential oil
½ cup fresh rosemary, or ¼ cup dried	½ teaspoon lemon grass essential oil
½ cup fresh sage, or ¼ cup dried	½ teaspoon lavender essential oil
½ cup fresh lavender, or ¼ cup dried	

Infuse the rosemary, sage, and lavender in the water for 30 minutes. Strain, and add the essential oils. To use, add 1 cup per wash bucket ⅔ full of water.

Little Spirit's Sacred Space

In welcoming a little spirit to the home, you will want to make special preparations that involve the elements and entice helpful spirits to take up residence. In certain West African communities, a newborn baby is laid on top of a banana leaf until his or her first cry is uttered. It is only after the first loud noise comes from the banana leaf that a baby is considered human. Early African Americans had several first customs that were designed to bring health, good luck, and prosperity to a newborn. One welcoming luck custom was to put a piece of fat into the child's mouth, and another one was to place a dime into his or her hand. As the child grabbed it, he or she gained luck and the mysticism inherent in dimes.

The emphasis on lucky rituals is not done lightly. Hoodoos know that the world is dangerous in every way imaginable, therefore we keep our babies extremely close to us. Baby carriers were used in Africa and by many indigenous cultures long before they came into vogue in the United States. Our Black sisters wrap their babies in a beautifully patterned piece of batiked or indigo cloth and snuggle their child close to their body. Typically the carrier is placed on the back, but whether you prefer a front or back carrier, use one. They are essential in the baby's adjustment to life outside the womb.

Sweetgrass and other types of woven baskets are another earth-embracing way to coddle your child. Traditionally, many of these baskets were made by our brothers and sisters, the Gullah people of the Sea Coast Islands, and to this day they continue the tradition. I kept every one of my babies in a small handwoven grass basket that could easily be carried from place to place. The baskets have the sweet smell of the prairie, grasses that embody the spirits of the earth. Blankets placed within the basket should be made of cotton or flannel.

Pillows are not desired within the basket, but a dream pillow containing rose petals, lavender, and chamomile can be placed in the bedroom to assist the child's sleep. Alum can be sewn on the outside of a sleep basket, blanket, or hat as an amulet of protection. A simple wreath of lavender, sage, bay, lemon balm, rose, balm of Gilead, and holly would also make a welcoming gift that is not only fragrant, but also soulful and protective for a new baby.

Honey has been an important tool for treating baby's difficulties in indigenous cultures for a very long time. Raspberry or strawberry leaf tea with a touch of honey makes a useful wash for cradle cap. It is also good for washing delicate skin.

Babies are also responsive to smell. If your baby is colicky, give him or her a whiff of lavender or a dab of chamomile essential oil placed at the temples. A blend of 1 cup powdered arrowroot, 1 cup cornstarch, ½ cup powdered calendula, and ½ cup powdered lavender also makes an effective baby powder with a light scent.

Mama's Plant Magick

Mama should not be forgotten, as she may envelop herself in her child and forget to heal herself. Many of the soothing treats listed throughout this book are useful during the transition from pregnancy through postpartum and motherhood. In addition to other pampering recipes, try a simple application of 3 to 4 drops of attar of roses, neroli, lavender, clary sage, geranium, or grapefruit essential oil added to an unscented body lotion or a massage oil.

AFTER-BIRTH HEALING COMPRESSES

Soak large cotton squares or strong paper towels in a prepared witch hazel tincture (available at most pharmacies). Place these in a sealable plastic bag and chill in the fridge. Use one square or folded paper towel placed on top of a sanitary pad to comfort the traumatized vaginal and perineal area after giving birth. This is also a good treatment for hemorrhoids that arise from the last stage of birthing.

Comfrey leaves can also provide relief. Gently roll clean leaves a few times in your hands to release their medicine. Then put them in the fridge or freezer until chilled (not frozen). Apply directly to perineal area.

AFTER-BIRTH HERBAL SITZ BATH

Barely cover the bottom of a bathtub with warm water. Add ¼ cup witch hazel (from the pharmacy or supermarket). Sit in this warm sitz bath for comfort from the trauma that is inflicted upon your body during birth.

Variation: Add 4 cups water to a pot. Bring close to a boil, then add 1 cup fresh calendula flowers or yarrow leaves (or ½ cup dried). Cover and turn off heat. Infuse for 20 minutes. Add 1 cup to a very shallow bath.

A Room of One's Own

As children grow older, they may get more frequent visitations from curious, playful, or evil spirits. This is a time to discuss spirits with the child and to increase protective measures. Children love quartz crystals, and simply gazing upon them can quell anxiety. Red agate and carnelian are protective stones that can be worn on a pendant or added to a mojo bag. Malachite rids the child of negative influences and clumsiness that can result in broken bones or worse.

Holly (*Ilex aquifolium* or *I. opaca*) water is sprinkled on newborn babies. Holly is an extremely protective, fatherly herb that can be hung in the child's room. Sweetgrass, juniper, and lavender bundles can also be placed in the child's room to bring similar protection and a feeling of well-being.

Dried corn contains the protective spirit of the goddesses of fertility and can be placed in the child's bedroom. As he or she grows, rose petals can be placed on the windowsill to entice good spirits to draw near, and water, cornmeal, and salt can be kept under the bed. Barley and wheat bundles should also decorate the room of a young one as they are fertility symbols.

Barley, wheat, and cornmeal can be thrown after the child as he or she embarks out into the world of school. This will assure that good spirits will travel along with the child. Calamus root or sweetgrass talismans act as protective charms and can be placed inside a flannel or hung on a piece of string or leather for a child.

Menarche and Manhood

Life in Africa is visualized as a circle, just as it is a wheel in Native American belief. The continuity and flow of life is even and swift. Before you know it, you'll have moved on from naming ceremonies, diapers, and baby carriers to a young person coming of age. Always include the ancestors and the spirits of the earth in these important passages of life.

Menarche

When a young girl becomes a young woman, it is a vivid, red experience. The shocking and swift onset of menarche is an important marker that should be celebrated and embraced by mother, daughter, and the family. Prepare a box for your daughter long before she approaches puberty. Place inside it a Tet, ankh, cornmeal, and a special pouch containing her first sanitary materials, which should be made of organic cotton. Wrap the pouch with a cowry necklace, which she can wear during her menarche ceremony.

When the special day arrives, snap the closure on the cowry shell necklace and take your daughter outside. Return a few drops of her menstrual blood through the center of the necklace, letting its fertile power fall back to the earth. This subtle act enhances your daughter's spiritual growth as she acknowledges her natural place on this earth as a young woman.

Manhood

For a young man, often hair and a changing voice are the major markers for the onset of puberty. Teach your son how to shave over a special handmade or metal bowl. Collect this first shaving and place it into a piece of red silk cloth. Tie it firmly and add it to the contents of his regular protective mojo hand.

TEA TREATS FOR TEENS

To soothe the nerves of adolescents, offer them a cup of tea with honey. Use peppermint for general purposes, or oat straw or pasque flowers to soothe the nerves and balance mood. Chamomile or lavender are used to relieve tension and aid sleep. St. John's wort helps alleviate depression. Steep the tea bag or dried herbs 15 to 20 minutes.

RITE OF PASSAGE BATH

Every child, regardless of gender, should enjoy a special bath ceremony as he or she comes of age (between 12 and 13). For this ritual, you can also prepare a special poem for your child that contains lessons of life to be contemplated as he or she washes away childhood and looks toward adulthood.

1 red candle

1 black candle

1 green candle

1 cup rose water, orange blossom water, or sandalwood water

1 cup Rhassoul mud or kaolin clay

3–4 drops sandalwood or lavender essential oil or attar of roses

Piece of red agate or lapis lazuli

1 cowry shell

Mud cloth (see note)

Coconut, vanilla, sandalwood, lemon grass, vetiver, patchouli, or lavender essential oil

Dram of sweet almond oil

2–3 bamboo charcoals

Sacred Incense Blend

6 pieces of frankincense

3 pieces of myrrh

1 piece of copal

½ cup dried rose petals

¼ cup dried lavender

3 teaspoons sandalwood

Grind the herbs and resins for the incense using a mortar and pestle or coffee grinder. Place a piece of petrified wood or a fish fossil in the bathroom and set the bamboo charcoals on top of it. Light the charcoals. When hot, sprinkle some of the incense blend on them. Also light the candles.

Run a bath of warm water. Add the rose, sandalwood, or orange blossom water. Add the mud or clay and swirl to mix well. Drop in the sandalwood or lavender essential oil or attar of roses.

Have your child get in and place the agate or lapis lazuli on his or her belly. Now would be a good time to have him or her read your poem and/or contemplate the transition from childhood to adulthood.

Have the mud cloth on the floor next to the bath. As your child dries off, encourage him or her to soak in the spirit of the ancestors from the motherland held within the earth-stained cloth.

At this time, give your child the essential oil to use as a personal scent. Tell him or her to add 6 to 7 drops of it to the dram of sweet almond oil.

Note: Make sure you select the mud cloth carefully, with full understanding of the proverb indicated by the pattern and the symbolism of the color. Rust mud cloth, although a bit more rare, is the perfect color because it is the color of Ogun, the warrior god, and Oya, the goddess of changes. In today's world, our children need to be ready for changes as they occur. They also need the power, prowess, and keen awareness of the hunter/warrior to survive. Rust and metal, as discussed in chapter 6, are used as symbols of power in Hoodoo.

Teach your children the wisdom of the elders. Encourage them to embrace the spirits and to know the pain and accomplishments of their ancestors. Equip your children with the mysticism and spirituality embodied in the magickal path of Hoodoo and conjur craft so your offspring can embark on the journey of life cloaked with the power of ancient wisdom.

chapter 13

The Conjurer's Dream

We discussed the implications, treatments, and goddesses and gods of war in chapter 6, but we did not discuss dreams, a fertile battleground for the warrior. Hoodoos have been fighting shapeshifters, spirits, and evil jobs and tricks in the bedroom since conjur craft took form. The reasons are varied, but one point that is central is that in dreams we have crossed a boundary. We have crossed over from the everyday into a magickal realm.

In *Folklore from Adams County Illinois*, numerous accounts by informants report evil deeds revolving around the dreamer that they were either a part of or witness to. Primarily, herbal mixtures are left in the bedding or mattress, but sometimes a deadly wreath is placed inside a feather pillow. The perpetrator(s) construct a wreath that they infuse with evil intent, using incantations that invoke evil spirits. Little by little, they build the malicious intent of the wreath. If the victim remains unaware until the wreath is a complete circle, death is imminent. The wreaths are not dangerous without three accomplices: (1) our lack of awareness, (2) our belief, and (3) evil intent.

We are also vulnerable to other types of attacks as we sleep. An adept conjurer can use juju during astral projection, the primary objects being to ruin your relationships, disturb the energy flow in your household, make you lose your job, or drive you crazy. To accomplish these objectives, the juju conjurer learns to do the following:

1. Go into a state of deep relaxation through controlled breathing.

2. Focus evil intentions.

3. Invoke ancestral spirits and the most formidable gods and goddesses.

It is difficult to defeat the evil conjurer with superior mind control who also enlists the aid of evil spirits and the strongest goddesses.

It is possible, however, to combat all of this evil intent through positivity and the grace of protective goddesses and gods. We will discuss some of these aspects later in the chapter. The key to protecting yourself, your family, or your clients during sleep is to stay in control of your mind and to develop keen awareness.

Rather than confronting the suspect directly, a psychic approach is preferred. Two key psychic dream defense mechanisms are (1) a serene mind, and (2) distance from the situation (the distance of dreamland is ideal).

WARRIOR'S TRICK WORKSHOP

Conjurer's dreamwork is presented here in a three-day-long workshop involving meditation, the laying of a trick, and a cleansing ritual. Once this is mastered, an advanced technique called "Attack of the Lucid Dreamer" can be tried (see page 213).

Day 1: Vision Quest

Visualization—See the situation in your mind through the eyes of a stranger. Realize that these things are not of your doing. They are outside of your realm of being, although they have been thrust toward you. The uneasy situation may be in the form of harassment at home, at work, or in society. Harassment may take the form of racism, sexism, homophobia, ageism, discrimination, lawsuits, gossip, or verbal or written attacks. Evil Hoodoo, incest, rape, or other physical violence are other possibilities.

Rebel Against the Notion of Your Enemy's Attacks—These things are happening to you, but you did not invite the perpetrators to perform the acts against your spirit.

Furthermore, you will not allow your energies to be drained on a daily basis by dealing with someone else's insecurities, bad judgment, or derangement. Realize with finality the actions are threatening and they must end so that you can live in peace.

Consult with a trained professional or spiritual advisor, but do not talk about what has been done with friends, especially if you do not know their full intentions. They might help perpetuate the problem through their own vibrations or gossip. You do not want this situation to continue, and you do not want to give your enemy allies, even if they are unwittingly corralled into fueling the flame.

Detach Yourself from Your Situation—See the situation for what it really is, without hysterics or emotional attachment.

Approach the Threshold of Clarity—If you know when your witching hour is (mine is at dusk and at midnight), look at the situation during these highly charged moments of your wakeful hours. (A witching hour is a time of day or night when you feel that your possibilities are endless, when you are supremely powerful, aware, enlightened, or at peace.) If need be, do this by gazing into a candle (scrying). You can also use a perfectly round crystal ball, the flickering flames of a fireplace, or running tap water—whatever it takes to see the problem clearly. The clarity that you seek is one that is nonjudgmental and lacks any emotion at all. It is what it is, nothing more or less.

Day 2: The Warrior's Trick

For this part you will need a fire. This could be consecrated lit candles (see chapter 5), a lit fireplace, chiminea, barbecue grill, or the flame from a gas stove.

Write the person's first and last name (if you know who is causing the harm) with a pencil on a piece of kraft paper or brown paper bag. As you do, say the following trick:

My three eyes are focused on you,
Each one is trained to see what is right and true.
I understand the evil in all that you do;
Your evil cannot, will not ever consume.
[*Name*], you will not win this war,
So from this day forward, may peace resume.
Your evil has flown off in the wrong direction,
but there are three more.

Life is but a circle;
A chain of collective events—now, as before,
Ricochet, bullet of evil,
Back from whence you came.
The circle has spun
And, I feel no shame!
As it is written, so it is done.

Repeat this three times, toss a pinch of saltpeter into the fire, and light the trick. Throw the flaming trick into the fire, or let it burn safely in a bathtub or cauldron.

Day 3: Meditation

Get into a lake, stream, ocean, or bathtub totally nude. Choose a place where it is highly unlikely that you will be disturbed or accidentally discovered. Float, relax, and breathe in through your nose and out through a slightly opened mouth on counts of four. As you develop your technique, you can extend your breaths to six or eight counts.

Pull in the cleansing vibrations of the water spirits. You will feel the strong presence of water spirits in the ocean or a fresh body of water in nature, however, you can simulate the experience in a bathtub using essential oils, salts, and natural incenses. Close your eyes and breathe in, two, three, four, and out, two, three, four. Continue this breathing pattern until you enter a deeply meditative, peaceful state.

Once you are feeling peaceful, focus on your third eye, the invisible, all-seeing eye in the middle of your forehead. Visualize the person (or people) and the situation they have thrust upon you. Again, I repeat, do not get passionate or involved in their evil intent. Remember, this isn't your situation; it is a drama that has been created to cause you and/or those you love misery.

Take a very deep, cleansing breath all the way from your solar plexus. If that concept is not in your consciousness, pull the breath from the soles of your feet. As you suck this breath up, imagine the situation coming up and moving through your body along with it. This ball of volatility is moving up from your soul into your belly, passing through your diaphragm and throat, and then *ka-pow!* you push it out of your mouth with an exaggerated gasp and exhale. You are releasing the entire situation to the wisdom of the ancestors and the water spirits. It is now out of your hands and placed safely in theirs. Relax for a few seconds as you resume breathing on counts of four. Repeat this each month until the situation improves.

ATTACK OF THE LUCID DREAMER

This is not for the dabbler or for those who desire a quick fix. It works well for the spirit wounded from years of abuse, such as incest, emotional abuse, harassment, or spousal abuse. It can work reasonably well for a protracted legal situation.

Step 1

Utilize the breathing techniques listed in the previous workshop. Work toward strengthening your ability to reach alpha waves (a supremely peaceful state while remaining awake). This will take at least a fortnight (two weeks) and may take a month. Be patient!

Step 2

Once you are able to reach that state at will, you are ready to approach the realm of lucid dreaming, which will lead to astral travel. A lucid dreamer controls the moment she falls asleep and the direction of her dreams. Her willful intent allows her entry into the world of the dreamer. The lucid dreamer is asleep and resting, yet she is fully attuned. She is in full control of the dream realm and the capacities of reason within it. Moreover, the lucid dreamer is as agile, limber, intellectual, patient, and strong as she chooses to be.

Each night, practice your meditation. Begin to understand, direct, and control your dreamscapes. Do the things you can't do while awake: try flying, try staying under water without breathing, try stepping outside of your body.

Step 3

You may begin to notice an animal who visits your dream. If this animal seems open, curious, and attentive, it is probably your spirit animal. Do not be afraid of this animal. Build a relationship of trust and mutual respect with it. Look into your animal's eyes, show compassion, and strike up a conversation. Allow yourself to hear his or her voice. Gradually, permit yourself to enter the spirit realm of the animal. Become one with your animal spirit ally. Common animal spirit allies include foxes, bears, wolves, rabbits, rats, birds, snakes, and dolphins.

Step 4

Learn everything you can about your animal while awake. This may include visiting them in the wild or at a zoo or reading about them. While asleep, experience life as your power animal. Give the issue that has brought you into a warrior state to your animal spirit. While you are asleep, deal with the evil intent of the person as a pure animal spirit would. Write in a journal about your animal experience immediately upon waking.

Protective Amulets

Another approach is to put deterrents in the way of evildoers who act through dreams. One of the most widely used amulets is a garlic braid. These are easy to make or find in local shops. You could also put a clove of garlic under your bed.

Making a small wreath of your own would also let the juju hoodoo know that you are on to him or her. Buy a ready-made wreath made from grapevine or straw. Wrap it with protective herbs such as willow sprigs, hyssop, rosemary, sage, lavender, and mugwort. Affix them firmly with a hot-melt glue gun or tie them on with simple hemp string. Leave this above the headboard of your bed or on his or her front door.

Divination and Prophetic Dreams

In Anthony Shafton's *Dream-Singers,* a landmark study of African American dream beliefs, Shafton tracks the relationship and correlation between African and African American beliefs about dreaming. He also points out the differences between White and Black culture concerning dreams. What he found through his extensive research is that Black people seem to have a very high regard for dreams. He verified the concept of lack of boundaries, a common thread in African spiritual belief systems. Shafton also found that the activities of the Black dreamer are as important to us as they are when we are awake.

There is a fascination in both African and African American cultures with what goes on in dreams. Both African and African diasporic cultures report ancestor visitations during dreams. There are also special people in each culture who know how to read signs, symbolism, and activities in dreams. These people in the Americas have used this ability to help their families know about covert activities, such as affairs, hexing, and Hoodoo, and also warned them to prepare for pregnancy, birth, illness, and death.

In various West African societies, spirits are seen as having a society complementary to our own. These spirits are misshapen and odd-looking to the human eye, but they have children, spouses, friends, enemies, and allies. Curiously enough, they move in reverse to humans. (For more on these wee folk, see chapter 3.) This is probably the reason that many serious Hoodoo tricks and jobs that take place at a crossroads require the hoodoo walk backwards away from the site where the magick takes place. Taking on the movements of the spirit helpers who are invoked makes them feel more comfortable. We are not rude outsiders who do not know the rules of the spirit world; walking and moving backwards allows us to temporarily become members of the other side.

Likewise, signs and symbols in dreams are read in reverse. The following are some examples of when the inversion or reverse is applied to interpreting dreams:

- A baby or birth would mean death, and vice versa.

- A funeral predicts a wedding.

- A sick person would indicate that healing is on its way for one who is sick.

- Eggs relate to death.

Incidentally, falling teeth also indicate death, while fish are a sign of pregnancy.

In my home growing up as a child, dreams were big business. My paternal grandmother could dream what number was going to come out in what was then simply called "the numbers." My grandmother would have her dreams, interpret them using a dream divination book (such as *Three Wisemen*), and then place her bet. She had an unusually high rate of success.

My mother learned as much as she could from Grandma and devised her own system of numerology. She not only studied dreams, dream books, and signs, but she also created a predictive system based on the frequency and occurrence of number combinations in the four nearby state lotteries. My baby sister came into the world with a type of caul as well. She regularly had dreams that the family used in placing their bets.

My area of dreamwork is shapeshifting, healing, and astral projection. I have devised a heavenly scented dream pillow and bath salts that assist in my dreamwork. Before we get to the recipes, let's explore the materials used.

About the Supplies

The following pertains to the Dream Pillow and Earth Mama's Delightful Bedtime Soak recipes. For this type of work, an invocation of the spirit of the ancient earth goddesses is most appropriate. According to Patricia Telesco in her comprehensive goddess encyclopedia *365 Goddess,* Gaia is the goddess who stretched herself out in the beginning of time and became our home. Black folk also know her as Isis, Inanna, and Geb. She is the earth—fertile, verdant, and lush, but also harsh and stormy. She is a giver of life, and a symbol of the abundant earth, graciousness, and providence. It is the Goddess's hair that we stroke as we tend our herbs and flowers. The Great Goddess provides the delightful scent of the Easter lily. Yet the Earth Mama is not all romance, for it is she who brings quick blood when we carelessly brush too closely to her precious rose.

The Earth Mama resides in the mountains, deserts, lakes, and seas. As patron goddess of gardeners, she offers us an opportunity for respite, healing, and renewal after a stressful day. Working creatively in concert with the Earth Mama using natural ingredients—her greatest gift—we can enjoy her soothing embrace before we drift off into the land of dreams.

Bay (**Laurus nobilis**)—Bay is used in dream pillows by those seeking prophetic dreams and also because it ensures protection and helps build strength.

Dead Sea Salt—Dead Sea salt is a natural substance from the Dead Sea in Israel used to encourage relaxation of muscles and reduce tension, bodyaches, and headaches when used as a bath salt. Salt is associated with spiritual cleansing, nurturance, and the mothers of the sea.

Egyptian Chamomile (**Ormenis multicaulis**)—In an effort to incorporate more African ingredients, the following recipes call for Egyptian chamomile or chamomile maroc. Egyptian chamomile is not related to chamomiles from Europe, such as Roman or German chamomile. Roman chamomile (*Anthemis nobilis*) is highly regarded as an aid for sleeping and for nerves. German chamomile (*Matricaria recutita*) is also good for insomnia, nervous conditions, and is an antiseptic and anti-inflammatory agent. Egyptian chamomile is not as expensive as German or Roman chamomile, and while it doesn't have all of the same applications, it does aid with relaxation and comfort at bedtime.

Epsom Salt—Epsom salts are recommended for relaxing strained or bruised muscles. The combination of salts in these recipes helps us reach a relaxed state. Salts are believed to be rejuvenating to the overworked body, mind, and spirit.

Hops (**Humulus lupulus**)—Hops are recommended for nervousness, sleeplessness, tension, and stress. They are popular in dream pillows or used to spread on a mattress as a sleep aid.

Jasmine (**Jasminum officinale** *or* **J. odoratissimum**)—For those healing from addictions, jasmine is a preferred substitute for hops. Jasmine aids sleep, attracts good spirits, and encourages prophetic dreams.

Lavender (**Lavandula officinalis**)—Used as an essential oil, lavender is an insect repellent (even fleas and mosquitoes don't like it). Lavender is also a relaxing herb when inhaled, so it is used for its aromatherapeutic action in soothing bath soak recipes. Lavender is a healing herb and pampers tired, abraded, or sunburned skin. Lavender has a calm, purple influence on the weary, and it is a specific herb for women especially when combined with borage oil or flowers. Lavender is a plant with an upright appearance and has a similar effect on the spirit.

Lemon Verbena (**Lippia citriodora**)—In a dream pillow, lemon verbena is used both for its citrus scent and because of its ability to strengthen other magickal herbs. Lemon verbena has cleansing and purification properties.

Mullein (**Verbascum thaspus**)—Mullein has many magickal uses. Mullein is worn on the body in a pouch or pockets to keep wild animals at bay while hiking in untamed areas. In a dream pillow, it is used to ensure a peaceful sleep by guarding against the appearance of night mares (particularly bothersome female sea spirits).

Orris Root (**Iris florentina**)—The orris root is derived from the rootstock of the Florentine iris. Hoodoos often refer to her as *Queen Elizabeth root*. Orris root powder has a slightly floral/musky scent. It is used as a scent preservative. In the world of magick, orris root powder is thought to have protective properties and to help in matters of love.

Rose (**Rosa** *spp.*)—The rose is a renowned healing herb known to calm personal stress. It has a heavenly fragrance, and is a symbol of beauty, eloquence, and romantic inclination. Rose petals lend a superior physical and mental soothing quality to our senses.

Spanish Moss (**Tillandsia usneoides**)—When growing, Spanish moss cascades downward like Rapunzel's locks, except it is a soft sage green rather than blonde. Soft to the touch when fresh, Spanish moss makes an ideal stuffing for dream pillows. Moss-filled pillows bring the spirit energy of nature into the bedroom. Spanish moss is best purchased cleaned and dried, otherwise it could contain troublesome insects.

DREAM PILLOW

This dream pillow is designed for protection, strength, restful deep sleep, and prophetic dreams. Allergy sufferers should wear a dust mask for this project and may want to leave out the hops. Substitute jasmine for the hops if desired.

Handful of dried bay leaves

Handful of dried Egyptian chamomile flowers

Handful of dried French lavender buds

Handful of dried hops or jasmine

Handful of dried lemon verbena

Handful of dried mullein

Handful of dried rose petals

Handful of dried Spanish moss

⅛ teaspoon chamomile essential oil

¼ teaspoon lavender essential oil

⅛ teaspoon attar of roses, or quality rose fragrance oil

2 teaspoons Queen Elizabeth root powder

2 9 inch squares of fabric, like gingham, linen, hemp, mud cloth, indigo adire, or kente

Purple cotton thread

Small scarab or Tet

Begin by making the botanical blend. Recite the following chant as you add each ingredient listed into one bowl. Except for the Spanish moss, crumble the ingredients into small, relatively fine pieces.

Geb, help me

[*Crumble bay leaves*]

Inanna, relax me

[*Crumble chamomile flowers*]

Isis, keep me safe

[*Crumble lavender buds*]

Gaia, direct my dreams

[*Crumble hops or jasmine*]

Geb, I thank thee

[*Crumble lemon verbena*]

Inanna, guide me to the truth

[Crumble mullein]

Isis, shield me

[Crumble rose petals]

Thanks be to Earth Mama for sharing your healing gifts.

[Break Spanish moss into 1" pieces]

Sprinkle the chamomile and lavender oils and the attar of roses over the botanicals and stir to mix well. Sprinkle the Queen Elizabeth root powder over the mixture and stir again.

Place mixture in a dark container and seal. Store away from direct light. Let mixture mature for 4 weeks, shaking contents daily. Each time you shake the mixture, reactivate the magickal quality of the herbs and flowers by reciting the following:

Geb, help me
Inanna, relax me
Isis, keep me safe
Gaia, direct my dreams
Earth Mama, I thank thee
Geb, guide me to the truth
Inanna, shield me
Thank you, Isis, for sharing your precious gifts!

While working the herbs each day and waiting for the mixture to mature, make a small pillowcase with the two squares of fabric and purple thread.

When the botanical blend has matured, stuff the pillowcase with it. Insert the scarab or Tet at the end, or save it to glue on the outside of the pillow.

To finish, sew 9 knots onto the pillow to magickally and physically fortify your stitchery: 2 knots near the middle of the top and sides, and 3 knots at the bottom.

When finished, put this dream pillow in your pillowcase.

EARTH MAMA'S DELIGHTFUL BEDTIME SOAK

2 cups Epsom salt
2 cups coarse Dead Sea salt
2 cups fine sea salt
1 tablespoon Egyptian chamomile
  essential oil

1 tablespoon lavender essential oil
Large glass or stainless-steel screw-
  top container
Handful of fresh fragrant rose
  petals, optional

Pour the salts into the container. Drop in the essential oils and stir. Seal container tightly and shake well. Let rest 36 to 48 hours.

To use, add 1 to 2 cups per bath. Also add a handful of fresh fragrant rose petals, if available. Soak in this bath for at least 20 minutes, but stay in longer if possible.

Yield: 6 cups
Shelf life: 1 year

The Spirits Who Ride

Throughout African American Hoodoo lore, there are accounts of folks being ridden by witches as they sleep. Hoodoos are so serious about this that they inspect people suspected of having fallen victim to this dark practice for the witches' stirrup marks. They also examine the victim to see if the hair is tangled from the wild night's ride.

Since my earliest recollections, I remember a peculiar sensation that has been beautifully described by Anthony Shafton in his book *Dream-Singers*. It is a feeling of being at a halfway point—a crossroads of sorts between everyday wakefulness and the land of dreams. A paralysis comes over me. I want to move, but I can't. Often this builds a deep anxiety within me. I feel as though I am suffocating; there seems to be a soft object over my nose, like a pillow or blanket. When I am finally able to break free from this frozen state, I awaken sweaty and gasping for air. I never thought I was ridden by a witch because I am one, yet I can relate to the idea of being ridden by something or someone.

If you are disturbed by sleep paralysis (the scientific explanation for witch rides) or are bothered by *night mares* (female sea spirits), it is useful to call on the power of the moon goddesses and old wise ones for assistance. Burning their preferred incenses, wearing certain amulets and charms, and sprinkling the powders of the goddesses in your bedroom can help alleviate distress so that you can awaken in the morning well rested.

Mythic Goddesses Who Inform Our Dreams

Quite often you will find references to the goddesses in Hoodoo shops and books. Many of the incenses, powders, and sachets are named for Isis, but who is she?

> Isis is the beginning.
> Her tears of passion tumbled down her breast and formed our great
>   oceans and seas.
> Isis is "She Who Weeps."
> She Who Weeps cried the Nile into existence. As the Nile rises and falls,
>   so, too, does the amount of her grief.
> Isis is goddess of revitalization, renewal, queen of sorcery, life of the
>   Nile, protectress, and she is Mother Moon.

Isis is a prototypical goddess drawn in part from the Phoenician goddess Astarte and other earth goddesses before her. Isis is sister to Nephthys (the invisible one) and daughter of Nut, the divine water jar that collects and then releases waters as rain from the heavens. As West Africans, our descendants transformed the image of Isis after their great migration from Khemet (ancient Egypt). They transformed her into Yemoya-Olokun, the Yoruban Great Mother.

Isis's legacy has captivated a variety of cultures, crossing racial and ethnic boundaries. She originated in the Neolithic Middle East as Inanna, the first complete goddess of sky, earth, and waters. The remnants from her followers were found at Catal Huyuk. In Sumeria and Assyria she was known as Ishtar, and in Greece she was Aphrodite. In Rome she was Venus, and in Christianity she has taken on epic proportions as Eve and the Virgin Mary, mother of Jesus.

Isis, Mother Moon and Great Mother, is the goddess of dreams. Invocation of Isis brings peaceful, prophetic dreams. With her gentle breath on our backs as we sleep, messages of love, compassion, hope, and renewal can be transmitted. When the moon goes through her various stages, it is important to realize the intimate relationship between Isis, the moon, the sea, and your *ka* (shadow or spirit self). When we want to do astral projection, it is important to remember that Isis and her archetypes have immense powers that transcend those of most deities.

The tools of Isis can be kept under our pillow, in a bowl near our bed, on our headboard, or wherever the spirit moves us. Her favorite musical instrument is the sistrum, which is somewhat akin to a rattle in sound and appearance. Rattles keep us on track, effect change, and stimulate our imaginations. Rattlesnake skin, which is also contained in Gopher's Dust, embodies Isis's sistrum and one of her incarnations. A bowl of salt or a salt circle in the kitchen (hearth area) or bedroom represents the protective spirit of Isis and all creator beings.

Isis is a milk-giving, nurturing goddess. Her nurturing quality was

Isis

condensed into mere sexuality in contemporary readings of Aphrodite and Venus, but they are all much more than goddesses of love in a sexual manner. Isis is a serpent when she wants to be, although she can also fly like a hawk and is usually depicted as a winged goddess. She is the ancient goddess of the Tree of Life. Her colors are white, silver, and deep blue—exactly the same as Yemoya-Olokun.

Stones associated with Isis are also moon stones: aquamarine, moonstone, sapphire, beryl, quartz crystals, and selenite. To charge these stones, put them in saltwater and then leave them outdoors for two or more days to allow them to drink in the power of the moon. You can then keep one or more of these charged stones of the moon in a mojo bag under your pillow or under your bed in a bowl of fragrant water. Make jewelry (or have it made for you) featuring these powerful stones. Setting them in silver evokes her power even more.

As you drift off to sleep, meditate on the myriad images of Isis. Conjure up dreams to answer your deepest questions, predict the future, inspire healing, or draw love. Invoke Isis also before journeys overseas, cruises, or vacations by the sea. Give Isis-inspired jewelry or amulets to fishermen or -women, flight attendants, sailors, and marines.

ISIS DREAM RITUAL

To invite the spirit of Isis, try this ritual before bedtime.

Coarse sea salt

1 cup whole or coconut milk

¼ cup Rhassoul mud or white kaolin

4–6 drops myrrh essential oil

½ cup white sand

Charcoal block

Large conch, abalone, or scallop shell

Loose incense (see note)

Charged clear crystal

Sheet of paper

Bowl of salt

Charged moonstone

Scrub the bathtub with the sea salt and rinse. Draw a warm bath.

In a small bowl mix together the milk, mud or clay, and myrrh oil. Add this to the running water.

As the tub is filling up, create a small altar. On a table near the bath or bathroom window place the sand. Put the shell on the sand and then the charcoal block on the shell. Light the charcoal block. When it is hot, sprinkle on some of the incense.

Get into the tub and place the crystal on your belly. Ask out loud the questions you want answers to, then chant *"Aung, shrang, shring, shraung"* or *"Dhum vam"* repeatedly until you can't go on any longer. Intersperse this chant with your questions, while deeply inhaling the incense. You have reached a higher plane where Isis can speak to you.

Once you get out of the tub, write the questions down on the sheet of paper. Put the moonstone in the bowl of salt and set this on top of the paper.

Go to sleep focused on your quest. In the morning write down your dream. Consult dream books for interpretations of the symbols. Remember that ancestral spirits like to speak to us indirectly using puns, metaphors, and opposites.

Note: Copal and cedar are sacred to several Native American groups and open the way to receive spiritual visions. Myrrh is Isis's favorite incense. Kyphi (see below) is an ancient Khemetian recipe that heals while also creating a sacred, loving environment.

Kyphi

Now, in your quest to invoke the dream goddesses, no doubt you will come across *kyphi*. Kyphi is a healing substance from Egypt that was popular there from the beginnings of the Old Kingdom through the last days of the New Kingdom. After that it was created in Greece, Rome, and various African empires. Kyphi is used for divination work, dreamwork, and to create a sacred space appealing to the goddesses. Kyphi was originally called *kapet*, which translates into a generic term for fumigation. Kyphi was also used orally for sore throats and colds.

Recipes for kyphi (also called *kupar*) were recorded by renowned ancient Roman physicians Rufus and Galen. Below are two ancient original recipes for kyphi, offered mostly for curiosity since the ingredients are fairly difficult to obtain.

SYRIAC RECIPE FOR KUPAR (SECOND CENTURY)

Base

168 g stoned raisins "cleaned inside and out"	Strong-smelling wine "Sufficient" honey

Resin

15 g frankincense	15 g myrrh

Herbs

4 g spikenard	8 g mastic tree flowers (*Pistacia lentiscus*)
4 g crocus/saffron	
8 g aspalathos	

Spices

4 g cinnamon	8 g cassis

Dissolve the raisins and soluble ingredients in the wine. Pound the dry ingredients in a mortar and "clean" them. Heat frankincense and honey. Mix it all together and store in a jar.

KYPHI OF RAMESSES III
(TWELFTH CENTURY BC)

Base
Raisins   Honey

Resin
Mastic (jed)   Pine resin (or wood)

Herbs
Camel grass   Mint
Sweet flag (calamus root)

Spices
Cinnamon

The Dreamer's Charms

Some hoodoos will recommend that those who are troubled in their sleep by malicious behavior or ill intent keep a pair of scissors under their pillow. To me this seems dangerous to the user. Other things folks have reported success with include water. Keep water under the bed—either plain tap water, rainwater, lightning water, rose water, lavender water, orange blossom water, or Florida Water. Reasons for this include the following:

- The spirits are drawn to pleasing aromas.

- The spirits get thirsty.

- Your *ka* (dream self) may get thirsty and wander dangerously distant from your body. If unable to return, this could result in a catatonic state.

- Lavender and rose water have a tranquilizing affect on the dreamer.

- Lightning water has a magickal charge and possesses some of the intensity and power of Shango, god of lightning, and Oya, goddess of storms and wind.

- Rainwater is the sustaining force for life on earth.

Some folk also spread salt or salt and pepper around the water. This way, only good spirits can come through the water—the evil ones will be burned.

Other amulets include the following:

- A scarab

- A garlic braid or clove of garlic under the pillow

- A gardenia plant, fresh roses, lilacs, or dragonsnaps

- John the Conqueror root hand

- Angelica root

- A Tet

chapter 14

Passin' On

Dreams give us a taste of the domain of the spirit, but there is a time when our families, loved ones, and friends pass on in earnest to that next plane. The following is an examination of African American attitudes toward grief, mourning, and burial beginning in West Africa and ending in the United States on the Atlantic coast.

The vast area encompassing the territory that scholars such as Professor Robert Farris Thompson call the Kongo and include Angola and Yorubaland were the lands heavily hit by slavery. African Americans descend from the Bakongo, KiKongo, Igbo, Fang, Djema, Bobangi, Luba, Kimbundu, Umbundu, Ibibio, Efik, Nupe, Beni, Ibo, Mande, Yoruba, Ewe, Fon, Popo, Ga, Akan, Ashanti, Fanti, and Bantu peoples. While many of these tribes are as different as, say, a Finnish person is from someone from Macedonia in appearance, language, and customs, Africans from the Kongo, Yorubaland, and Angola do share a fundamental set of beliefs, some of which were enhanced during the slave trade and brutal Middle Passage.

> *Oh, freedom*
> *Oh, freedom*
> *Oh, freedom over me*
> *And before I'd be a slave*
> *I'd be buried in my grave*
> *And go home to my Lord*
> *And be free.*
>
> —Traditional, "Oh Freedom"

The Bantu, Ibo, and Mande people in particular left an indelible mark on the southeastern United States. Remnants of the Mande language, cultural practices, and beliefs still thrive in the Gullah and Geechee people of the Georgia coast and South Carolina lowlands. For sheer numbers of people distributed in the Americas, the Yoruba of Nigeria are a key culture, and their beliefs have flourished. As we examine distinctive, traditional African American customs and beliefs regarding grief, mourning, death, and burial, we will consider the cultures that spawned the beliefs. We will also discover useful ways to adapt and incorporate these belief systems into our own grieving and attitudes toward death and dying.

As we consider the striking qualities of African American ways of dealing with loss, mourning, and sorrow, it is important to keep in mind the impact that slavery had on Black culture. Africans who were transplanted in the Americas came from well-developed societies. Within a group described with the blanket term *slave* there were craftsmen, metalsmiths, musicians, teachers, midwives, medicine women and men, warriors, and children of noble birth. For many of these people, being stripped of both their community and their role within society was a fate much worse than death. To the mind of a slave, surely death must be better than a half-life as the property of an alien culture.

It was Igbo warriors who perhaps made the most vivid statement regarding an unwillingness to accept what fate had imposed upon them. When the slave ship filled with Igbo (many of whom were warriors) arrived on the coast of Georgia, the entire human cargo, still in chains, walked into the Atlantic Ocean and never were seen again. This mass suicide has taken on epic proportions in African American lore. The warriors are believed to have walked through the waters back home to Mother Africa and I am certain that is exactly what their spirits did.

Folklore and song became a rich source of hope as well as a reservoir for our culture. We became the masters of the double-entendre, as evidenced in our Negro spirituals. We sang of "home"—sometimes meaning Africa, but most often referring to the realm of the spirit. The following was included in the 1867 compilation *Slave Songs of the United States* by William Francis Allen, Charles Pickard Ware, and Lucy McKim Garrison.

"I Want to Go Home"

I want to go home
Dere's no rain to wet you,

O, yes, I want to go home,
Want to go home
Dere's no rain to wet you,
O, yes, I want to go home,
Want to go home

Dere's no sun to burn you
Dere's no hard trials
Dere's no whips a-crackin'
Dere's no stormy weather
Dere's no tribulation
No more slavery in de kingdom
No evil-doers in the kingdom
All is gladness in de kingdom

Animism, the idea that nature is animated with significant spirits, is a unifying belief among the various tribal groups transported to the Americas. In the animistic pantheon there is as much purpose for us as humans as there is when we journey into the spirit realm. We continue to be honored by our family and ancestors. We continue to have a role in our communities. We live free of the constraints of society or even a corporeal body.

In *The Healing Wisdom of Africa*, author Malidoma Patrice Some speaks about how he, as a Dagara, dealt with grief and mourning. For Some, sadness was greatly reduced once he realized that community offers immortality. A *kontomble* (spirit messenger) that he calls the "Green Lady" taught him how to recognize the presence of the ancestors as they exist in nature and work within our community. He came to recognize the interdependence of the living and the dead.

Malidoma Some stresses that sorrow and grief are natural and that these emotions should never be denied full expression. The healing wisdom of the Dagara teaches us how to unite ritual with community in order that we might live a richer life.

The jazz funeral popular in New Orleans, Louisiana, is a dramatic manifestation of the Dagara grieving concept. At the inception of the ceremony, solemn music sets the tone echoed by friends, family, and communal procession. Somber music encourages reflection, solemnity, and memories. Tears (note the water element) run freely. In the end, the ceremony takes on an upbeat note. Hand-clapping, dancing, and sometimes singing lend an air of hope while also inviting camaraderie. Participants in the New Orleans jazz funeral become one, a community united by the ritualistic acting-out of grief followed by a joyous, jubilant celebration.

FUNERAL RITUAL

This grieving ritual marries the Dagara's principle of communal sharing with some of the spirit of a New Orleans jazz funeral.

Gather a circle of friends, associates, family, or neighbors. Chant, clap, and act out the directions.

Half of group: [*chanting*]
                                     Done laid your burden down

Other half of group: [*chanting*]
                                     Laid your burden down

Leader: [*Lay down an offering wrapped in a piece of kente
                    cloth or banana paper: a photograph, favorite food,
                    letter, article of clothing, or other memento.*]

Half of group: Now, go on to the next plane

Other half of group: Don't turn yourself around
                        Don't turn yourself around

Group: [*Form a circle and grab hands. Slowly
                    walk clockwise around the offerings.*]

Leader:	[*Sets the offerings on fire.*]
Half of group:	[*Chanting*] Light as a feather
Other half of group:	[*Chanting*] That's how things gonna be
Leader:	[*Lights sage/lavender smudge stick and smudges members of group. At the same time, half of the group continues.*]
Half of group:	Missin' you, lovin' you
Other half of group:	[*Chanting and clapping joyfully*] So happy that you're free Happy that you're free! [*Repeat as desired.*]
Leader:	[*Pours cool water, vodka, rum, or gin libation around perimeter of the fire, then douses the fire with the libation. Buries the burnt offering remains.*]
Group:	[*Everyone sits down to reflect on the person who is the cause for the ritual. Conversation, tears, and hopefully some laughter complete the ceremony. Slowly, everyone leaves the circle.*]

The elements of fire and water play important roles in this ritual. The emotional states of grief include fiery feelings like anger and remorse. Fire is a positive element because it brings warmth, purging, an opportunity for renewal, and focus for hope. Water, as represented in our tears, represents the cosmic womb of the Great Mother. At the same time it symbolizes rain, the substance that cleanses, regenerates, and feeds life on earth. Water or spirits poured as a libation on a fire brings fire and water together while saluting the spirits. The spirits' thirst for acknowledgment, remembrance, and continuity is quenched by water. We acknowledge the ancestors, demonstrating to them that we know they are still with us.

Water plays an important role in West Africa, as it does universally. Bodies of water harbor precious sustenance; they are places for cleansing the body and soul and the homes of revered water spirits. It was also the water of the Atlantic that brought Africans to the New World. To the Yoruba who participate in Ifa beliefs, water embodies the angelic forces (or orisha) of Yemoya-Olokun. Yemoya-Olokun are honored as a dual deity. Yemoya is associated with the oceans and seas, while Olokun gives life to fresh water in the form of rivers, lakes, and streams. As the Great Mother, Yemoya is closely associated with nurturance of the womb and amniotic fluid, and Olokun symbolizes clarity and fluidity. The two are looked to for their healing powers and cool heads.

In New Orleans, because of high water levels, the dead are buried above ground in tombs. Traditional African American tombs demonstrate a clear connection to West African Ifa by incorporating surface decorations such as seashells (totemic symbols suggestive of Yemoya-Olokun). The tomb is not only a marker, but it also becomes a charm and a symbol for the unification of humans with angelic water spirits. It is a tangible symbol for the departed, and as such, it is lavished with care and attention.

Water is gentle, soothing, and cool. We embark on journeys to new lands—both earthly and spiritual—over water. The flow of salty tears is a physical manifestation of sorrow, mourning, and grief; it is the river that runs down our face. This natural expression of our emotions must not be dammed; instead, it should be allowed to run its course. Malidoma Patrice Some describes the importance of water in ritual as a crucial survival mechanism among his people. The coolness of water is an equalizing force that reduces the sharper, hot emotions, such as anger, hostility, and passionate holding-on.

As discussed previously, the Yoruba call medical herbs *ewe*. The angelic forces have corresponding numbers, colors, and ewe. Considering the Yoruban reverence for the water spirits Yemoya-Olokun, I created the following bath ritual, built around the two water spirits and their ewe. Yemoya-Olokun's ewe offer comfort from loss and grief.

"ON WITH LIFE!" BATH RITUAL

This ritual is good for dealing with any type of loss, such as loss of employment, friendship, love, animal companion, theft, or loss of self-esteem. Begin making the bath soak on a Friday evening of a waning moon.

Gardenia petals or plant
Silver or white silk cloth
2 cups Dead Sea salt
2 cups fine sea salt
2 cups Epsom salt
⅛ cup dried orange rind
¼ cup crumbled peppermint leaves
2 tablespoons myrrh essential oil

2 tablespoons sweet orange essential oil
2 tablespoons sandalwood essential oil
Charged crystal
Release Incense (recipe follows)
Charcoal block
Seashell

To begin, take a spirit-cleansing bath in cool water. Fresh or ocean water is best, but a cool indoor bath will work. Before the bath, place the gardenia petals or plant on the silk cloth on your bathroom windowsill or table.

Focus your intention to create powerful healing brews. Clear your head of clutter and confusion. Dip your head under the cool water several times.

To make the bath soak, combine the salts in a large, nonreactive bowl. Recite the following:

Precious gift from the Mothers of the river and sea.

Grind orange rind in a mortar and pestle, food processor, or clean coffee grinder, and say:

Uplift my spirits with your blessed fruits.

[*Mix the orange powder into the salts*]

Release your powers. Heal my grief.

[*Stir in the peppermint*]

In honor of Yemoya-Olokun, sweet spirits, hear my plea!

In a small, separate bowl, combine the three essential oils and swirl to blend. Pour this over the salt-orange-peppermint blend and mix well.

Place the charged crystal in the bottom of a container with a screw-top lid. Add the bath soak blend and seal. Store for 3 days, shaking contents daily.

To use, add 2 cups to running bathwater. Burn the Release Incense over the hot charcoal that has been placed in the seashell. Release your grief, sorrow, despair, or whatever you are feeling into the water and into the smoke. As you watch the tub drain and the smoke drift upward, visualize your anguish or sorrow moving along with them.

Yield: Approximately 6½ cups, or enough for 3 washes
Shelf life: 1 year

RELEASE INCENSE

5 bay leaves
3 anise stars
2 small cinnamon sticks, or ¼ cup cinnamon chips
Handful of dried uva ursi leaves
Handful of dried mint leaves and stems
Handful of dried rosemary leaves and stems
Handful of dried chamomile flowers
12 myrrh tears
7 frankincense tears
⅛ teaspoon myrrh essential oil
⅛ teaspoon bay essential oil
⅛ teaspoon ylang ylang essential oil
Charged aquamarine
Charged tourmaline

Using a coffee grinder or mortar and pestle, pulverize the bay, anise, and cinnamon until they are a coarse powder. Crumble in the uva ursi, mint, rosemary, and chamomile.

Stir in the myrrh and frankincense tears. Sprinkle the essential oils over the mixture.

Put the aquamarine and tourmaline in a container with a lid. Add the incense blend and seal. Store for 3 days, shaking contents daily.

Yield: Approximately 1 cup
Shelf life: 1 year

Traditional Burial Customs

African and traditional African American burial, death, and grieving rituals are not only concerned with the living, a great deal of consideration is given to the spirit of the departed as well. Traditional graves found in Louisiana (New Orleans), Missouri (St. Louis), Mississippi, Florida (Jacksonville), Virginia (Richmond), Georgia, and the South Carolina lowlands all bear witness to African ancestor reverence.

In the early days of life in the Americas, African slaves, sharecroppers, and freemen insisted that a tree be planted on the burial site. The tree was usually an evergreen (conifer) and it served as a reminder of the duality and persistence of life. The cycles of growth (spring leaves), maturity (fall color), and death (winter) is easy to grasp when one gazes upon a tree. The trunk, branches, and leaves are in the realm of the humans while the life force of the tree—the roots—lie beneath the earth. This duality of human and spirit serves as a useful metaphor for the interaction between departed spirits and their living community.

Pine and spruce trees in particular play a key role in traditional southern U.S. burials—this owing to their availability and ability to flourish in the region. To early Black Americans, the green scent of evergreen trees contained medicine to heal the body and the spirit. In Faith Mitchell's book *Hoodoo Medicine,* she goes into great detail about the variety of ills pine tar (*pinus* spp.) was used for, including congestion, fever, stomachache, whooping cough, germs, and parasites. In South Carolina it was used as a spring tonic. The use of pine sap was greatly influenced by African American interaction with the Native American community. The indigenous people on the coast of the Southeast used pine sap (tar) for swelling, burns, itching, sore throats, colds, and consumption.

To the present day, pine tar enjoys a special place in the Black community. Pine soap is used for bathing and scalp disorders (it is believed to help strengthen the hair and combat baldness), while pine oil is used for cleansing floors. Pine oil used in this manner is antibacterial. The scent serves as a spiritual and systemic tonic. In the winter when my spirits are grieving the lively spirits of summer and autumn, I put a teaspoon of white pine essential oil directly on a wet mop with a dash of Castile soap and clean the floors. This appears to have a marked influence on the spirits in my home. This floor wash is also recommended for wakes and to help combat depression.

"LIFT ME UP" PINE FLOOR WASH

This recipe is for the down-home folk with access to trees on their property. If you do not, see the variation.

Enough pliable young, green shoots from spruce, pine, and/or cedar trees to fill a stockpot ¾ full
Tap water
¼ teaspoon fir essential oil (see note)

¼ teaspoon cedar essential oil
½ teaspoon white pine essential oil
Unscented liquid Castile soap or concentrated lemon-scented dish detergent

Fill a stockpot with the shoots and tap water. Set on medium heat and bring to a boil. When the water starts to boil, turn heat down to medium-low. Cover and continue to simmer 25 minutes.

After 25 minutes, remove pot from heat. Let cool, then strain into a wash bucket. Add the essential oils and a squirt or two of the soap.

Sweep your floors. Then sprinkle some of the pine water on your broom and mop your floors with it.

Note: Use any combination of these oils or just one, depending on your stash, so long as the total amount comes to 1 teaspoon.

Variation: Fill a large bucket ¾ full of rainwater or tap water. Add the essential oils—again, in any combination—and a squirt or two of the soap. Sweep and then mop your floors.

In addition to evergreen trees and seashells, white bathroom tiles (a contemporary adaptation on seashells) are sometimes seen on traditional African American grave sites. Plates, cups, lanterns, flashlights, and sometimes even shoes are also featured. Sometimes these were the last objects used by the deceased or they were favorite objects. This custom is derived from the Kongo belief that the last object touched has the intent and power of the deceased person's spirit. It is considered dangerous to keep these things in the home lest a troubled spirit would be led back to the home. Bringing the objects to the graves encourages continuum in the journey of the spirit. This custom also bears a resemblance to aspects of Egyptian burial during the Old Kingdom. Egyptian kings were provided utensils and familiar objects to take with them to the next life. This was witnessed clearly

Bottle tree at crossroads

with the pristine discovery of King Tutankhamen's tomb in the Valley of the Kings in 1922.

The purpose of the placement of the objects was quite different for the ancient Khemetians because the objects assured comfort to the ka (spirit double). For West Africans and their American descendants, the familiar objects served as an anchor to hold the spirits in the spirit world. These objects were to keep the spirits properly situated, thus preventing them from wandering into the human realm. The term *kanga mfunya* is used to describe the "tying" of spirits to objects that guide them to the spirit world.

Another device used both to engage spirits and keep them from wandering is the *bottle tree*. Bottle trees have been seen in places as diverse as Suriname, Trinidad, Texas, Virginia, Alabama, Arkansas, Mississippi, and the Dominican Republic. Bottle trees stem from the Bantu tradition of tying bottles and other objects to trees to protect a residence or vacant land from thieves. The shimmery vibrancy of the bottles is attractive to spirits. The bottles draw and then trap wayward spirits inside. Within the bottles, our ancestors can safely be useful to the community, for their presence scares off potential thefts or other wrongdoing. Bottle trees are a new home for our departed loved ones where we can visit them and be close to them.

The domain of the spirit is visualized as being white and having a glasslike shimmer. Kaolin, a pure-white clay found at the bottom of riverbeds, is used on masks and medicine bundles to symbolize the spirit realm. In the Caribbean, tombs are whitewashed on Christmas morning to honor the spirit realm. The white rooster (*nsusu mpembe*) embodies the power of the white, or spirit, realm, so in many African and traditional African American burial rituals, a white cock is sacrificed to help the spirit stay in its own domain. A candle and then a lamp helps light the way from earth to the spirit world. Pipes are sometimes laid on the burial site to represent the impending voyage through the tunnel from one world to the next.

There are many ways for us to honor and engage our ancestral spirits in the world of the living. Tossing coins around the home and on the altar keeps money available to departed spirits. In turn, they bring us good luck and prosperity. Placing fruit, fragrant flowers, and seashells on the burial site and home altar is pleasing to the spirits, as is the color white. The spirits enjoy sweet cakes, honey, candy, wine, vodka, gin, and rum. Incense—especially that which contains a bit of tobacco, frankincense, pine, and sage—are also very pleasing to the ancestors. The ancestors get thirsty and they can be channeled into your dreams through water. Placing a bowl of fresh water under the bed draws spirit ancestors who then manifest themselves as symbolic messages in dreams. They also enjoy Florida Water, kananga water, orange blossom water, rose and lavender water. In *Magical Herbalism,* author Scott Cunningham suggests burning crushed willow bark/sandalwood incense to draw the spirits near. Yew and willow leaves and bark are also sometimes burned to call up the spirit of a departed loved one.

ANCESTRAL ALTAR

This altar is a useful place for private reflection, communion, and healing the soul. Arrange the following objects on a table that has been cleansed with kananga water and a little Castile soap. Place the objects on top of a piece of silver or rich blue silk.

Crystal bowl filled with kananga water	Loose tobacco
Copper container filled with graveyard dirt (from the burial site) or other soil	A glass of water
	Small shot glass of spirits (vodka, wine, etc.)
1 white candle	Fresh fruit
Gardenia or fragrant rose petals	Hard candy
Coins (dimes and pennies)	Photograph of the deceased

Replenish perishables as needed; remember, empty glasses and spoiled food insult the spirits. Burn some of the Release Incense (page 236) at the altar when you are ready to let go.

Ylang Ylang

The healing scent of ylang ylang (*Kananga odorata*) invites warmth and joyfulness back into the life of the bereaved. Kananga water has a twofold purpose: it pleases the spirits while it also uplifts, soothes, and comforts during the grieving process. The gentle nervines in ylang ylang also help reduce anxiety, inhibition, and stress. A recipe for kananga water can be found on page 83.

Hoodoo for the Terminally Ill

In the West we have begun to reclaim many aspects of our lives that had previously been taken over by societal norms. We are learning about our heritage—learning that it is not dark, backwards, or evil. We incorporate elements of our ancient customs into our wedding ceremonies, dress, and decor. Many women have taken birthing back by creating a community of sisters around them to help facilitate a more gentle birth. Women who assist with birth may be doulas, midwives, mothers, and sisterfriends. Whoever it is, we seek them out to make sure our birthing environment is loving and personalized—but what about death?

Dream Pillows

One of our first duties is to make a terminally ill community or family member as comfortable as possible. We can do that by lovingly creating a Restful Sleep Dream Pillow to encourage more restful sleep. I would suggest mixing together some chamomile buds, mullein, hops, lavender, and an angelica root. Prepare about ⅛ cup of powdered calamus or Queen Elizabeth root with 2 to 3 drops of chamomile essential oil and attar of roses mixed in. Pour the scented powder over the herbs and mix together. Stuff this mixture into a 4" x 6" ready-made muslin drawstring bag, and then stuff this inside the patient's pillow.

You can also make a Spiritual Healing Dream Pillow in a similar way. Skip the scented powder and stuff the muslin bag with lavender, mullein, and rose petals. Sprinkle the herbs beforehand with a few drops of ylang ylang and lavender essential oils.

Sandalwood

Sandalwood (*Santalum album*) has been used as a spiritual aid for over four thousand years. Chunks of sandalwood are ground and used as an incense or prepared into oil for soaps, candles, perfume, and creams. The special quality of sandalwood useful at this tender juncture is that it is a calming herb; it opens the way to wisdom. Products containing sandalwood are used to initiate rituals, curb depression, and comfort. Sandalwood is the preferred root for aiding the crossing-over of the spirit, while also helping those in mourning.

Sandalwood only grows in a few forests. It is a tree very resistant to tampering with by humans, so it has not been successfully farmed. *Mysore* is considered to be the best type, but it is extremely hard to get a hold of, and it is poached heavily. There are also mature trees found in Tamil Nadu, other parts of India, and Indonesia. Ethical harvesting is done by Scents of Earth (listed in appendix B). Ethically wildcrafted sandalwood is typically done by uprooting a tree during the monsoonal rains, tapping the root, and then replanting. This does not damage the health of the tree.

Herbal Teas and Honey

Teas made with chamomile, pasque flowers, and St. John's wort are soothing alone or in combination, especially with raw lavender honey. They help alleviate the depression that arises with serious illness. To create lavender honey, add 2 to 3 tablespoons of lavender buds to a jar that is ⅔ full of raw, unprocessed honey. Let steep for 3 to 4 weeks, turning the jar upside down every few days.

Supplementary Treatments

Supplementary treatments with peace-loving, immunity-boosting olive leaf extract may be helpful. Decoct ¼ cup dried olive leaves in 2 cups water for 25 to 30 minutes. Combine it with the sacred bark *pau d'arco* from Brazil, along with vinegar and garlic tonics.

Blankets

Handmade woven blankets made with natural fibers like wool, silk, or cotton bring warmth on many levels while also helping those who suffer with fevers or chills.

Touch

Massages with warmed olive, almond (sweet oil), or grapeseed oil, as well as tender hugs are very comforting.

Talking

Talking about happy times can bring joy in the last days. In (so-called) sophisticated societies, death seems to burn the lips and so we avoid it—but it doesn't avoid us. Discussions about plans for a special funerary ceremony, although painful, let the person know that his or her life will be celebrated in the way he or she would find most pleasing.

ASHES TO ASHES, DUST TO DUST RITUAL

White ashes (see appendix B) or white sand	Charcoal block Powdered sandalwood

Spread out the ashes or sand to form a small circle. Light the charcoal block and place it on the ashes. After 3 to 5 minutes, sprinkle on the sandalwood. Allow this spicy root that smells of the earth and rain to replenish your spirits. Reflect and contemplate.

Sandalwood is a root that brings release. It even brings sensual satisfaction to those practicing celibacy (hence its use in temples and sacred jewelry such as rosaries). If tears flow, allow them to put out the charcoal block. Collect the residue of the burnt sandalwood, ash, or sand and place all in a mojo healing bag.

Rituals and Ceremonies

So what shall we do when the loved one decides to move on? Well, in the olden days there was time to "set-up," or arrange for, a death ceremony (funeral). Families would set-up and hold vigil over their loved one, making sure he or she felt comfortable to leave his or her body and go on to the next world. This was our "wake"; we stayed awake until the wee hours of the morning sipping sweet coffee and eating rum cake, gingerbread, and cornbread biscuits accompanied by hearty soul food. We would reminisce, remember, connect, cry, comfort others, and watch for "the signs" concerning the deceased person's passage.

Sometimes the burial would take place first in an almost perfunctory manner, but the funeral and celebration of the life of the deceased was well planned. Folks waited until their relatives had the means to contribute and travel to the location of the ceremony.

Death can be sudden or lingeringly slow until our resources are completely drained. Funeral homes seem to step in and just take over, and that is really not how it should be. There are several steps you can take to integrate African heritage and traditional African American customs back into funerals and burials. A simple way would be to bury a few of the deceased person's things with him or her so that his or her spirit will be comfortable on its journey yonder. You could also bury items that might assist in the journey: a flashlight, money, incense, or hard candies as an offering. To add an African touch, you could carefully select an appropriate handwoven West African textile to wrap the person's body in for safe passage home (see chapters 9 and 11 for specifics on fabrics). You could also anoint his or her head with a holy oil, such as a mixture of rosemary, hyssop, angelica, frankincense, and myrrh in an olive-oil base. In the United States it was customary in some areas to place daisies or other flowers on the eyes of the loved one. For others, pennies were placed over the eyes to both keep them shut (so the deceased wouldn't try to see this world any longer) and as good-luck charms.

If you don't want to ruffle feathers in the family, you could prepare a discreet lucky or love mojo bag and hide it in the coffin. In light of the historic reverence for pine discussed earlier, you might consider a coffin made from simple pine. Try also to plant a tree near the burial site, or choose a site with a tree already growing near it. You can also plant a new young tree on your property as a memorial, or if you live in an apartment or condo, you can grow a potted palm, ficus, corn plant, or Norfolk Island pine tree. There are so many things that can be done, but you need to think ahead. Plan, and be prepared in the same way you are for births or weddings. Taking control is an important element of overcoming the powerless feeling and anger that death awakens.

FUNERARY WREATH

This wreath is helpful to the departed, folks attending the funeral, and the loved ones of the deceased. Therefore it can be brought to the funeral, placed on the grave, or brought back home and hung on the front door. The flowers and leaves are symbols of spirituality, peace, strength, courage, luck, and love. Don't feel bad if you can't find all of these, as even as few as three types will be sure to do the trick. If you are too overwhelmed, you can have a florist or friend prepare this wreath for you.

1. Myrtle, willow leaves, yarrow sprigs, juniper, and Norfolk Island pine
2. Angelica, bay leaves, linden leaves, lavender, and heather
3. Carnations, roses, sweet pea, cockscombs, snapdragons, and gardenia

1 medium or large grapevine wreath
Hot-melt glue gun
White, blue, or purple ribbon or lace for accents

Place the wreath on newspaper. Arrange the #1 items as the bottom and side layers of the wreath. Affix with glue sparingly.

Next, layer on an assortment of the #2 items. Affix with glue.

Arrange the flowers listed as #3. Try to have a strong, showy flower at the north, south, east, and west, with smaller flowers between them. Affix with glue.

You can use the ribbon or lace to hold together the arrangement, as well as for hanging the wreath up.

Lavender Bundles and Sachets

Lavender (*Lavandula officinalis*) is specific to the emotions. Lavender buds were prepared into a sachet and held by women during childbirth, and they were also used for controlling fits of hysteria, rage, or depression. Lavender is gentle and uplifting without being overly stimulating.

One way to use lavender is to give out small bundles of it held together with a wide purple ribbon to the immediate family at the wake and/or funeral. A second idea is to make sachets; see below.

GRIEF TRICK

1 pound lavender buds

2 teaspoons lavender essential oil

⅛ cup calamus root powder

⅛ cup Queen Elizabeth root

Purple flannel or muslin tea bags

Stir the essential oil into the lavender buds. Sprinkle the calamus and Queen Elizabeth root onto the mixture and blend.

Put ¼ to ½ cup lavender mixture into each flannel or muslin tea bag. Pull the string tightly. Place the sachets in a pretty basket and make them available to people during the wake and funeral.

The day we die
The wind comes down
to take away
our footprints.

The wind makes dust
to cover up
the marks we left
while walking.

For otherwise
the thing would seem
as if we were
still living.

Therefore the wind
is he who comes
to blow away
our footprints.

—Southern African
Bushman proverb

In closing, one of the saddest parts about death is the new American way of handling funerals. African cultures, and indeed many indigenous cultures, spend a long time preparing for death ceremonies. Some cultures, like the Melanesian people of New Ireland, seem to dedicate their entire lives to the preparation of death ceremonies. In Africa, the finest cloths are prepared from raffia and other natural fibers to shroud and salute departed members of the community. Incorporating natural materials, herbs, and African traditions offer solace and comfort during times of loss.

At-Risk & Endangered Materials

At-Risk and Endangered Plants Used in Hoodoo

Consider the fragile status of the following plants and use substitutes or purchase from ethical wildcrafters.

Bearberry (*Arctostaphylos uva ursi*)

Bearberry is used in kinnikinnik blends for ancestor contact and promoting higher awareness. The oil and leaves are used in Hoodoo candlemancy and mojo bags. Bearberry is used medicinally for urinary tract infections and as a mild diuretic. Bearberry has suffered from mass marketing as a pharmaceutical and its habitat and growth are in decline.

Black Cohosh (*Cimicifuga racemosa*)

Black cohosh is used magickally to build courage and draw love and luck.

Bloodroot (*Sanguinaria canadensis*)

Bloodroot, also known as *king root* and *he root,* is used to draw positive spirits and love.

Blue Cohosh (*Caulophyllum thalictroides*)

Blue cohosh is used for love, impotence, and courage.

Cascara Sagrada (*Rhamnus purshiana*)

Indigenous to the Americas, this plant is harvested for its strong laxative properties. The translation of *cascara sagrada* is "sacred bark." It is mass-marketed for a wide variety of medical purposes, some of which are not supported by solid research. The bark of the tree is the part that is harvested for medicinal and magickal work. The bark is burned as an incense and it is used in various Hoodoo formulas. The key with cascara sagrada is buying it from a source that is ethical. See the suggested suppliers in appendix B.

Goldenseal (*Hydrastis canadensis*)

Goldenseal is used magickally to ensure prosperity and for blessings. It grows on the East Coast in woodland habitats. Goldenseal has mass appeal and has steadily gained popularity for its medicinal quality as an effective antimicrobial in treating upper respiratory ailments. This plant is not grown as a crop; instead, it is taken from the wild places where it grows naturally (wildcrafted). Since the root itself is harvested, the demand exceeds the supply. Use ginger as a substitute.

Sandalwood (*Santalum album*)

See sidebar on page 242.

Solomon's Seal (*Polygonatum biflorum*)

Solomon's seal is used for agreements, money draw, and wisdom.

Trillium (*Trillium* spp.)

Trillium, also called *Indian balm* and *bethroot,* has been used in Hoodoo for luck- and love-draw mojos and tricks.

White Oak Bark (*Quercus alba*)

White oak bark is used in ancient tree magick, healing, and retrieval.

White Sage (*Salvia apiana*)

White sage is often used in smudging ceremonies for house clearings and as an incense. In this capacity, white sage provides us with clarity by encouraging the presence of positive spirits and higher spiritual development. White sage has a very specific, small area where it grows naturally within a segment of California used for development. White sage also suffers from her popularity. So smudge with other types of sage, sweetgrass, lavender, or juniper blends.

Our Animal Companions

It may be a new concept to think of certain plants as being endangered or at-risk species, but this doesn't hold true with animals or sea creatures. A variety of animal parts—fur, teeth, bones, horns, and claws—have been useful in Hoodoo and similar paths in Africa and the Americas. For the sake of curiosity, let's examine a few of the more prominent animals used so that we can understand why they were revered and what substitutes can be used.

Badgers' teeth were—and in some cases, still are—used in mojo bags. The badger is an awesome creature; it is low to the earth, adept at digging, and extremely aggressive when crossed. Badgers are very good symbols of the warrior, as they can take on animals as ferocious as bears or dogs.

There are about fifteen subspecies of the badger in the Americas. In West Africa there is the species *Mellivora capensis,* also called a *honey badger* or *ratel.* These creatures appear almost skunklike; they have brown or black fur with a distinct white, pale-yellow, or gray covering on top. Honey badgers are found in the Ituri forest of northern Zaire.

A characteristic useful to consider when regarding all species of badger is that their skin is so tough that a porcupine quill, African bee, or dog bite can barely penetrate it. They appear to be completely devoid of fear. They attack animals such as horses, antelope, cattle, and even buffalo even though they are no larger than a raccoon.

Alligator and crocodile teeth have also been used in mojo bags. Crocodiles are in a group of reptiles called *Crocodylidae,* which populate both the Americas and West Africa (in the form of *O. t. tetraspis* and *O. t. osborni,* also called *West African dwarf crocodile* and *Congo dwarf crocodile*). The American alligator and the West African dwarf crocodiles are *crocodilians* that share key characteristics admired by warriors, hunters, and hoodoos: they are tough, tenacious, cunning, and heavily armored.

Raccoons are omnivores whose species live in Europe, Asia, and the Americas. There is a great deal of folklore surrounding the raccoon in Native American folklore. The name *raccoon* is derived from the Algonquin word *arachun,* or "he who scratches himself." Other Indian words for raccoons indicate that they are considered witches, sorcerers, or even demons. The raccoon is another cunning survivor. The penis of the raccoon has become sought after for love-drawing tricks because the raccoon is associated with virility and manhood.

Snakes of various types have played a large role in the imagination of Africans, largely due to the myths surrounding them learned during childhood. The admired qualities of the snake include its ability to survive on land and in the water, its ability to camouflage itself and blend quietly into its environment, its ability to hunt and eat much larger and more powerful prey, and the potency of its venom.

Dr. Buzzard, the hoodoo of Gullah heritage from Georgia's Sea Coast Islands, is remembered as being able to implant snakes and other reptiles into his human victims with the power of his mind, a handshake, or a blow of dust.

The rattle of the rattlesnake is an emblem of ancient Egyptian goddesses Hathor and Isis, two venerable Great Mother goddesses. Isis used her sistrum, a rattlesnakelike rattle, to motivate gods and humans to become active rather than passive. Isis, or *Auset* as she was called in Egyptian, brought the cobra into being. Snakeskin and rattlesnake rattles are used in various Hoodoo formulas, including the infamous Gopher's Dust.

Fascinating histories, traits, and mythology aside, my advice on utilizing animals in Hoodoo is to work with the animal without taking life. Using the Hoodoo foot track magick concept, you can take dirt from specific types of tracks for the job at hand.

Fallen feathers, snakeskin, found skulls, teeth, or parts from animals that have met with a natural or accidental death is one thing; contributing to animal endangerment, overuse, or cruelty is quite another. An additional benefit of gathering magickal ingredients in this manner is that you become more aware and your sense of intuition is sharpened. If you eat meat, fish, or fowl, you can use their parts (such as bones or feathers) in your mojo bags and other types of rootwork.

Another element fertile for exploration is using representations of animals to enhance your Hoodoo. I have heard of folk using manufactured plastic toys or metal casts of spiders, scorpions, snakes, and tigers symbolically in their magickal work. Even fossils, which I speak about in relation to altars and incense censors, are rich with possibility.

In South Africa there is a lively tradition of creating power animal sculptures out of clay. This is a form I particularly enjoy, as they are hewn from the Earth Mother and then submitted to the fire element in the dramatic firing process called *raku*. Successful raku glazes are unpredictable and rely heavily on chance and fate; in other words, they embody the spirit of magick. I have a very small rhinoceros on my altar, but many other types of animals made by South African potters are available.

My favorite of all is working with the generous purity within the life force of various animal spiritual companions and messengers. I do this by having them indoors and encouraging wild creatures like birds, butterflies, and bees to live by my home in my garden. West African tribes, ancient Khemetians (Egyptians), and various magickal paths within the African diaspora in the Americas strongly support the notion of working with totemic animals. In Wicca and witchcraft, working closely with animals is aligned with the concept of the familiar.

Remember that the ultimate goal of the hoodoo is to cultivate positivity. We seek to draw positive spirits, helpful ancestors, and luck or love. Most significantly, it is nearly impossible to build something positive on a foundation of negativity, therefore restrain from harming animals (including humans).

Substitutes for animal blood as an offering, sacrifice, or to enhance the power of a trick include:

- carnelian stone

- garnet

- ruby

- apple cider

- cranberry juice

- pomegranate juice

- tomato juice

Sea Creatures

A great deal of Hoodoo revolves around the veneration of water, water spirits, and water goddesses. Consequently, we look to the sea for ingredients to enhance rootwork. Cowries (and other seashells), Irish moss, sea kelp, and sea salt are useful in invoking the purifying, protective, loving presence of the Sea Mothers.

There are two sea creatures that you should think hard about before using as a hoodoo: coral and pearls. Pearls are extracted from living creatures in a violent way. Using pearls may cause your tricks or jobs to backfire negativity or send bad karma your way.

Coral is alive. If you can find a piece washed up on the beach or in an antique shop, it may bring some benefits to your magick work. Buying commercially harvested contemporary coral encourages the endangerment of these fragile, yet beautiful and important creatures.

Resources

Botanical Arts and Herbal Suppliers

Liberty Natural Products, Inc.
8120 SE Stark Street
Portland, OR 97215
ph: (503) 256-1227; fax: (503) 256-1182
sales@libertynatural.com
http://libertynatural.com/index.html

Source for pure, direct-from-the-source, inexpensive essential oils. All sizes of glass and plastic storage containers. Talcum and other bottles, floral waters, droppers, wands, salts, clay. $50 minimum per order.

Penzeys Spices
http://www.penzeys.com

Many locations. Excellent source of exotic, fresh, high-quality spices for incenses and mojo bags. Wide variety of pepper for making Stay Away and Hot Foot Powders. Recipes, bottles, jars. Does mail order.

Richters Herbs
357 Highway 47
Goodwood, ON LOC 1A0
Canada
(905) 640-6677
http://www.richters.com

Huge selection of herbs from seeds or young plants. Books.

San Francisco Herb Co.
250 14th Street
San Francisco, CA 94103-2420
1-800-227-4530
http://www.sfherb.com

Rose petals and buds, frankincense, myrrh, spices, dried botanicals, potpourri ingredients, and fragrance oils.

Scents of Earth
PO Box 859
Sun City, CA 92586
1-800-323-8159
info@scentsofearth.com
http://www.scents-of-earth.com/info.
html

Incense-making supplies, lotus oils, attar of roses. Baked Earth Attar, Queen of Sheba Incense, sandalwood (choice quality), frankincense, myrrh, white ash, and pure bamboo charcoals.

Snowdrift Farm, Inc.
2750 South 4th Avenue, Suites 107–108
South Tucson, AZ 85713
ph: 520-882-7080; fax: 520-882-2739
http://www.snowdriftfarm.com

Packaging, salts in bulk, and recipes. Sells perfume-grade alcohol (formulator's or perfumer's alcohol), which can be used instead of vodka.

SoapCrafters Company
2944 S. West Temple
Salt Lake City, UT 84115
(801) 484-5121
http://www.soapcrafters.com

Blank incense sticks, fragrance and essential oils, packaging for incense storage, jars, bottles, and more.

Sun Burst Bottle Company
5710 Auburn Blvd., Suite 7
Sacramento, CA 95841
(916) 348-5576
http://www.sunburstbottle.com

Lip balm tins, blue and brown glass bottles, jars, and storage bins in all sizes and many shapes.

SunFeather Natural Soap Co.
1551 State Highway 72
Potsdam, NY 13676
(315) 265-3648
http://www.sunsoap.com/

Soapmaking specialists. Good for supplies that are unusual and hard to find. Plus recipe books and herbal housecleaning books and ingredients. A club and website. High-quality materials.

Taos Herb Company
PO Box 3232
710 Paseo del Pueblo Sur, Suite J
Taos, NM 87571
1-800-353-1991
http://www.taosherb.com

Smudging supplies, sage, sweetgrass, copal, frankincense, myrrh.

Wholesale Supplies Plus
1-800-359-0944
http://www.wholesalesuppliesplus.com

Soap and candlemaking supplies, packaging, labels, and quality fragrance oils.

Hoodoo and Spiritual Supplies

The Broom Closet
3 Central Street
Salem, MA 01970
ph: (978) 741-3669; fax: (978) 745-3028
http://www.broomcloset.com

Excellent blessed candles and incenses.

Lucky Mojo Curio Co. Catalogue
6632 Covey Road
Forestville, CA 95436
(707) 887-1521
http://www.luckymojo.com

Good source for original Hoodoo formulas, herbs, lodestones, magnetic sand, flannels, and Hoodoo books. Candles, talismans, and amulets, including scarabs.

New Orleans Mistic
2267 St. Claude Avenue
New Orleans, LA 70117
http://www.neworleansmistic.com

Amulets, charms, Hoodoo herbs, African diasporic books, candles, baths.

Ritual Adornments
2708 Main Street
Santa Monica, CA 90405
http://www.ritualadornments.com

Semiprecious stone beads, clasps.

Specialty Paper

Paper Source
http://www.paper-source.com

Many locations. Carries banana paper, fig bark paper, coconut paper, etc.

Pearl Art and Craft
http://www.pearlpaint.com

Many locations. Good variety; great prices.

Broommakers

Friendswood Brooms
8 Willow Road
Leicester, NC 28748
http://www.friendswoodbrooms.com

Some of the best broommakers in the U.S.

Justamere Tree Farm and Soapworks
Patterson Road
Worthington, MA 01098
(413) 238-5902
info@justameretreefarm.com
http://www.justameretreefarm.com

Dan Mordhorst
112 Doris Avenue
Franklin Square, NY 11010
(516) 326-9520
dan@danshandmadebrooms.com
http://www.daveamason.com/dan/home.
html

Broommaker historian.

Handmade-Paper Kits

Dieu Donné Papermill
133 Broome Street
New York, NY 10013
1-877-337-2737
http://www.dieudonne.org

One of the most prominent papermaking institutions in North America. Does special orders, classes, workshops, exhibitions, kits, and sells specialty papers.

Magnolia Editions
2527 Magnolia Street
Oakland, CA 94607
(510) 839-5268
http://www.magnoliapaper.com

Lee S. McDonald, Inc.
PO Box 290264
Charlestown, MA 02129
ph: 1-888-627-2737; fax: 617-242-8825
http://toolsforpaper.com

Papermaking, prepared pulps, kits, and instructional books.

African Textiles

Adire African Textiles
161 Faringdon Avenue
Harold Wood
Romford, UK
duncan@adire.clara.net

Printed woven raffia cloth from the Kuba people of Congo, adinkra cloth by the Ashanti of Ghana, bogolan (mud cloth) from Mali, and ewe cloth (kente cloth) from the Ewe people of Ghana and Togo.

The Niger Bend
5264 Irish Ridge Road
Chittenango, NY 13037
(315) 655-8989

African cloth, sculptures, drums, information, artifacts.

Organizations

Following is a list of organizations that relate to the text of this book. Support and research foundations concerning the rich cultures of the Gullah and Geechee people of the Sea Islands. Their herbal and magickal practices are derived largely from West African tribes, which in turn informed Hoodoo practices and African American herbalism. Resources for herbalism are also listed.

The Gullah/Geechee Sea Island Coalition
PO Box 1207
St. Helena Island, SC 29920
1-888-TRY-ISLE
GullGeeCo@aol.com

To support a memorial to honor the Ibo warriors who landed on St. Simon's Island but refused to be enslaved. Inquiries can also be made to Hunnuh Home for tours, authentic Gullah arts, crafts, food, books, archives, and research.

Sapelo Island Cultural and Revitalization Society
PO Box 1
Sapelo, GA 31327
(912) 485-2126

Sightseeing, tours, crafts, and accommodations within the Hog Hammock community of the Gullah community.

United Plant Savers (UpS)
PO Box 77
Guysville, OH 45735
(802) 479-9825
http://unitedplantsavers.org

Guide to herbal information, plant preservation, endangered and at-risk plants. Resources for herbal schools, herbalists, supplies.

Apprenticeships, Workshops, and Initiations of the African Diasporic Traditions

Stephanie Rose Bird

Workshops making elixirs, soaps, and healing balms and painting with the author. See "To Write to the Author" on page ii.

Ifa Foundation
PO Box 3516
DeLand, FL 32721-3516
http://www.ifafoundation.org
iyalawo@yahoo.com

Spiritual marketplace, initiations for priests/priestesses, and information on orishas.

The School of Ancient Mysteries and Sacred Arts Center
Luisah Teish and Associates
5111 Telegraph Avenue #305
Oakland, CA 94609
(510) 595-1471
teishsamsac@aol.com

Luisah Teish is the author of several books. Features Oshun studies, rituals, ceremonies.

Sage Mountain
PO Box 420
E. Barre, VT 05649
(802) 479-9825
sagemt@sagemountain.com
http://www.sagemountain.com

Herb wisdom classes, workshops, women's conference, apprenticeships, field trips abroad. See also United Plant Savers information above.

Malidoma Patrice Some
"Into the Heart of African Shamanism"
Echoes of Ancestors
28704 S. Meridian Road
Aurora, OR 97002
echoes@onemain.com

Three-year-long apprenticeship in African shamanism and workshops with book author Malidoma Patrice Some. Foundation to benefit African communities.

Glossary

Absolute—A solvent-extracted essential oil frequently made from fragrant flowers such as carnation, jasmine, hyacinth, and narcissus.

Ade iko—A crown made entirely of raffia worn by devotees of Obaluaiye.

African diaspora—Places where people of African descent live; for example, North America, the Caribbean, South America, and parts of Europe.

Africanism—A carryover of an African behavior, custom, or tradition outside of Africa.

Afro-Brazilians—People of Brazil who are descendants of Africans.

Agrarian culture—A culture that is sustained largely by farming.

Alchemists—An influential group to hoodoos that came into prominence during the Middle Ages. Alchemists sought to transform ordinary materials into extraordinary and valuable materials such as gold. Books by alchemist Albertus Magnus are used by hoodoos.

All Saints' Day—November 1; a day to honor the souls of departed youth.

All Souls' Day—November 2; a day to honor and welcome spirits of departed adults.

Altar—A sacred place that honors spirits, ancestors, loved ones, or the self.

Amulet—A piece of jewelry or sculpture that is symbolic and protective.

Ancestor—A relative of an earlier, and sometimes distant, generation.

Animism—The idea that inanimate natural objects have a spirit.

Ankh—Ancient Egyptian symbol of everlasting life.

Anointing oil—Sacred oil used to enhance the inert magickal power of candles and other objects.

Aphrodisiac—A substance that arouses sexual desire; usually organic foods that are ingested.

Aromatherapy—Using scents and aromas of a natural plant-based origin as a therapeutic treatment.

Ase—West African word roughly translated to "spiritual blessings."

Ashe—West African word that describes magickal forces and energies of the universe.

Asperger—Tool used to magickally dispense precious substances during spellwork, rituals, or ceremonies.

Astral travel—Allowing your spirit to be released from your body so that it can journey and do work either in dreams or through meditation.

Attar—A pure oil-based scent made from rare, precious, or unusual organic substances. Attar of roses, for example, is created from steam-distilled rose petals.

"Aung, shrang, shring, shraung" ("Dhum vam")—A mantra recommended by spiritualist Anna Riva designed to induce tranquility to aid magickal work.

Badenya—Component of West African duality meaning the mother-child aspect.

Bak—Moringa oil used by ancient Nubians and Khemetians as a pregnancy belly rub.

Banganga—Priest/priestess or magickal specialist called a rootworker or conjurer in Hoodoo.

Banishing—A trick to get rid of something negative.

Barracao—Meeting place used during Candomble practices.

Bilongo—Medicine in bags used by the Bamana people of western Sudan used for addressing various ills.

Binah—Spiritual, loving, stable, highly aware, divine mother who is the third sephirah in the Tree of Life. Associated with myrrh. *Binah* means "The Understanding."

Blessings—Positive thoughts usually having a spiritual component.

Breathwork—Using breathing in a meditative way to relax or bring focus.

Candlemancy—The art of using candles magickally.

Candomble—A magicko-herbalist tradition primarily practiced by people of African descent in Brazil.

Carolina lowlands—South Carolina islandic cultures.

Catal Huyuk—Neolithic European village thought to be a remnant of matriarchy and goddess worship.

Caul—The covering on the eye of a newborn that usually predicts psychic ability.

Cauldron—Cast-iron pot used for creating herbal brews, burning incense, and other magickal work.

Chant—Repetitive statement used to enhance the spiritual aspect of ritual, ceremony, or worship.

Charging—Energizing or strengthening.

Charms—A collection of symbolic objects designed to meet a specific purpose, such as luck, love, protection, or remembrance.

Chicomecoatl—Mexican goddess of the hearth and fire who wears the sun as a shield.

Chiminea—Portable outdoor clay stove useful for burning incense and conducting rituals.

Conjur craft—Author's term for the contemporary practice of Hoodoo.

Conjure—To collect (draw) magick, spirits, or energy.

Cool—Ideal character in West Africa; balanced, not showy or withdrawn—just right.

Correspondences—Magickal coordinates that help tricks, spells, and rituals, such as the cycle of the moon, specific herbs or minerals, and gods and goddesses.

Cosmic womb—The center of creation in women's spirituality.

Crossroad—A magickal, mystical place where four roads intersect.

Curse—Negative energy cast upon someone.

Daliluw—Recipes and techniques used for mixing various parts of mojo bags or herbal bundles in Africa.

"Dhum vam"—see *"Aung, shrang, shring, shraung."*

Dibia—Igbo wisemen healers.

Didgeridoo—A piece of wood carved by termites used as a musical instrument by Aborigines from northern Australia.

Divination—Seeing the future.

Dominant hand—The hand that yields the most power. Used in spells, tricks, rituals, etc.

Dressing candles—To bring additional power to candles using herbal or mineral oils.

Earth Mother—A goddess that embodies nurturing, kindness, and fertility.

Elegba—Orisha of gateways, forests, and crossroads. Associated with Oya and Shango. Considered a trickster.

Erinlé—Hermaphrodite hunter who lives in the forest and in the sea. Orisha of herbalism.

Essential oil—A pure plant essence extracted from flowers, leaves, stems, berries, or roots. Used medicinally in aromatherapy and Hoodoo and as a perfume.

Ewe—Yoruban herb corresponding to an orisha.

Ewu iko—A gown made of raffia worn by devotees of orisha Obaluaiye.

Fadenya—Akin to yin-yang in Asia, fadenya means "father-child" and is juxtaposed against badenya ("mother-child") to create a balance of character.

Feeding powder—Herbal or mineral substance used to charge and sustain the life of a powerful object.

Feng shui—In Chinese, "wind-water." The Chinese art of powerful and purposeful spatial arrangement designed to control cosmic energy called *chi*.

Fixing tricks—Doing spellwork.

Flannel—A small fabric bag often made of cotton flannel used to construct a mojo.

Folhas de pisar—Sacred leaves strewn on the floor of a barracao to absorb negative energy and dispel evil in the practice of Candomble.

Foot track magick—Magickal element of Hoodoo that involves the physical tracks and footprints.

Fragrance oil—A synthetic perfumed oil used in certain recipes, rituals, and ceremonies.

Ga Wree Wree—A fierce masked performer representative of the power of the forest.

Geechee—Another term for a Gullah person of the Sea Coast Islands or Carolina lowlands.

Gopher's Dust—A magickal dust used in foot track magick that traditionally incorporates snakeskin or the rattle of a rattlesnake. Used to motivate and enforce changes.

Graveyard dirt—Dirt taken from a graveyard. Especially potent if gathered from a grave at a crossroads. Mullein is an herb that is used as a substitute.

Great Mother—Goddess of all goddesses; creator being.

Gris-gris—Synonym for mojo bag.

Ha—Dahomean word for a ceremonial broom. Called *ja* in Spanish in Brazil by followers of Candomble.

Hand—Synonym for mojo bag, charm.

Hant—Southern usage for a spirit or ghost. Often refers to a troubled, wandering spirit.

Hara Ke—Fertility goddess from Ghana associated with rain and sweet water.

He and she—Male and female lodestones that have been matched by size and shape. A he is phallic-shaped whereas a she is rounded. The he has a negative charge while the she has a positive charge. See also *lodestone*.

Herbal bundle—Dream pillow, mojo bag, or other collection of herbs in fabric used for a magickal purpose.

Hex—Negative energy cast upon a victim. This concept originated in Pennsylvania Dutch culture.

High priestess—Can mean a seer, leader, oracle, holy woman, or wisewoman.

Holy water—Used in religious ceremonies and in magickal spirituality as well. It is water taken from the river Jordan and/or blessed by a high priest.

Hoodoo—An eclectic group of multicultural practices heavily influenced by the Angola, Kongo, and Dahomey people of Africa. In the Americas, Hoodoo has been influenced somewhat by Native American spirituality, Qabalah, the Pennsylvania Dutch, early spiritualists, and European magick.

Hunter shirt—See *warrior shirt*.

Ifa—Belief system of the Yoruba and other people of African descent that combines ancestor veneration with honor of the orisha, herbalism, magick, and healing.

Invocation—A song, poem, or chant designed to call upon the spirits or ancestors.

Isis—The Great Mother goddess of ancient Egypt from whom life is thought to have sprung.

Iwa—In Africa it means "cool" and is symbolized by the color white.

Ja—See *ha*.

Jazz funeral—Type of funeral service practiced primarily in New Orleans that uses live Dixie-style jazz.

Jiridon—The West African science of trees practiced by hunters, shamen, and warriors. Masters of jiridon are master herbalists and adept ecologists. See also *tree-talking*.

Joe mows—Inversion of the word *mojo*; used as a playful synonym.

John the Conqueror—A Hoodoo root named for a mythic, heroic, escaped slave.

Juju—Magick, sometimes with bad intent.

Ka—Shadow self.

Kanga mfunya—The binding or tying of spirit to objects so they can go on to the spirit world.

Kente cloth—A vibrant, symbolic type of fabric historically created by the Asante people of Ghana. Used to express folklore, proverbs, and clan affiliations through geometric depiction of people, history, household objects, and circumstances.

Khemet—Ancient Black Egyptian civilization.

Kinnikinnik—Algonquin word for a special botanical mixture used in rituals often containing the herb tobacco. It can be smoked in the peace pipe or burned in ancestor veneration rituals.

Koran—The holy book of Islam.

Kush—Ancient kingdom in northern Africa. Kushites were Black people who lived near Egypt.

Kwanza—"First fruits." Late December celebration of harvest, community, and health.

Kyphi—Ancient Egyptian incense containing dried fruit, herbs, red wine, etc. Used to create a healing, sacred, loving environment conducive to the goddess Isis.

Las ofrendas—Spanish for "the offerings."

Laying of tricks—Hoodoo term for performing spells.

Lexicon—A particular group of practices united by mythology, folklore, stories, and belief.

Libation—The pouring of a liquid on the earth to appeal to the spiritual world.

Liturgical palms—Palms used in religious or spiritual rites (Candomble).

Lobi singi—Moralizing tales and proverbs used to communicate in Suriname.

Lodestone—A stone whose use is traced back to the early alchemists. Also called a *he* or a *she*. Lodestone is made from magnetite. See also *he and she*.

Los Dias de los Muertos—Spanish for "The Day of the Dead." Practiced in Mexico and the U.S.

Loy Krathong—Annual Thai ritual that combines the elements of fire and water to aid with renewal and change.

Lucid dreaming—Controlling your own dreams while sleeping and being aware that you are dreaming.

Mae de santo—High priestess of Candomble.

Magickal herbalism—Herbalism used with magickal or spiritual intent.

Makadi—Leaflets from a palm tree used for creating costumes and rituals (Kuba of Zaire).

Mariuo—Similar to a garland, a mariuo is created by sacred leaves from the heart of liturgical palms and placed above windows in Afro-Brazilian barracao (meeting places) for the practice of Candomble.

Mbari—African earth goddess Ala of Ghana resides in or near a special house built for her called a *mbari*. It literally translates to "crown her."

Medical herbalism—Using plants, roots, berries, seeds, and barks to heal.

Medicine bag—A bag or pouch that contains healing energy from a wide range of cultures, including Native American, African, and African American.

Menarche—When a young girl transforms into a young woman. Usually marked by the first menstrual period.

Mesopotamia—Ancient Middle Eastern civilization where Iraq is currently located.

Middle Passage—The height of African slave trade to the Americas.

Minkisi—Singular form of the term for a Kongo power figure. See also *nkisi*.

Mojo—A small bag of charms that serves as an amulet for a wide range of purposes.

Mooyo—The soul of a charm bag, believed to be the forerunner of a Hoodoo mojo bag from the Kongo and Angola.

Mother Earth—The planet Earth cast in a feminine goddess light.

Mud cloth—Cloth properly called *bogolanfini* and created by the Bamana people of Mali. Hunters and warriors wear this cloth to collect their power and to serve as a shield. It reflects important symbols, proverbs, and tribal affiliations. Created using dye-and-resist and the reactions between root sap, soap, and river mud.

Mujaji—A line of southern African fertility rain goddess queens; the embodiment of the godly in human form (sacred leadership).

Nana Buku—Orisha Obaluaiye's mother. Her image is a conical mound of earth that wears a grasslike raffia skirt.

Nation sack—A female-owned mojo bag. Originated in Memphis, Tennessee.

Native Americans—Asiatic people who are the original settlers of the Americas.

Ne Kongo—A cultural healer of the Kongo that carried the first healing medicines from heaven to earth.

Ngama—See *nyama*.

Nganga—Spiritual herbalist healer from the Kongo.

Night mares—Mischievous sea spirits that inhabit dreams.

Nkisi—Kongo charms powered by nature spirits, as they contain a wide variety of natural objects and ephemera. See also *minkisi.*

Nkisi nkondi—Figurative sculpture from the Kongo that has nails inserted into it to bind its powers.

Nsusu mpembe—"White rooster."

Nubian—Ancient Black civilization.

Nut—Goddess of the sky, sun, moon, and stars; the mother to the gods.

Nyama—*Ngama* in Hoodoo. Unpredictable energy and action that flows through everything in the universe; can be helpful or dangerous.

Nyi-ji—An amulet used by hunters and warriors that contains the tears of animals.

Obaluaiye—Fierce orisha with the power to create smallpox or heal epidemics if he sees fit.

Ogun—Akin to war god Mars, Ogun is the Ifa orisha of metal, power, fire, and war.

Opening the way—Enhancing psychic abilities.

Oracle—A person or object that can divine the future.

Orisha—Angelic beings often compared to gods or goddesses.

Oya—Orisha of changes, her domain is the cemetery. Associated with wind, tornados, changes, and edges. Consort to Shango.

Pai de santo—High priest of Candomble.

Poppet—A small, stuffed doll or other organic object used to represent a human. Sometimes called a "voodoo doll."

Prophetic dreams—Dreams that predict the future.

Qabalah—Jewish mysticism and ancient Hebrew spiritual practice that contains many different types of numerological correspondences and written incantations.

Raffia—A natural fiber in the palm family used in African ceremony, ritual, and art.

Rhassoul mud—A reddish-brown clay with therapeutic properties that comes only from the Atlas Mountain range in Morocco, Africa.

Rites of passage—Defining moments in one's life usually marked by age or life cycle.

Rootwork—Magicko-herbalism; also called *Hoodoo*.

Rosicrucian—American spiritualist tradition that influenced Hoodoo.

Sacred space—A special space used for rituals, ceremony, reflection, or meditation.

Sacudimento—Leaf-whipping used by priests or priestesses in the Afro-Brazilian practice of Candomble.

Sakpata—People of Benin, Cuba, and Brazil who celebrate Obaluaiye.

Santeria—A unique hybrid of Western and non-Western rituals, ceremonies, prayers, and invocations primarily practiced in South America.

Scarab—Based on *Scarabeus sacer,* an Egyptian dung-eating beetle, scarabs are sculptures or jewelry used as an amulet to absorb evil.

Scarification—Scars deliberately made on the body, often to mark a rite of passage or to mark an honor. Can be patterned or elaborate like tattoos.

Scrying—Gazing at an object such as a flame, water, crystal ball, or mirror to see into different worlds and times.

Sea Coast Islands—Islands off the coast of Georgia and South Carolina where Gullah culture flourishes.

Secret society—A group united by gender, age, and covert magickal or healing activities. Usually made up of associates within a single tribe or clan.

Seven Powers of Africa—This refers to seven powerful Yoruban Ifa orisha: Shango, Elegba, Obatala, Oshun, Ogun, Orunmilla, and Yemoya-Olokun. Together the seven bring a well-balanced array of gifts including wisdom, life, love, eloquence, messages, and protection.

Shamanism—A type of healing practiced by a variety of indigenous groups that combines knowledge of herbalism and natural medicines with deep spirituality. Shamen sometimes use trance that may be induced by hallucinogenics such as peyote. Most are adept at shapeshifting.

Shango—Fiery and fierce orisha who is also stately and noble.

Shashara—The broomlike tool of orisha Obaluaiye.

Shrine—An arrangement of objects in a specific space to honor gods, goddesses, orisha, spirits, or nature.

Sisterfriends—A term used in Black culture, and primarily in America, to refer to a close circle of female friends.

Sistrum—Egyptian musical instrument connected with Isis that has a side similar to a rattlesnake, thus it is used to motivate and incite.

Sitz bath—Very shallow bath used for therapy or comfort using minerals or herbal medicines.

Sleep paralysis—A halfway point between wakefulness and sleep that can render the body unable to move.

Smudging—Submitting a person or thing to fragrant smoke with spiritual or magickal energy. A practice attributed to Native Americans who smudge with sage, lavender, mugwort, and other indigenous herbs. A practice similar to smudging called *perfumo* was done in ancient Egypt and continues to be done by Chinese healers.

Sticking—An adaptation of piercing from traditional scarification rituals. Sticking a poppet or other object such as a candle is used to insert intent and energy into the subject.

Strewing—To toss or spread, usually referring to confetti, flower petals, or sacred plants in Hoodoo.

Tet—Also called *Thet, Tit, Knot of Isis, Belt of Isis,* and *Buckle of Isis.* Emblem of Isis, the Egyptian Great Mother. A Tet is believed to embody feminine power, fertility, and the strength of blood. Made of carnelian, jasper, or red faience, a Tet symbolizes female reproductive organs.

Tisane—Herbs whose medicine is extracted by pouring boiling water over leaves or flowers.

Toby—Another name for a mojo, especially used in Maryland.

Tree-talking—A practice recorded in the Bayou Pierre swamplands in Mississippi. Called *jiridon* in Africa. See also *jiridon.*

Trick—The name for a spell in traditional Hoodoo.

Veve—Drawing made with cornstarch on the earth or floor used to invoke the spirit of gods or goddesses in Haitian Vodoun.

Vodoun—A spiritual path influenced by West African Ifa, often mistakenly called *voodoo.*

Voodoo—Misnomer for the West African practice Vodoun. See *Vodoun.*

Warrior shirt—A shirt worn by Mande and Asante (as well as a few other groups) hunters and warriors. It has pockets filled with amulets, knotted cords, animal teeth, claws, horns, cowry shells, and glass. Also called a *hunter shirt.*

Water jar—A jug or amphora that is the symbol of the Egyptian goddess Nut.

Wildcrafting—To harvest plants, berries, nuts, or roots from wild, open spaces.

Witching hour—A powerful time for conducting rituals.

Wohpe—Lakota goddess of pleasure, wishes, cycles, beauty, meteors, and time.

Wo Puh Gle—A talking entertainer clad in grassy costume of the Dan people of the Ivory Coast.

Yamoti—Sesame seeds.

Yeh to Gle—An authority figure clad in grassy costume of the Dan people of the Ivory Coast.

Yemoya-Olokun—Great Mother in Ifa cosmology, goddess of ocean and rivers, and all-knowing, compassionate giver and taker of life.

Yoruba—The people of southeastern Nigeria.

Yorubaland—Countries or territories where the Yoruba live. Many Yoruba were sold into slavery, thus their descendants populate parts of the Americas and the Caribbean.

Yowa Cross—Symbol from Kongo culture that resembles the crossroads. Represents the intersections of the world of the living and the world of the dead as well as the center of the four winds.

Bibliography and Recommended Reading

Items marked with an asterisk (*) are recommended by the author.

Amen, Ra Un Nefer. *Metu Neter.* Vol. 1. New York: Kamit Publications, 1990.

Anderson, Martha G., and Christine Mullen Kreamer. *Wild Spirits, Strong Medicine: African Art and the Wilderness.* Edited by Enid Schildkrout. New York: The Center for African Art, 1989.

Bass, Ruth. "Mojo." In *From My People: 400 Years of African American Folklore,* edited by Daryl Cumber Dance, 586–96. New York, Norton Books, 2002.

Baring, Anne, and Jules Cashford. *The Myth of the Goddess: Evolution of an Image.* New York: Penguin Group Publishers, 1991.

"Beliefs and Customs Connected with Death and Burial." In *From My People: 400 Years of African American Folklore,* edited by Daryl Cumber Dance, 613–15. New York: Norton Books, 2002.

*Berger, Judith. *Herbal Rituals.* New York: St. Martin's Press, 1998.

Best, Michael R., and Frank H. Brightman, eds. *The Book of Secrets of Albertus Magnus: Of the Virtues of Herbs, Stones & Certain Beasts, A Book of the Marvels of the World.* Oxford, UK: Oxford University Press, 1973.

Bremness, Lesley. *The Complete Book of Herbs.* New York: Viking Studio Books, 1994.

Bremness, Lesley, and Marie Pierre Moine. *Crabtree and Evelyn Fragrant Herbal: Enhancing Your Life with Aromatic Herbs and Essential Oils.* New York: Bulfinch Press, 1998.

Brown, Simon. *Practical Feng Shui.* London: Ward Lock Books, 1997.

Carawan, Guy, and Candie Carawan. *Ain't You Got a Right to the Tree of Life?: The People of Johns Island, South Carolina—Their Faces, Their Words, and Their Songs.* Athens, GA: University of Georgia Press, 1989.

Cole, Herbert M. *Icons: Ideals and Power in the Art of Africa.* Washington, DC: Smithsonian Institution Press, 1989.

Courlander, Harold. *A Treasury of Afro-American Folklore: The Oral Literature, Traditions, Recollections, Legends, Tales, Songs, Religious Beliefs, Customs, Sayings and Humor of Peoples of African Descent in the Americas.* New York: Marlowe and Company, 1976.

Cunningham, Scott. *Cunningham's Encyclopedia of Crystal, Gem & Metal Magic.* 2nd ed. St. Paul, MN: Llewellyn Publications, 2002.

———. *Cunningham's Encyclopedia of Magical Herbs.* St. Paul, MN: Llewellyn Publications, 1985.

Cunningham, Scott, and David Harrington. *Spell Crafts: Creating Magical Objects.* St. Paul, MN: Llewellyn Publications, 1993.

Dance, Daryl Cumber, ed. *From My People: 400 Years of African American Folklore.* New York: Norton Books, 2002.

Darish, Patricia. "Dressing for the Next Life: Raffia Textile Production and Use among the Kuba of Zaire." Chap. 4 in *Cloth and Human Experience,* edited by Annette Weiner and Jane Schneider, 118–37. Washington, DC: Smithsonian Institution Press, 1989.

Diallo, Yaya, and Mitchell Hall. *The Healing Drum: African Wisdom Teachings.* Rochester, VT: Destiny Books, 1989.

Edwards, Victoria. *The Aromatherapy Companion.* Pownal, VT: Storey Books, 1999.

Franklin, John Hope. *From Slavery to Freedom: A History of African Americans.* 7th ed. New York: McGraw-Hill, 1994.

Gamache, Henri. *The Master Book of Candle Burning: How to Burn Candles for Every Purpose.* 1942. Reprint, Old Bethpage, NY: Original Publications, 1998.

Gleason, Judith. *Oya: In Praise of an African Goddess.* San Francisco: HarperCollins, 1987.

Goodwine, Marquetta L., and Clarity Press Gullah Project, eds. *The Legacy of Ibo Landing: Gullah Roots of African American Culture.* Atlanta, GA: Clarity Press, Inc., 1998.

Hartt, Frederick. *A History of Painting, Sculpture, Architecture: Prehistory, Ancient World, Middle Ages.* New York: Prentice-Hall Inc., 1976.

Hearn, Lafcadio. "New Orleans Superstitions." In *A Treasury of Afro-American Folklore,* edited by Harold Courlander, 159–64. New York: Marlowe and Company, 1976.

*Hiebert, Helen. *Papermaking with Plants: Creative Recipes and Projects Using Herbs, Flowers, Grasses and Leaves.* Pownal, VT: Storey Book, 2000.

Hyatt, Harry Middleton. *Folklore from Adams County Illinois.* New York: Memoirs of the Alma Egan Hyatt Foundation, 1935.

*Illes, Judika. *Earth Mother Magic: Ancient Spells for Modern Belles.* Gloucester, MA: Fairwinds Press, 2001.

*Karade, Baba Ifa. *The Handbook of Yoruba Religious Concepts.* York Beach, ME: Weiser Books, 1994.

Knishinsky, Ran. *The Clay Cure: Natural Healing from the Earth.* Rochester, NY: Healing Art Press, 1998.

Lust, John. *The Herb Book.* New York: Bantam Books, 1974.

Mack, Carol K., and Dinah Mack. *The Field Guide to Demons, Fairies, Fallen Angels and other Subversive Spirits.* New York: Owl Books / Henry Holt, 1998.

*Manniche, Lise. *Sacred Luxuries: Fragrance, Aromatherapy, and Cosmetics in Ancient Egypt.* Ithaca, NY: Cornell University Press, 1999.

McClusky, Pamela, and Robert Farris Thompson. *Art from Africa: Long Steps Never Broke a Back.* Seattle, WA and Princeton, NJ: Seattle Art Museum / Princeton University Press, 2002.

Mickaharic, Draja. *Spiritual Cleaning: A Handbook for Psychic Protection.* York Beach, ME: Weiser Books, 1982.

Mitchell, Faith. *Hoodoo Medicine: Gullah Herbal Remedies.* Columbia, SC: Summerhouse Press, 1999.

Rhyme, Nancy. *More Tales of South Carolina Low Country.* Winston-Salem, NC: John F. Blair Publishers, 1984.

Riva, Anna. *Magic with Incense and Powders: 850 Rituals and Uses with Chants and Prayers.* Los Angeles, CA: International Imports, 1985.

Roberts, Elizabeth, and Elias Amidon, eds. *Earth Prayers: From Around the World.* San Francisco: HarperCollins, 1991.

Scheub, Harold. *A Dictionary of African Mythology: The Mythmaker as Storyteller.* Oxford, UK: Oxford University Press, 2000.

Shafton, Anthony. *Dream-Singers: The African American Way with Dreams.* New York: John Wiley and Sons, 2002.

Some, Malidoma Patrice. *The Healing Wisdom of Africa: Finding Life Purpose Through Nature, Ritual and Community.* New York: Jeremy P. Tarcher / Putnam, 1998.

*Stoller, Paul, and Cheryl Olkes. *In Sorcery's Shadow.* Chicago, IL: University of Chicago Press, 1987.

Tarostar. *The Witch's Formulary and Spellbook.* Las Vegas, NV: Original Productions, n.d.

*Teish, Luisah. *Jambalaya: The Natural Woman's Book of Personal Charms and Practical Rituals.* San Francisco: Harper and Row, 1985.

Telesco, Patricia. *365 Goddess: A Daily Guide to the Magic and Inspiration of the Goddess.* San Francisco: HarperSanFrancisco, 1998.

*Thompson, Robert Farris. *Flash of the Spirit: African and Afro-American Art and Philosophy.* New York: Vintage Books, 1987.

Trevelyan, Joanna. *Holistic Home: Creating an Environment for Physical & Spiritual Well-Being.* New York: Sterling Publishing, 1998.

Umeh, John Anenechukwu. *After God Is Dibia: Igbo Cosmology, Divination and Sacred Science in Nigeria.* Vol. 2. London: Karnak House, 1999.

Van Sertima, Ivan, ed. *Black Women in Antiquity.* Piscataway, NJ: Transaction Publishers, 2002.

*Voeks, Robert A. *Sacred Leaves of Candomble: African Magic, Medicine, and Religion in Brazil.* Austin, TX: University of Texas Press, 1997.

Walker, Barbara. *The Woman's Encyclopedia of Myths and Secrets.* Edison, NJ: Castle Books, 1991.

Worwood, Valerie Ann. *The Complete Book of Essential Oils and Aromatherapy.* Novato, CA: New World Press, 1991.

———. *The Fragrant Heavens: The Spiritual Dimension of Fragrance and Aromatherapy.* Novato, CA: New World Press, 1999.

Yoder, Don. "Folk Medicine." In *Folklore and Folklife,* edited by Richard M. Dorson, 201–15. Chicago, IL: University of Chicago Press, 1972.

Yronwode, Catherine. "The Lucky W Amulet Archive." *Lucky Mojo.* http://www.luckymojo.com/luckyw.html.

Index